FEMALE-PERPETRATED SEX ABUSE

Female-Perpetrated Sex Abuse is a groundbreaking study into gender, sexuality, and victimhood. It examines the cultural conditions of possibility for female-perpetrated sex abuse (FSA) victimhood as a means to advance contemporary critical understandings of the role of gender and sexuality as instruments of modern power. As the first direct exploration of FSA victimhood, this book analyses:

- why victims of FSA remain so underexplored and invisible as objects of human science knowledge;
- the limited and overly rigid discourses in local and global psychological theory and practice that continues to treat particular subjects as 'victim worthy' through paradigms that construct victimhood as gendered; and
- the possibility of new discourses that could disrupt normative understandings of gender, sexuality and power in sex abuse, and as constitutive to the beginnings of a counter-knowledge on transgressive sexualities.

By tracing the historical and cultural conditions of the emergence of FSA broadly and FSA victimhood specifically, Kramer illustrates how deeply engrained constructions of gender and sexuality both produce and constrain the possibilities for reporting, disclosing and self-identifying victimhood.

Female-Perpetrated Sex Abuse is essential reading for academics, researchers and students alike, in the areas of psychology, sociology, gender studies, criminology, counselling and social work.

Sherianne Kramer holds a PhD from the University of the Witwatersrand in South Africa, where she is a registered research psychologist and lecturer in the Department of Psychology. Her research interests are primarily focused within the critical psychology discipline and include crime, violence and injury prevention, female- and child-perpetrated physical and sexual violence, gender identity, and performativity and knowledge productions.

Concepts for Critical Psychology: Disciplinary Boundaries Re-thought
Series editor: Ian Parker

Developments inside psychology that question the history of the discipline and the way it functions in society have led many psychologists to look outside the discipline for new ideas. This series draws on cutting-edge critiques from just outside psychology in order to complement and question critical arguments emerging inside. The authors provide new perspectives on subjectivity from disciplinary debates and cultural phenomena adjacent to traditional studies of the individual.

The books in the series are useful for advanced-level undergraduate and postgraduate students, researchers and lecturers in psychology and other related disciplines such as cultural studies, geography, literary theory, philosophy, psychotherapy, social work, and sociology.

Most recently published titles:

Rethinking Education through Critical Psychology
Cooperative schools, social justice and voice
Gail Davidge

Developing Minds
Psychology, neoliberalism and power
Elise Klein

Marxism and Psychoanalysis
In or against Psychology?
David Pavón-Cuéllar

FEMALE-PERPETRATED SEX ABUSE

Knowledge, Power,
and the Cultural Conditions
of Victimhood

Sherianne Kramer

 Routledge
Taylor & Francis Group
LONDON AND NEW YORK

First published 2017
by Routledge
2 Park Square, Milton Park, Abingdon, Oxon OX14 4RN

and by Routledge
711 Third Avenue, New York, NY 10017

Routledge is an imprint of the Taylor & Francis Group, an informa business

© 2017 Sherianne Kramer

The right of Sherianne Kramer to be identified as author of this work has been asserted by her in accordance with sections 77 and 78 of the Copyright, Designs and Patents Act 1988.

British Library Cataloguing-in-Publication Data
A catalogue record for this book is available from the British Library

Library of Congress Cataloguing-in-Publication Data
A catalog record for this book has been requested

ISBN: 978-1-138-21108-7 (hbk)
ISBN: 978-1-138-21109-4 (pbk)
ISBN: 978-1-315-45361-3 (ebk)

Typeset in Bembo
by Apex CoVantage, LLC

CONTENTS

FIGURES AND TABLE

Figures

Table

ACKNOWLEDGEMENTS

This book is a product of many research endeavours, many conversations and debates over coffee and wine, and many chance meetings that have left lasting imprints on both my heart and my mind. The contributions to this book thus reach far beyond the four corners of my little writing space, and I would like to take the opportunity to thank all those extraordinary people in my life that influenced the shape and life of this text. First, I have been fortunate enough to receive various grants from the University of the Witwatersrand, the Faculty of Humanities and the National Research Foundation, all of which made my research endeavours possible. I am so grateful for these contributions to my work, and I hope that I have made good use of these resources. I want to thank Professor Ian Parker for offering me the opportunity to write this book and for providing me with invaluable feedback in the early stages of the writing process. I also want to thank Elizabeth Rankin, Russell George, Eleanor Reedy, Alex Howard, Kristin Susser, Donna Moore and Autumn Spalding on the editorial, project management and marketing teams for my book – you all assisted me so effortlessly at every stage of the write-up. My colleague and dear friend, Professor Brett Bowman – over the last decade you have given so much of your intellectual spirit. As my supervisor, you always provided indispensable advice and stood firmly by my side to meet every research-related challenge. As my colleague and mentor, you have guided me, supported me, and advocated for me, envisioning a research potential in me long before I could. As the first reader of this text in its original form of my Doctorate, you gave so much time, energy, and life to the various conceptualisations and ideas taking shape, and I am so grateful for all of the wisdom that you shared so generously with me. To my parents, Peter and Arlainé, thank you for a lifetime of encouragement. You have constantly and unwaveringly supported my academic journey and provided me with sound advice and reassurance when I have felt uncertain. Thank you to my brother, Justin, and my sister, Bianca, for being my most ardent supporters and for showing me how to dream big through your own work. My lifelong friends, Olivia, Jade, Julie, Tenielle, Hayley, Claudia, and Shani, thank you for all the wine, coffee, lunch, and running dates that helped to get me through this — it is so meaningful to have you by my side at every milestone. Thank you to my best friend and best legal advisor, Marc, for always so selflessly giving of your time. To my colleagues, Clare and Aline, thank you for the writing retreats, the hours of diagram drawing to make sense of my ideas, and the friendship throughout the writing process (and beyond). To my partner in everything, Jean-Claude. Your intellectual insight and brilliant mind have contributed so much to the thinking behind this book, and behind my academic career in general. You are endlessly patient and supportive, and I am so blessed to be able to share my life with a person of your calibre. Thank you for your wisdom, for your love, and for you. Finally, this book could not exist without the various people that came forward with their stories. Thank you for giving life to this text and for sharing your lives so openly.

INTRODUCTION

Female-perpetrated sex abuse (FSA) has recently become the object of increased interest in the international academic literature (Gannon & Rose, 2008; Kramer, 2010; Kramer & Bowman, 2011; Sandler & Freeman, 2007, Vandiver & Kercher, 2004). While some global work has provided broad overviews of general female sex abuser characteristics, manifestations, and circumstances—and to a lesser extent, specific case studies—to date, there is very limited academic information about FSA victims (McMahon, 2011). Likewise, the media is currently peppered with images and stories of women who have committed a variety of sex crimes; however, the victims of these women are mostly invisible. The visibility of FSA victimhood is largely contingent on the cultural, social, and historical conditions in which an FSA event takes place. The 'problem' of FSA victimhood is illustrated in this text through the use of specific examples from South Africa that are mirrored, compared, and contrasted to global FSA incidents. The political landscape of South Africa provides an interesting entry point into understanding victimhood as it occurs at the intersection of multiple and contesting fragments of identity comprised of race, class, ethnicity, gender, and sexuality.

The unfathomable nature of FSA victimhood is particularly significant in a country such as South Africa, where trauma and victim discourses are frequently embedded in almost daily reports of child sex abuse, rape, and sexual violence (Jewkes & Abrahams, 2002). Additionally, the country's promotion of a national human rights discourse (The Bill of Rights of the Constitution of the Republic of South Africa, 1996) recognises that every citizen has the right to be treated humanely. In so doing, this discourse inadvertently acknowledges that every citizen – regardless of gender, sexuality, or race – is capable of being subject to inhumane victimisation. This is further amplified by post-Apartheid crises framed as drivers of victimisation such as xenophobia, the crime wave, the HIV/AIDS pandemic, and the failure of democracy to erase the fissures, violence, and sufferings of Apartheid (Boehmer, 2012). However, despite the fact that the country is finely tuned to a history of suffering and abuse, and ongoing inequalities that are often flagged as vehicles for sexual and gender-based violence, FSA victims in South Africa, and globally, continue to remain unfathomable. This, regardless of the fact that sexual abuse and rape have recently been re-defined by the South African legal system to include males as potential victims and females as potential perpetrators. Whilst this definition is not yet entirely pervasive in the public imagination, it has, at least in the case of South Africa, been reconceptualised as such in various legal documents (Minister for Justice and Constitutional Development, 2007). It thus becomes increasingly important to explore this apparent tension. How and why do victims of FSA remain virtually invisible within widespread constructions of trauma and victimhood? In response to this question, this text attempts to surface the discursive coordinates by which persons involved in FSA are able or unable to occupy a victim subject position. Consequently, this process attempts to reveal the way conditions of possibility for such a subject position are contoured.

Given the often shameful and sensitive nature of sexual abuse, many victims resist reporting the incident, and numerous sexual offences go undetected. This is even more significant in cases of female abusers, where reporting is likely to be less accurate due to gender stereotypes, research limitations, and professional biases (Freeman, 1996; Giguere & Bumby, 2007) made possible by a vast network of widely circulated gendered discourses that imply that female-perpetrated sex crimes are unlikely. FSA is therefore often registered as obscene conduct rather than as sexual assault by legal systems across the globe, and so the extreme disparities in the reported prevalence rates between male and female sex abusers are often misleading (Bourke, 2007; Denov, 2003). This discrepancy is exacerbated by definitional problems associated with the term 'obscene conduct' which, at least in the United States of America, refers to any verbal, pictorial, written, or behavioural phenomena deemed immoral or indecent. This vague description, coupled with the facts that it is not necessarily sexual and that obscenity has no standard legal definition (Hatch, 2012), results in very ambiguous reporting patterns for FSA. Nonetheless, there are some international indications of FSA prevalence. The percentage of FSA cases across all reported sexual abuse is 10.7% in Canada (Peter, 2008), 2% in New York (Sandler & Freeman, 2007), and 1%

to 8% internationally (Denov, 2003). These percentages increase up to 58% when victim self-reports are taken into account (Denov, 2003; Strickland, 2008), although this may depend upon the definitions used in self-report studies. The self-reports identified by Denov (2003) are based on large-scale qualitative and quantitative analyses of six American studies which included surveys of both female and male college students who were exposed to sexual abuse during childhood, as well as data representing surveys conducted on convicted male rapists and sex offenders to detail their sexual victimisation backgrounds. Self-reports indicated being subject to a range of FSA behaviours including oral, vaginal, and anal penetration; sexual molestation, and sexual coercion. Despite these self-reports, legal, medical, and psychological experts continue to insist that female sex crimes are rare regardless of the fact that "when various individuals are surveyed about their sexual victimization experiences, the incidence of female-perpetrated sex crimes is often higher and much more variable" than expected (Giguere & Bumby, 2007, p. 2). While we know that only 17 of the 2,759 incarcerated sentenced female offenders have been categorised as sexual abusers in South Africa (Department of Correctional Services, 2011), there is no 'evidence-based' indication of South African FSA prevalence rates as per victims' self-reports.

The question therefore arises as to what accounts for the continued invisibility of FSA victimhood and, in turn, how and in what ways self-identified victims construct their victimhood. Foucault (1978) provides an important framework for beginning to respond to this question. In his *History of Sexuality*, Foucault (1978) argues that sexuality is a privileged site in the historical production of the human subject. He uses the term 'apparatus of sexuality' to denote a system of relations between particular elements that are comprised of "discourses, institutions, architectural forms, regulatory decisions, laws, administrative measures, scientific statements, philosophical, moral and philanthropic propositions" where the non-discursive elements make up the institutionalised structures, and all utterances and behaviours informed by this apparatus make up discursive practices (Foucault, 1980, p. 194). Foucault (1978) argues that sexuality and the self are both products of historicised and institutionalised discursive practices which function as forms of knowledge that are relayed and circulated through modern power. Here, power refers to all those apparatuses of knowledge imbedded in religious, political, economic, and legal practices, and the organised hierarchical cluster of relations between them such that subjects and social practices are both the vehicles for and the effects of power (Digeser, 1992). For Foucault (1978), this power/knowledge coupling emerges at a particular historical and cultural moment and operates to produce and regulate bodies, constitute subjects, and reify sexualities.

Foucault's (1978) *History of Sexuality* is indispensable for any investigation of how subjects are constituted and in what ways this constitution is subject to the power/knowledge coupling. The unique nature of FSA is that it is constituted at the intersection of gender (female), sexuality (sex), and several forms of power (abuse). Foucault (1978) does not foreground theorising about gender, and thus using only his theoretical framework would compromise the important role of gender in any critical engagement with gendered abuse. It is therefore necessary to complement Foucault's (1978) account of power, production, and subjection with Butler's (1989, 1999, 2004) work on gender-identity formation. Butler's (1989, 1999, 2004) gender theory is of particular relevance given its emphasis on gender performativity as a driver of both the reproduction of and resistance to heteronormative gendered constructions. Accordingly, the use of Foucauldian theory as a primary framework will be complemented by, and at times pitted against, theories on the hegemony of masculinity (Bartky, 1988; Connell, 1993; Hearn, 2004); postmodern feminist deliberations on sexual violence (Anderson, 2007; Anderson & Doherty, 2007; Cahill, 2001; Cohen, 2014; Doherty & Anderson, 2004; Gavey, 1989, 2012, 2013; McCaughey & King, 1995); and Butler's (1989, 1999, 2004) theory of performativity, all of which provide specific examples of the way that sexuality and gender are socially constituted. The aforementioned theories are all based on poststructuralist conceptualisations of the subject and seek to demonstrate the limits of available and circulated discursive categories (Miller, 1998). This overall theoretical framework allows for a demonstration of how deeply engrained constructions and regulations of sexuality and gender render particular objects of knowledge (such as FSA victimisation) (un)thinkable. This hybrid theoretical framework is useful for a conversation about the ways that the subjection of the individual to various cultural, material, and historical discourses and conditions produces and/or limits particular possibilities for the FSA victim subject position, and in turn restricts possibilities for sexuality, gender, and identity (see Figure I.1).

By exploring the intersections between power, sexuality, and gender in the production of FSA victimhood, this text aims to reveal the ways that power/knowledge provides the discursive coordinates by which FSA victims are able or unable to occupy a victim subject position. Consequently, this text intends to expose the role of modern power in the way victimhood is able to be produced or not be produced in a particular historical and cultural moment and, in turn, call for a more complex, variable, and dynamic understanding of both gender and sexuality as instruments and effects of modern power.

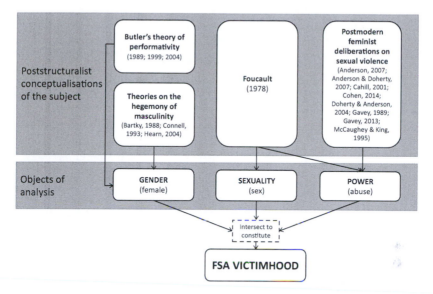

FIGURE I.1   Hybrid theoretical framework used to explore FSA victimhood

Where are the victims?

Despite the current increased academic interest in FSA, there remains a sense of disbelief and doubt amidst the general public and within the legal and mental health care domains concerning FSA (Giguere & Bumby, 2007; Kramer & Bowman, 2011; Lawson, 2008). Inconsistent patterns of interest amongst different professionals are typical in the area of sexual abuse. Given the sensitive nature of the subject, denial and suspicion are common reactions that have characterised the history of sexual abuse research and practice. For example, sexual violence as a real and relevant research subject was only consolidated and broadly taken up in the 1960s, at which time previous misdemeanours such as sexual coercion and sadism were categorised as sexual violence. Even women, the most emphasised category of vulnerability in the current discursive framework for sexual violence, escaped the victim 'surveillance radar' prior to the 1970s (Fisher & Cullen, 2000). The production of sexual violence as a category of knowledge set off a very gradual interest in the area; however, particular segments of society continue to rely on discourses that exclude certain acts, such as marital rape and the rape of sex workers, from the category of sex abuse (McMahon, 2011). In fact, most sexual violence incidents are still frequently framed by the public in terms of typical myths and 'types', such as the indisputably (often black) male aggressor, the female victim who precipitated her attack with her seductive dress code or excessive alcohol consumption, and/or the likelihood of the perpetrator being a stranger rather than an acquaintance (Du Mont, Miller, & Myhr, 2003; Muehlenhard & Kimes, 1999). Furthermore, sexual violence is defined strictly in binary terms – between men and women, between the public and the private space, and between victim and perpetrator (Richardson & May, 1999). These binaries, made possible by widely circulated global gendered and racialised discourses that uphold masculine-feminine gender and black-white race dichotomies, result in limited definitions for sexual abuse, which in turn result in fewer reports of incidents. This means that both sexual abuse prevalence rates and the ability to occupy a victim status is always somewhat contingent on historical and cultural conditions (Fisher & Cullen, 2000) as well as what is deemed socially appropriate within these conditions (Richardson & May, 1999). For example, rape was previously defined exclusively as requiring vaginal penetration, limiting rape victims to women and girls. This cohort was then further constrained because self-identified sexual abuse experiences could only be classified as sexually violent if the description thereof mirrored the normative constructions of sexual crime. Thus, women subjected to an act of sexual violence rarely occupied a victim subject position unless their experiences echoed legal, medical, and scientific productions of sexual abuse. These productions focused primarily on non-consensual penile-vaginal penetration, resulting in most other forms of sexual violence remaining invisible (Koss, 1992). Recently, at least in middle- and higher-income contexts, gendered discourses have become slightly less rigid, allowing for broader conditions of possibility for the production of sexual abuse definitions that extend beyond vaginal penetration, thus reconstituting women as sexual agents (Gavey, 2013) and adding men to the list of possible victims in the lexicon of sexual abuse. These men are, however, often associated with homosexuality (Anderson, 2007), thus diminishing the capacity of the male rape victim to occupy any kind of heterosexual position. In addition, Doherty and Anderson (2004) have demonstrated that where men are able to occupy both a heterosexual and male rape victim subject position simultaneously, a 'hierarchy of suffering' is instituted whereby heterosexual men are treated as far more psychologically damaged by rape than their female or homosexual counterparts. This is framed in phallocentric terms whereby, given the apparent penetrability of both women and gay men, rape is constructed as not necessarily traumatic or even different from consensual intercourse for these subjects. Whilst this framework minimises rape experiences for women and homosexual men, the rape of heterosexual men who are discursively organised as impenetrable is also deemed as a departure from hegemonic masculinity and thus has other kinds of implications for these subjects.

The above-mentioned expansion of the sexual abuse catalogue of meanings is evidenced by the surge in research about sexual violence – prior to the 1970s, research on rape was limited to 100 publications in the PsycINFO and Social Sciences Citation databases. This is in acute contrast with Rutherford's (2011) recent literature search of the same databases, which yielded 22,808 publications. This growth has not extended to the production and categorisation of FSA victims (McMahon, 2011). However, given the historical pattern of the gradual increase in the constitution of various forms of sexual abuse (Rutherford, 2011), it is likely that the current academic interest will begin to produce the category and consolidate the research area of FSA victims.[1]

While academic and professional conversations and research concerning FSA are gaining momentum in areas such as the United Kingdom, Canada, and the United States of America, limited work has been conducted in South Africa in this area. The few studies that I have conducted have investigated FSA from South African academic, legal, and mental health care professionals' perspectives (Kramer, 2010), as well as explored self-perceptions of incarcerated female sex abusers (Kramer, 2011) and a number of self-identified victims (Kramer, 2014), to which this particular text primarily responds. These studies demonstrated that South African mental health professionals, academics, and police workers cannot yet fully conceive of a woman that sexually offends (Kramer & Bowman, 2011). Consequently, incarcerated South African female sex abusers receive light sentences and are not considered in need of the comparable levels of rehabilitation that their male counterparts receive. This has the effect of ensuring that FSA continues to be unthinkable, even by the abusers themselves, which inevitably reduces the possibility for the surfacing of their victims (Kramer, 2011). Across these studies, incarcerated female sexual offenders relied heavily on gendered constructions in producing their subject positions such that key markers of femininity such as passivity, victimhood, maternity, and tenderness were emphasised in their descriptions of their crimes. These women therefore seemed incapable of perceiving themselves as anything other than characteristically maternal, nurturing, and feminine, despite being convicted for sex crimes. Other studies have demonstrated that those female sex abusers who have attempted to express themselves through discourses that are not solely reliant on heteronormative constructions of femininity are most often silenced by 'expert' discourses that draw on dominant understandings of men and women and ensure that "women are relegated to limiting, narrow frames of reference" (Denov, 2003, p. 312). These 'expert' discourses, usually grounded in legal and mental health institutions, explicitly mute the voices that may provide counter-knowledge and alternative discourses for the expression of sexuality and gender in this context. Sexual violence is then to a great extent socially determined, and so certain behaviours escape public, legal, and medical attention simply by virtue of their nonconformity to 'normative' understandings of violence (Muehlenhard & Kimes, 1999). These studies imply the need to understand how such 'escape' is possible at the intersection of gender and sexuality. This implication is also a noteworthy academic advance as very little work on FSA has been conducted from a critical or constructionist perspective, and to date there are no international (McMahon, 2011) and only my one South African study (Kramer, 2014) that takes FSA victimhood as an object of analysis.

A number of recent studies have focused on the characteristics of victims sexually abused by a female (see Faller, 1987; Sandler & Freeman, 2007; Vandiver & Kercher, 2004; Vandiver & Walker, 2002; Wijkman, Bijleveld, & Hendriks, 2010). However, most of the work on FSA typically reasserts proposed FSA typologies that are more often than not based on the very gender constructions FSA would seem to subvert. The current literature base is primarily comprised of research on small samples of female sex offenders, proposals for various FSA typologies, and suggestions for interventions and treatments (see Elliot, 1994; Gannon & Cortoni, 2010; Hislop, 2001). Additionally, these studies are based on information provided by the abusers rather than the victims, and remain focused on victim demographics based on statistical data. While this generalised information is an important means of understanding patterns of victim abuse in FSA, it does not meaningfully engage with the discursive dimensions of FSA victimhood that make the object of its description possible (see Bowman et al., 2015). Such engagement may provide novel and alternative understandings of gender and sexuality. It is likely that the academic and public invisibility of FSA victimhood is based on the circulation of gendered, sexualised, and criminal discourses that imply that FSA is both improbable and harmless (Denov, 2001). By exploring how power produces a speaking FSA victim subject as a function of particular social and historical conditions, the current critical text attempts to understand the politics of the FSA victim literature. This is particularly accomplished by using a Foucauldian understanding of the subject as constituted by and within language and power. Thus, victimhood does not pre-exist language and power, but rather it exists only in as much as it is constructed by social, psychological, and scientific paradigms as an object of knowledge (Butchart, 1997). In this text, I therefore take discourse and material conditions, as they circulate within forms of power, as targets for understanding how, under certain historical and social conditions, a particular category of victimhood is produced. In so doing, this text, while specific to FSA victimology, also provides innovative understandings of the gendered and sexualised human subject.

Finally, because "sex is seen not just as a means of biological reproduction nor a source of harmless pleasure, but, on the contrary . . . as the central part of our being [including more perverse and 'problematic' parts of our being], the privileged site in which the truth of ourselves is to be found" (Weeks, 1981, p. 6), engaging in conversation about FSA victimology represents a strategic point of entry into understanding the way sex, gender, and identity intersect to produce a form of modern social transgression that, constituted through discourse, is itself an instrument and effect of power (Foucault, 1981). The counter-knowledge surfaced in this text aims to contribute to critical accounts of the way that power/knowledge produces, reifies, and naturalises human subjects through technologies of sexuality, and how psychological theory and practice have been instrumental in this reification process. At this point, it is important to note the predicament that I faced in compiling this manuscript. Given my objective to identify particular discursive coordinates as a means to (re-)produce FSA victimhood, this text is centred on the con-struction of a specific object of knowledge, and in doing so is itself a relay for power and knowledge. Throughout this book, I treat FSA victimhood as a discursively emergent object and as a historical product. However, if this text aims to make visible FSA victimhood and thus, in some sense, contrib-ute to its 'invention', then how can the object be understood outside of its own constitution? More specifically, the acts of investigation, exploration, and examination not only surface the object of knowledge (Bowman & Hook, 2010), but they also serve to solidify, define, make visible, and thus reify a particular phenomenon as a psychological and scientific object of knowledge. Through this inescapable reification process, I perform the very discursive function I critique, and so this text inevitably also defines, demarcates, and limits the parameters of FSA victimhood. In fact, the use of the FSA acronym (and later others, such as CSA to abbreviate child sex abuse) further supports this discursive delimitation. The text cannot, therefore, be extracted from the body of human science from which it departs and to which it will contribute new possibilities for the production of FSA and victimhood.

Note

1 A key paradox to this text is that it cannot be extracted from the body of human science knowledge from which it departs, and it will thus form part of the emerg-ing apparatus of discourses, scientific statements, and theoretical propositions that give rise to the productive possibility of FSA victimhood. It is recognised that this text thus contributes to the production of the FSA victim category.

References

Anderson, I. (2007). What is a typical rape? Effects of victim and participant gender in female and male rape perception. *British Journal of Social Psychology, 4*(1), 225–245.

Anderson, I., & Doherty, K. (2007). *Accounting for rape: Psychology, feminism and discourse analysis in the study of sexual violence.* London: Routledge.

Bartky, S. L. (1988). Foucault, femininity, and the modernization of patriarchal power. In I. Diamond & L. Quinby (Eds.), *Feminism and Foucault: Reflections on resistance* (pp. 93–111). Boston, MA: Northeastern University Press.

The Bill of Rights of the Constitution of the Republic of South Africa. (1996). *Government Gazette, 378*(17678), Chapter 2.

Boehmer, E. (2012). Permanent risk: When crisis defines a nation's writing. In E. Mengel & M. Borzaga (Eds.), *Trauma, memory, and narrative in the contemporary South African novel: Essays* (Vol. 153) (pp. 29–46). Amsterdam: Rodopi.

Bourke, J. (2007). *Rape: A history from 1860 to the present.* London: Virago Press.

Bowman, B., & Hook, D. (2010). Paedophile as apartheid event: Genealogical lessons for working with the apartheid archive. *Psychology in Society, 40,* 64–82.

Bowman, B., Stevens, G., Eagle, G., Langa, M., Kramer, S., Kiguwa, P., & Nduna, M. (2015). The second wave of violence scholarship: South African synergies with a global research agenda. *Social Science & Medicine, 146,* 243–248.

Butchart, A. (1997). Objects without origins: Foucault in South African socio-medical science. *South African Journal of Psychology, 27*(2), 101–110.

Butler, J. (1989). Foucault and the paradox of bodily inscriptions. *The Journal of Philosophy, 86*(11), 601–607.

Butler, J. (1999). *Gender trouble.* New York, NY and London: Routledge Press.

Butler, J. (2004). *Undoing gender.* London: Routledge.

Cahill, A. J. (2001). *Rethinking rape.* Ithaca, NY: Cornell University Press.

Cohen, C. (2014). *Male rape is a feminist issue: Feminism, governmentality and male rape.* New York, NY: Springer.

Connell, R. W. (1993). The big picture: Masculinities in recent world history. *Theory and Society, 22*(5), 597–623.

Denov, M. S. (2001). A culture of denial: Exploring professional perspectives on female sexual offending. *Canadian Journal of Criminology, 43*(3), 303–329.

Denov, M. S. (2003). The myth of innocence: Sexual scripts and the recognition of child sexual abuse by female perpetrators. *The Journal of Sex Research, 40*(3), 303–314.

Department of Correctional Services. (2011). *Women per crime category.* Retrieved from www.dcs.gov.za/AboutUs/StatisticalInformation.aspx

Digeser, P. (1992). The fourth face of power. *The Journal of Politics, 54*(4), 977–1007.

Doherty, K., & Anderson, I. (2004) Making sense of male rape: Constructions of gender, sexuality and experience of rape victims. *Journal of Community and Applied Social Psychology, 14*(2), 85–103.

Du Mont, J., Miller, K. L., & Myhr, T. L. (2003). The role of "real rape" and "real victim" stereotypes in the police reporting practices of sexually assaulted women. *Violence Against Women, 9*(4), 466–486.

Elliott, M. (Ed.). (1994). *Female sexual abuse of children.* New York, NY: Guilford Press.

Faller, K. C. (1987). Women who sexually abuse children. *Violence and Victims, 2*(4), 263–276.

Fisher, B. S., & Cullen, F. T. (2000). Measuring the sexual victimization of women: Evolution, current controversies and future research. *Criminal Justice, 4*, 317–390.

Freeman, M. (1996). Sexual deviance and the law. In I. Rosen (Ed.), *Sexual deviation* (3rd ed.) (pp. 399–451). New York, NY: Oxford University Press.

Foucault, M. (1978). *The history of sexuality: An introduction.* Canada and New York, NY: The Penguin Group.

Foucault, M. (1980). *Power/knowledge: Selected interviews and other writings, 1972–1977.* New York, NY: Random House LLC.

Foucault, M. (1981). The order of discourse. In R. Young (Ed.), *"Untying the text": A post-structuralist reader* (pp. 48–78). London and Boston, MA: Routledge & Kegan Paul Ltd.

Gannon, T. A., & Cortoni, F. (Eds.). (2010). *Female sexual offenders: Theory, assessment and treatment.* West Sussex: John Wiley & Sons.

Gannon, T. A., & Rose, M. R. (2008). Female child sexual offenders: Towards integrating theory and practice. *Aggression and Violent Behaviour, 13*(6), 442–461.

Gavey, N. (1989). Feminist poststructuralism and discourse analysis: Contributions to feminist psychology. *Psychology of Women Quarterly, 13*(4), 459–475.

Gavey, N. (2012). Beyond "empowerment?" Sexuality in a sexist world. *Sex Roles, 66*(11–12), 718–724.

Gavey, N. (2013). *Just sex? The cultural scaffolding of rape.* New York, NY: Routledge.

Giguere, R., & Bumby, K. (2007). *Female sexual offenders.* Silver Spring, MD: Center for Sex Offender Management.

Hatch, O. G. (2012). Fighting the pornification of America by enforcing obscenity laws. *Stanford Law and Policy Review, 23*(1), 101–118.

Hearn, J. (2004). From hegemonic masculinity to the hegemony of men. *Feminist Theory, 5*(1), 49–72.

Hislop, J. (2001). *Female sex offenders: What therapists, law enforcement and child protective services need to know.* Ravensdale, WA: Idyll Arbor.

Jewkes, R. K., & Abrahams, N. (2002). The epidemiology of rape and sexual coercion in South Africa: An overview. *Social Science & Medicine, 55*(7), 1231–1244.

Koss, M. P. (1992). The underdetection of rape: Methodological choices influence incidence estimates. *Journal of Social Issues, 48*(1), 61–75.

Kramer, S. (2010). *Discourse and power in the self-perceptions of incarcerated South African female sex offenders.* Unpublished Masters thesis. University of the Witwatersrand, Johannesburg.

Kramer, S. (2011). "Truth", gender and the female psyche: Confessions from female sexual offenders. *Psychology of Women Section Review, 13*(1), 2–8.

Kramer, S. (2014). *Surfacing (im)possible victims: The role of gender, sexuality and power in constructing the conditions of possibility for victims of female sex abuse.* Unpublished PhD dissertation. University of the Witwatersrand, Johannesburg.

Kramer, S., & Bowman, B. (2011). Accounting for the "invisibility" of the female paedophile: An expert-based perspective from South Africa. *Psychology and Sexuality, 2*(3), 1–15.

Lawson, L. (2008). Female sexual offenders' relationship experiences. *Violence and Victims, 23*(3), 331–343.

McCaughey, M., & King, N. (1995). Rape education videos: Presenting mean women instead of dangerous men. *Teaching Sociology, 23*(4), 374–388.

McMahon, S. (2011). *Changing perceptions of sexual violence over time*. Harrisburg, PA: VAWnet. Retrieved from www.vawnet.org/applied-research-papers.html

Miller, P. A. (1998). The classical roots of poststructuralism: Lacan, Derrida and Foucault. *International Journal of the Classical Tradition, 5*(2), 204–225.

Minister for Justice and Constitutional Development. (2007). *Criminal law (Sexual offences and related matters) amendment bill*. Republic of South Africa: Creda Communications.

Muehlenhard, C. L., & Kimes, L. A. (1999). The social construction of violence: The case of sexual and domestic violence. *Personality and Social Psychology Review, 3*(3), 234–245.

Peter, T. (2008). Exploring taboos: Comparing male- and female-perpetrated child sex abuse. *Journal of Interpersonal Violence, 24*(7), 1111–1128.

Richardson, D., & May, H. (1999). Deserving victims? Sexual status and the social construction of violence. *The Sociological Review, 47*(2), 308–331.

Rutherford, A. (2011). Sexual violence against women: Putting rape research into context. *Psychology of Women Quarterly, 35*(2), 342–347.

Sandler, J. C., & Freeman, N. J. (2007). Typology of female sex offenders: A test of Vandiver and Kercher. *Sexual Abuse: A Journal of Research and Treatment, 19*(2), 73–89.

Strickland, S. M. (2008). Female sex offenders: Exploring issues of personality, trauma, and cognitive distortions. *Journal of Interpersonal Violence, 23*(4), 479–489.

Vandiver, D. M., & Kercher, G. (2004). Offender and victim characteristics of registered female sexual offenders in Texas: A proposed typology of female sexual offenders. *Sexual Abuse: A Journal of Research and Treatment, 16*(2), 121–137.

Vandiver, D. M., & Walker, J. T. (2002). Female sex offenders: An overview and analysis of 40 cases. *Criminal Justice Review, 27*(2), 284–300.

Weeks, J. (1981). *Sex, politics and society: The regulation of sexuality since 1800*. Essex and New York, NY: Longman Group Limited.

Wijkman, M., Bijleveld, C., & Hendriks, J. (2010). Women don't do such things! Characteristics of female sex offenders and offender types. *Sexual Abuse: A Journal of Research and Treatment, 22*(2), 135–156.

PART I

Surfacing (im)possible victims

1

FEMALE-PERPETRATED SEX ABUSE

An object of power/knowledge

Female-perpetrated sex abuse has recently emerged as an object of scientific inquiry and is gradually gaining momentum and visibility in various fields of study. This chapter traces this emergence by first thinking through definitional and construct-related issues in relation to sexual abuse generally, and then by identifying previous studies and their theoretical and practical implications in the FSA area more specifically. In so doing, an overview of current typological and aetiological FSA formulations is provided. Through the identification of the function of gender and sexuality in underwriting these formulations, the chapter outlines reasons for the continued conceptualisation of FSA as both rare and innocuous. It furthermore emphasises how engrained and widely circulated discourses on men, women, and children continue to delimit the sexual and gender lines in which FSA is thinkable. The chapter concludes with a proposal for how these theoretical formulations, embedded in gender and sexual discourses, give shape to South African specific aetiologies and typologies in the disciplines of psychology and the social sciences more broadly.

Sex abuse: vague constructs and varied meanings

Sex abuse has been variously defined. These definitions are malleable enough to include a number of apparently different types of abuse such as sexual coercion, sexual victimisation, rape (attempted and completed, marital, date, acquaintance, punitive), assault, molestation, forced intercourse, sexual harassment, trafficking, verbal sexual threats, stalking, forced fondling, overt and threatening sexual advances, extrafamilial, intrafamilial and mixed sexual abuse, pornographic use of sexual material, exhibitionism, and voyeurism (Barth, Bermetz, Heim, Trelle, & Tonia, 2013; Finkelhor, 1979, 1984; Fisher & Cullen, 2000; Koss, Heise, & Russo, 1994; Russell, 1983; Wyatt & Peters, 1986). Furthermore, these definitions are contested according to their 'fit' to a particular academic, scientific, legal, or political agenda. Thus, in some cases sex abuse is defined broadly to include non-contact *and* contact abuse (which may or may not include penetration and forced intercourse), whereas in other cases the definition is narrowed to exclude non-contact (Barth et al., 2013; Wyatt & Peters, 1986). Additionally, different forms of sexual violence have been studied and theorised in isolation from one another, resulting in divergent definitions that lack integration (Gidycz, 2011). Sex abuse is also differentiated from other forms of sex crimes if it occurs with a child. Thus, child sex abuse (CSA) would involve abusive sexual activities with a child whereby the child's perpetrator has maturational, age, or authoritative advantage. However, again there are multiple definitions for CSA with little agreement across disciplines, theories, and the broader field of sex abuse. Arguments concerning the age of both perpetrator and victim, peers as perpetrators, the child's ability to consent, and whether exposure to sexual images can be considered abusive, are some of the key controversies that have continued to make securing a global CSA definition impossible (Finkelhor, 1994; Wyatt & Peters, 1986).

The lack of clear and distinct sex abuse definitions and their endless mutations and reproductions according to different temporal and cultural contexts is testament to the fluidity of the sex abuse construct. In fact, across the course of history, sex abuse definitions have had a mutually constitutive relationship with prevalence rates whereby an apparent increase in sex abuse victims has led to the adaptation of sex abuse definitions. This has consequently widened the scope of sex abuse and therefore allowed for a further increase in prevalence rates. The abundance of different definitions across the area of sex abuse thus directly impacts on the statistical representation of sex abuse prevalence (Wyatt & Peters, 1986). This pattern is evident in FSA whereby the current academic focus on the phenomenon has resulted in a seemingly increased FSA prevalence rate and, in turn, a production of discourses concerning FSA. A key example would be the recent adaptation of the South African Criminal Law (Sexual Offences and Related Matters) Amendment Act (Minister for Justice and Constitutional Development, 2007), which was rewritten to include women as potential sexual perpetrators and men as potential victims. As indicated by the Institute for Security Studies (2015), in effect, this

Amended Act constructed a range of 'new' sex offences, rendering any comparison of prevalence rates before and after the Act's adaptations futile. In addition, the use of a broad category termed 'sexual offences' cannot account for the multifarious, blurred, and often contradictory sub-categories that this overall classification is supposed to represent, and thus trends reported based on this category are meaningless.

Finkelhor (1994) suggests that increased sex abuse prevalence rates are merely due to an increase in public awareness. However, public consciousness is dependent on circulated popular, scientific, or political discourse, which suggests that awareness-raising is directly impacted by any discursive framework applied to sex abuse definitions. This is reflected in Finkelhor's (1994, p. 49) claim concerning CSA in the early 1990s:

> The past 20 years have seen a revolution in public and professional knowledge about child sexual abuse. Most of the prevailing beliefs of a generation ago concerning its nature and prevalence have turned out, in the light of subsequent research, to be wrong or greatly oversimplified. But the knowledge is neither complete nor fully disseminated. In the context of such a rapid revolution, new myths or oversimplifications have undoubtedly been adopted in place of the old.

CSA is often only reported during late adolescence or adulthood, despite the average age of its occurrence being earlier. This demonstrates how, with increased access to circulated discourse, children (or rather now adults) are able to construct their experiences as abusive retrospectively. This is evidenced by the tendency of adults reportedly abused as children to justify their late reporting with claims that they only started to understand the seriousness or abusive nature of the situation when they became older, and often only as a result of media exposure or a conversation with someone older (Schaeffer, Leventhal, & Asnes, 2011). Given that sex abuse is replete with 'discourses of damage' (Levett, 1990), the identification of a particular experience as sexually abusive simultaneously results in the occupation of a victim subject position. This echoes Furedi's (1998) claims that victimhood is dangerous not so much in that victimisation results in emotional or physical suffering, but rather in its capacity to be identity-defining. This victim identity is then further reinforced by social codes that insinuate that an experience of victimisation should be invested with special (non-normative) meanings. CSA is thus a powerful example of the way that historical and social conditions and discourses align to produce sexual violence as an intractable experience for the subject and, in turn, an object of psychological and scientific study.

In a similar fashion, the term rape has been subject to a number of revisions. In its early conception, rape simply referred to the act of a man (usually a stranger) forcibly penetrating a woman without her consent and was thus viewed as a crime of masculine power (Fisher & Cullen, 2000; Koss, 1992). This view was most likely an outcome of Koss and colleagues' (1987) early study on sexual victimisation, which resulted in the widely circulated hypothesis that sexual aggression is the result of masculine hostility (Gidycz, 2011). Consequent definitions of rape therefore bound femaleness to victimhood (see Koss et al., 1994) and emphasised early feminist sociocultural theories of rape. Rape was understood as an outcome of patriarchy, the social control of women and masculine expressions of dominance through female-targeted violence (Muehlenhard & Kimes, 1999; Murnen, Wright, & Kaluzny, 2002). In fact, the women's liberation movement ironically created the conditions of possibility for the construction of rape as an effect of patriarchal power and female vulnerability. This was particularly with regards to the transformation of rape from a personal and private incident to a public and political one. The creation of a public forum and agenda for rape prevention by second-wave feminists resulted in scientific inquiry and historical analyses into the area, thus allowing for the conceptualisation of rape as a key concern for women, who were now constructed as an increasingly vulnerable population. Given that many of these historians and scholars formed part of the feminist movement, rape was produced as an inevitability in women's and girls' lives (Rutherford, 2011). This has resulted in three decades of rape research being devoted to women's safety and thus primarily focusing on female victimisation and male perpetration. In turn, rape definitions have generated a range of well-established biological and social theories relating to the aetiology of masculine sexual aggression (Weiss, 2010). Significantly, these feminist theories, amongst others, were also key to the surfacing of girls and women as objects of knowledge to be scientifically analysed and documented. This shift resulted in endless 'revisions' of established 'truths' about women and contributed to female-focused psychological questions and theories that, in effect, meant women became increasingly surveilled sexual subjects (Worrell & Etaugh, 1994).

Later, as a result of increased feminist scholarship and legal reforms in the area, the definition of rape was broken down into typologies (marital rape, date rape) so that it was no longer confined to strangers, and it was expanded to include forms of penetration other than the penile-vaginal penetration type so that both heterosexual and homosexual rape, and all of their oral and anal variants, were made possible. Variations on the ability to consent were also included in the broadened definition so that contingencies were made for unconscious, mentally disabled, mentally ill, or intoxicated victims, as well as other elements of force such as psychological and physical coercion (Fisher & Cullen, 2000; Koss et al., 1994). However, these extensions and variations have resulted in the use of a range of words associated with sexual victimisation to describe the experience of rape (sexual assault, sexual battery, criminal sexual conduct) (Koss, 1992), thus blurring the concept further. More significantly, the term 'rape', with all of its 'new' and various meanings, gave rise to counterclaims from critics who argue that the term is now too broad and has thus produced a phantom epidemic of rape incidents (Koss, 2011). These critics argue that if rape were determined by victims' perceptions as opposed to laws and statutes that are over-inclusive, the rape prevalence rates would be massively reduced. Consequently, seminal researchers such as Koss (1985, 2011) have been severely criticised for conducting research that demonstrates that, despite the broad definition of rape, self-reports continue to show that rape is under-reported.

It is only very recently that the term has been re-defined to include males as potential victims and females as potential perpetrators. In South Africa, this reconceptualisation has been implemented at the level of the legal system, although this has not yet permeated entirely into public consciousness (Minister for Justice and Constitutional Development, 2007). The same cannot be said for international standards – in the United States of America, the Federal Bureau of Investigation (FBI) continues to define rape as the non-consensual penile penetration of a woman (Federal Bureau of Investigation, 2004). Even so, its reconceptualisation in South Africa, coupled with the constant (and dramatic) adaptations to the term 'rape', is a prime example of how both sexuality and violence are dynamic and socially produced, serve a particular function in history, and are given particular weight because they are mobilised as an outcome of new research. Additionally, with each reconceptualisation, the criteria for both perpetration and victimisation shift (Muehlenhard & Kimes, 1999), thus ensuring that more and more social bodies become subject to regulatory surveillance mechanisms. This unfolding of definitions and increase in scope of the possibilities of sex abuse is evident in the ebb and flow of crime reporting.

More recently, postmodern feminists such as Ann Cahill (2001) have criticised the second-wave feminist construction of rape as a metaphor for male dominance in patriarchal cultures. She further dismisses more liberal feminist understandings of rape as gender-neutral and argues that gender and sexual constructions cannot be ignored in the way that rape has been produced and reproduced. Cahill (2001) thus calls for an understanding of rape as an 'embodied' experience whereby sexuality and gender are central to its possibility. Further, rape, sexual violence, and sex abuse are political and powerful because they shape social productions of both the female and male body (Martin, 2002) and, in turn, demarcate well-defined and constrained possibilities for victimhood and perpetration. Whilst we may no longer view women solely as passive and inescapable recipients of sexual violence and men as merely active and aggressive instruments of their inevitable sex drives, sex abuse and violence are still embedded in strong heterosexually driven discourses that imply that rape is something that happens to women, and often a particular type of woman (chaste, vulnerable, and usually white). Whilst sex abuse is now open to multiple contestations and academic and political debates, the continued discursive framing of sexual violence in heteronormative terms means that certain kinds of sex abuse will fall outside of these parameters (Gavey, 2013) and will thus remain unlikely, unfathomable, and sometimes completely invisible.

The emergence of female-perpetrated sex abuse

> Theoretical linkages between sexual aggression and masculinity, or hypermasculinity . . . are so well established in the ways in which rape and sexual assault have been conceptualized over the years that to envision men as victims (or women as aggressors) requires a conscious bracketing of preconceived notions about both sexual violence and gender.
>
> *(Weiss, 2010, p. 276)*

Sex abuse discourses are rooted in constructions of the male aggressor and the female victim, and sexual violence has historically been essentialised as a masculine behaviour emanating from a 'natural' or innate aggressive sex drive (see Gidycz, 2011; Koss, Gidycz, & Wisniewski, 1987). Traditional sexual and gender codes endorse the image of an oversexed dominant male and an unassertive female succumbing to the male's needs, thus maintaining the legitimacy, 'normality', and social acceptance of male-to-female sexual coercion (Murnen et al., 2002). As a response, existing sexual victimisation programmes aim to decrease vulnerabilities in women and aggressive tendencies in men (Gidycz, 2011; Koss et al., 1994), without any consideration of alternative interventions. Sex abuse is thus constructed as a predominantly male activity and sex abuse victims are treated almost exclusively as objects of male sexual violence. In turn, FSA is considered rare, trivial, and harmless (Denov, 2001), and the FSA victim remains mostly invisible. These prevailing discourses are central to most understandings of sex abuse, including those of the medical system, the legal system, the media, and the scientific literature – and consequently the popular imagination. Of course, this relationship is bidirectional such that the prevailing discourses in the popular imagination further reinforce the medico-legal discourses. In addition, these discourses are strengthened by scientific and psychological studies that acknowledge the existence of FSA yet continue to rely on statistics that demonstrate that it is nonetheless rare (Cooper, Swaminath, Baxter, & Poulin, 1990; Davin, Hislop, & Dunbar, 1999; Higgs, Canavan, & Meyer, 1992). However, these studies are in direct conflict with self-reports that have led to suggestions that FSA is, in fact, "not rare, but rather under-recognized" (Denov, 2001, p. 306) – a suggestion that provides at least a platform for beginning to uncover the discursive coordinates that contour the conditions of FSA victimhood. This disparity results in conflicting prevalence rates of female sex abusers which, in some cases, range from 1% to 8% in research conducted directly with female sex abusers, as opposed to the approximately 58% reflected in victim self-reports (Denov, 2003). This discrepancy was reflected in a study conducted by Denov (2003), which attempted to address questions concerning FSA prevalence where sex abuse broadly included all forms of unlawful sexual contact, assault, and/ or penetration. Specifically, the former rate reflects official law enforcement reports of offenders in America, the United Kingdom, and Canada, whereas the latter percentage reflects self-reports by both female and male victims collected from child abuse hotlines, college surveys, and self-identified victims undergoing therapeutic treatment. Whilst Denov's (2003) observations are important, it is equally significant to note that self-reports tend to fluctuate according to the definition used. In South Africa, only 0.6% of all currently incarcerated sentenced female offenders have been categorised as sex crime offenders (Department of Correctional Services, 2011), with total cases amounting to 215 over the last decade (Department of Correctional Services, 2013). More importantly, despite international recognition that sub-Saharan Africa has some of the highest sexual abuse prevalence rates worldwide (Barth et al., 2013) and South Africa's research, medical, and judicial institutions' focus on vulnerable populations, trauma, sexual violence, and victimhood, South African FSA victims are not at all represented as a category in the country's health and criminal justice statistics. As a consequence, there is no robust statistical information available concerning South African FSA victims.

Despite the continued debate about both the prevalence and nature of FSA, there is currently an increased scientific interest in the area (Lawson, 2008). The possibility for the construction of FSA as a category of sexual violence arose in the late 1970s as a result of sex abuse becoming a central social issue. It was also due to the debates accompanying several variants of the feminist view that male aggression and a dominant male sexuality lead to female sexual victimisation. Even so, research on FSA continues to be limited to a few sporadic studies. More significantly, most studies remain focused on the abusers, and this has resulted in limited research being conducted on FSA victims directly (McMahon, 2011). The few studies that have focused directly on FSA victims are either based on sexual coercion and/or abuse within lesbian relationships (Renzetti, 1992; Waterman, Dawson, & Bolagna, 1989), or they indicate national data concerning male victims of FSA (Mendel, 1995; Tjaden & Thoennes, 2000; Weiss, 2010) or survey-based self-reports by daughters concerning their sexually abusive mothers (Rosencrans, 1997). Whilst the above-mentioned studies do begin to surface the FSA victim, they are all based on Euro-American data that most likely will not resonate with the more diverse and multicultured contexts (such as South Africa) that make up a greater portion of the globe. In addition, all of these studies are restricted to quantitative data that cannot present detailed FSA victimhood experiences. More recently, Ristock (2003) interviewed victims of interpersonal violence (including sexual violence) in lesbian relationships. Significantly, Ristock's (2003) study draws on discourse analysis to explore data gathered through interviews and focus groups, thus providing in-depth insights into female sex crimes. This is especially regarding the power dynamics inherent in these crimes and how sexual violence continues to be negotiated in gendered and dichotomised terms. However, given the study's broad focus on interpersonal violence and narrow focus on lesbian relationships, only a small part of this study is devoted to actual FSA. Similarly, Girshik (2002) explores female-to-female sexual violence by paying special attention to how these instances challenge and disrupt heteronormative laws in the justice system and heteronormative practices in the social provider system. Whilst both of these studies go a long way to visibilise FSA victims, they remain restricted to female victims without considering the possibility of male victims.

The continued exclusion of FSA victims (and especially male FSA victims) from social scientific study reflects the way that instruments and effects of modern power, represented through discourse, materiality, and history (Hook, 2001), limit historical and social conditions and discursive possibilities for the construction of the FSA victim. Thus, while female sex abusers have recently been produced as real criminal subjects that sexually coerce men, children, and other women, the objects of their coercion remain nameless, uncategorised, and therefore peripheral to the scientific and psychological discourse on sexual violence. The current increased awareness of FSA is a slight move away from the previous outright denial of female sex crimes, especially with regards to rape (Freeman, 1996). Again, this is evidence of the way objects of social knowledge shift according to historical and social conditions. In a similar respect, the expansion of surveillance of new subjects in recent years means that new possibilities for deviance emerge such that contemporary definitions of men, women, and sexuality may provide the discursive conditions for the production of FSA victimhood.

FSA as an object of knowledge in academia emerged in the 1980s (see Finkelhor & Russell, 1984). One of the earliest studies involved the development of a proposed outline of female sex abuser characteristics based on research conducted with a clinical sample of 40 female sex abusers (Faller, 1987). The sample was comprised of mostly young white women who had sexually abused victims that were most often white females ranging from six to seven years old. This study found that most of the women had abused multiple victims who were usually their own children. It also found that up to 73% of the sample had co-offended with a male accomplice. However, the study detailed instances of single-parent maternal child sex abuse, too. In addition, Faller (1987) found that the most often reported type of abuse was group sex. Some of the abusers in Faller's (1987) sample were reported to have poor psychological, social, or mental functioning, whilst others abused various substances or were exposed to sexual abuse during their own childhood.

Faller's (1987) study initiated a gradual interest in FSA as a significant and potentially complicated type of sex crime. By the early 1990s, Finkelhor (1994, p. 46), a seminal author in the field of CSA, stressed that "there is no question that women do sexually abuse children, that much of this abuse goes undetected, and that, until recently, it received little professional attention". However, the focus on female sexual perpetration was, and still remains, on CSA. A possible explanation for this narrow focus is that, due to the discursive conditions of possibility for the construction of the female sex offender as 'predisposed' to child molestation, a woman who sexually abuses a child is still conceivable despite the horror it invokes in the public imagination. In addition, the child has historically been constructed as innocent, naïve, and vulnerable (Ariès, 1973) as well as desexualised and passive (Bhana, 2006), which presents the child with the opportunity to more readily occupy a victim subject position (Kramer, 2011). This is emphasised by the construction of the modern family as child-centred and contemporary cultural values that assert that the child requires ongoing protection (Carrington, 1991). It is also more difficult to deny female child sex abusers because women, by virtue of their gender stereotyping, have more access to children, and are also most likely to be engaged in child-rearing activities such as bathing and dressing (Vandiver, 2006). However, given the global and gendered discursive practices which imply that women are victims of male aggression, the possibility of a female sexually abusing an adult male challenges our current conceptualisation of the gendering of females (Kramer, 2010). Furthermore, discourse on gender implies that masculinity is incompatible with a victim identity, leaving men that are subjected to any form of violence, sexual or other, a limited range of discursive possibilities to make sense of their experiences (Eagle, 2006). Nonetheless, there has been some documentation of adult male victims of FSA. For example, the National Violence Against Women Survey conducted on 8,000 American men and 8,000 American women recorded a number of men that had been raped by their intimate female partners. These victimised men were less likely than their female counterparts to report the incident or to seek assistance (Tjaden & Thoennes, 2000). Likewise, the most recent National Crime Victimization Survey, conducted nationwide in 2010 in the United States, found that up to 9% of sexual assault and rape victims are men. Significantly, 54% of these sexual offences were perpetrated by men and 46% by women (Weiss, 2010). In South Africa, the most recently available crime report by the South African Police Services (2012) indicates that up to 11.4% of all sexual offence victims in 2012 were adult males. This number increased to 28.7% in 2014, with men between the ages of 30 to 34 and 40 to 44 experiencing the largest proportion of these offences (Statistics South Africa, 2016). These statistics, although not necessarily representative given reporting biases in sexual offences, nonetheless show at least the conditions for surfacing a potentially sexually transgressive woman that victimises a man.

The denial of FSA, and in fact all types of sex abuse, is likely to be pronounced in sub-Saharan Africa, where patriarchal discourses and silencing of transgressions of taboos are common features of daily life (Shumba, 2001, 2004). This trend is exacerbated by gendered practices whereby, at least in many 'lower-income contexts', women are regarded as victims and passive recipients of male authority. This is typically reinforced by discourse that endorses the male breadwinner; women and children as dependents; and masculine aggression as normative, which in turn promotes gender inequalities, economic disparities, and women's reliance on their male partners for food, shelter, and their children's financial access to education (Jewkes, Levin, & Loveday, 2003). These discourses serve as vehicles for the continued denial of FSA. Given these issues and the resultant limit on the range of available subject positions for both abusers and victims of FSA, in South Africa particularly (Kramer, 2010) and across the globe more broadly, it is useful to identify and explore the discursive conditions of possibility for the production of an FSA victim subject position. The coordinates provide at least the beginnings of counter-knowledge rooted in attempts to offer new understandings of the way that gender, sexuality, and victimhood are related and produced through modern forms of power. This counter-knowledge will, of course, be surfaced through the identification of theories, discourses, and scientific knowledge that stand in opposition to it.

Female-perpetrated sex abuse: current scientific formulations and limitations

The primary challenge in researching female sexual abusers is that, compared to their male counterparts, very few women that commit sex crimes are actually convicted and sentenced (Atkinson, 1996). Furthermore, at least in the case of South Africa, those that are convicted tend to receive extremely light sentences, with over half (51.2%) of all convicted female sexual offenders receiving sentences of zero to six months' incarceration across the last decade (own calculations based on raw data from the Department of Correctional Services, 2013). This is the case despite the provisions set up by the South African Criminal Law Amendment Act 105 of 1997, which imposed mandatory minimum sentences for particular crimes, including rape. This amendment resulted in offenders convicted for rape and other sexual offences receiving longer sentences (Neser, 2001). This has not, however, extended to female sexual offenders. It is therefore difficult to access these women and their victims. Additionally, as a result of engrained and socialised beliefs that men are aggressors and women are victims, reports of FSA are often dismissed by police and mental health services (Brockman & Bluglass, 1996) or withdrawn by the victims themselves. Significantly, convicted perpetrators are likely to embody behaviours reflective of legal definitions of sexual violence (Muehlenhard & Kimes, 1999). This limits FSA research samples to circulated (and thus gendered) understandings of sexual violence, making the ability to draw conclusions difficult and findings repetitive of earlier traditional scientific studies that promote heteronormatively gendered interpretations of sex crimes. For example, those women that are apprehended and researched by the justice and mental health systems tend to have committed a sex crime against a child and are most often an accomplice to a male offender (Vandiver, 2006). This does not necessarily indicate that women only act under the coercion of a male accomplice and that they only sexually abuse children. Rather, given the conventional construction of the male aggressor and the female victim, women acting outside of this 'acceptable' framework for their gender are often ignored, dismissed, or denied (Kramer, 2010). This results in conditions for reporting being limited to these 'mainstream' FSA events, and in consequence, research being conducted only on those female sex abusers that have male accomplices and child victims – thus narrowing the already constrained scope and range for describing female sex crime.

The current FSA literature is marked by discrepancies, controversies, and inconsistencies. Most studies that attempt to answer questions on the 'nature' of FSA are often left with more questions. While some studies claim that female sex abusers are a heterogeneous group (Brockman & Bluglass, 1996; Gannon, Rose, & Ward, 2008; Sandler & Freeman, 2007), others have attempted to construct generalisable profiles, typologies, and classifications (Sandler & Freeman, 2007; Vandiver & Kercher, 2004) in order to identify any existing similarities across female sex abuser samples. Over the last two decades, the traditional means of understanding FSA has been to place the abuser into one of three categories.

Typologies

These FSA categories were originally constructed from a study conducted by Mathews, Matthews, and Speltz (1989) whereby qualitative data from interviews conducted with 16 convicted American female sex offenders were used inductively to develop FSA typologies. The first constructed category is the *Lover/Teacher* type, who is framed as rarely inflicting physical harm and viewing herself as a sexual educator. Her victims are primarily male children and adolescents (Higgs et al., 1992). Both prepubescent and adolescent male victims seldom view an incident of FSA as traumatic, and subsequently criminality in this category of abusers is often overlooked. The tendency to disregard perpetration in these cases is in line with the prevailing belief that sexual interaction with an older woman provides "the ultimate educational experience" (Travers, 1999, p. 36). This has obvious implications for the ability of prepubescent and adolescent males to occupy an FSA victim subject position. Portrayals of these 'sexual educators' are often eroticised and men are constructed as always desiring and enjoying sexual interaction with a woman, even under forced circumstances (Bourke, 2007), and so it is unlikely that these subjects are able to take up a victim position.

The second category is the *Predisposed* type. These women are constructed as arising from "a long transgenerational familial history of sexual abuse . . . [resulting in] intense feelings of worthlessness" (Higgs et al., 1992, p. 136). This type is "described as very emotionally disturbed, psychotic or sociopathic" (Travers, 1999, p. 35). Such pathologising discourse is often used by the medico-legal system as a means to justify and rationalise FSA crimes. It also fails to recognise that there are cases where sexually transgressive women were raised in homes with positive emotional climates or come from families that have never been abusive (Bourke, 2007). Even more significant is that these pathological explanations are rarely applied to male sex abusers, whose actions are rather understood as emanating from a 'naturally occurring' inclination towards sexual aggression. This contrast is a key example of the heteronormative gendering of sex abuse.

Finally, the third category encompasses the *Male-Coerced* type, which describes female sex abusers that act under the often-abusive instruction of a male accomplice (Higgs et al., 1992). In most of these cases, the female abuser is romantically involved with or married to the male abuser, and the victim is usually a family member or their own child. Resonating with second-wave feminist understandings of rape as a metaphor for patriarchal dominance, the accomplice type is most commonly tied to 'battered woman syndrome' and is often accompanied by justifications that such perpetrators are "victims of a patriarchal rule and should be absolved of responsibility for their actions" (Bourke, 2007, p. 228). While the majority of these relationships are described as abusive, there are cases where the female accomplice is an aggressive rather than a coerced participant (Vandiver, 2006). Either way, this typology reinforces traditional sexual and gender codes and roles, which implicate females as passive victims of male sexual aggressors (Denov, 2003). It also ensures that accountability for the sexual violence is placed on the male rather than the female accomplice, and that the female perpetrator is reorganised into the female victim (Bourke, 2007). Consequently, the persons subjected to the sexual violence are perceived exclusively as objects of male sex abuse. For Denov (2003), the use of female victimisation and passivity to explain FSA ultimately relies on the same traditional heteronormative gendered discourses that constrain the possibilities of generating alternative conceptual frameworks for these women's behaviours. In turn, these constraints limit the possibilities for persons subjected to FSA. Although there is a growing public and academic interest in the area, it appears that the image of a woman capable of sexual perpetration is still implicitly unfathomable and is sustained as one of the greatest taboos in many areas (Travers, 1999). Female sexuality remains a culturally ambivalent subject (Denov, 2003) and, in consequence, female-perpetrated sexual violence becomes a highly sensitive and uncomfortable issue that ensures "deliberate avoidance" (Bourke, 2007, p. 215).

More recently, Nathan and Ward (2002) have further differentiated the *Male-Coerced* type with the category *Male Accompanied – Rejected/Revengeful* to indicate female sex abusers that experience anger or jealousy in their primary relationship and act with a male accomplice without being subject to his forceful coercion. Additionally, another two categories, namely the *Experimenter/Exploiter* type and the *Psychologically Disturbed* type, have been added to the list of FSA typologies (Vandiver & Kercher, 2004). However, the *Experimenter/Exploiter* characteristics appear to resonate with the *Lover/Teacher* type, and the same can be said of the *Psychologically Disturbed* and *Predisposed* types, these overlaps thus rendering distinct categorisation redundant.

In much the same way that the aforementioned typologies contribute to the production of FSA as an object of human science and psychological knowledge, so do various studies that aim to delineate categories of, risk factors for, and statistics describing it. A study conducted by Vandiver and Kercher (2004) demonstrates that distinct categories for FSA do exist; however, it was emphasised that further clarification for each is required. These constructed categories include *heterosexual nurturers* (coincides with the original *Lover/Teacher* type) who target only male victims with an average age of 12; *noncriminal homosexual*[1] *offenders* who target mainly female victims with an average age of 13 and are the least likely group to have subsequent arrests; *female sexual predators* who have the highest number of offences and rearrests and tend to victimise younger males; *young adult child exploiters*, the youngest group of offenders, who target both male and female children (average age of seven); *homosexual criminals* who target females with an average age of 11 years old for prostitution and forced sexual performance rather than for sexual assault; and finally, *aggressive homosexual offenders* who tend to target older female victims (average age of 31). Vandiver and Kercher's (2004) study was specific to a population in Texas and thus Sandler and Freeman (2007) replicated the method with a population of female sex abusers in New York. Their study indicates that female sex abusers are a 'heterogeneous group' and that while there do indeed seem to be distinct categories, these were different from the categories indicated by Vandiver and Kercher (2004). Sandler and Freeman's (2007) categories include *criminally-limited hebephiles*, where hebephelia indicates this group's exclusive preference for pubescent children (between 11 and 14 years old); *criminally-prone hebephiles* who are more likely than the former group to be rearrested and have multiple offences; *young adult child molesters* who target young (average age of four years) male and female victims; *high-risk chronic offenders* who have the highest number of arrests and tend to target young female children; *older non-habitual offenders* who have no other offences outside of the registered sex offence; and *homosexual child molesters* who target young female victims exclusively. Similarly, Gannon and colleagues (2008) developed a descriptive model of the FSA offence process that provides a concise and detailed explanation for female sex crime by taking into account the cognitive, affective, behavioural, and context contributing factors. However, this study was conducted on a small English sample of 22 female sex abusers, which limited applicability to other contexts. It also does not address FSA victims directly.

Despite these research limitations, the outcomes of these studies have provided the building blocks for a discursive construction of the female sex offender. Research conducted on the basis of the aforementioned categories maintains that most female sex abusers are white women aged between 20 and 30 who target both male and female victims that are usually younger than 12 years old. Additionally, solo abusers are more likely to engage with a male victim, while abusers acting with a male accomplice seem to target female victims (Vandiver, 2006). The victims are also usually their own children or a close relative or acquaintance (Vandiver & Kercher, 2004). Key risk factors constructed as part of these categories include "social isolation, maladaptive coping strategies, passive or aggressive personality styles, and mental health problems" (Gannon et al., 2008, p. 370). Previous studies that attempt to 'profile' the female sex abuser have implied some limited characteristics of the victims of abuse (see Faller, 1987; Nathan & Ward, 2002; Sandler & Freeman, 2007; Vandiver & Kercher, 2004; Vandiver & Walker, 2002; Wijkman, Bijleveld, & Hendriks, 2010). These studies suggest that the victims are usually young, ranging from three to seven years old (Faller, 1987; Vandiver & Walker, 2002). Additionally, up to 75% of FSA victims are relatives or acquaintances of the abuser (Wijkman et al., 2010). There also seems to be little gender discrepancy with victim choice – female sex abusers tend to abuse males and females equally (Vandiver & Kercher, 2004). However, the race of the victims tends to be less equivalent across racial categories, with up to 94% of victims being white in Faller's (1987) study. It should, however, be noted that this study took place in Michigan, which, at the time, was comprised of up to an 80% white majority in the population (U.S. Census Bureau, n.d.). Rather than any reflection of 'real' victim numbers or of perpetrator characteristics, these results may then be due to the hegemony of whiteness in these areas, and the consequent treatment of white children as the primary objects of surveillance and intervention (Bowman, 2010).

These patterns and demographic descriptions are useful in outlining which conditions, types, and risks are thinkable in the context of FSA victimhood; however, they have been produced from research with incarcerated perpetrators in Global North contexts that are dissimilar from South Africa and other Global South countries.[2] Indeed, while South African female sex offenders reflect the global pattern pertaining to age at time of offence, with 71.6% of offenders being below 35, the racial patterns are in stark contrast with the vast majority of apprehended offenders being black (61.9%) rather than white (own calculations based on raw data from the Department of Correctional Services, 2013). This said, statistics based on race in South Africa should be interpreted with caution, as this large percentage of black female sexual offenders may simply be reflective of the demographic composition in

South Africa, where black citizens make up 79.5% of the population (Statistics South Africa, 2011). These particular racial patterns may also be proxies for other risks linked to violence, such as socioeconomic inequality, unemployment, poverty, and gender inequality (Kramer & Ratele, 2012). These proxies are an outcome of the same gender and sexual discourses that are being surfaced and examined in this text.

Aetiologies

There are also a number of common theories of aetiology in the literature. These aetiological proposals further construct the female sex abuser by providing psychological explanations for her existence. The construction of a psychological or social 'cause' for FSA provides a particularly powerful condition for its possibility. For example, some abusers' behaviours are constructed as a function of socioeconomic disadvantage or poverty. This is particularly pronounced in mothers who sell their children for prostitution. These women are characterised as both impoverished as well as compromised by an underprivileged lifestyle. Other perpetrators are either framed as mentally ill, or as hypersexual, or as suffering from menstruation or hormonal effects. These theories are, however, limited, as most of the evidence is developed from samples that are already in psychiatric care for other reasons. Female sex abusers are also far more likely to be sent for psychiatric help than their male counterparts (Bourke, 2007) and are also often regarded as alcoholics or drug abusers (Vandiver, 2006). More recently, Latent Profile Analysis has been used to typologise female sex offenders based on measurements of their personalities. These studies argue that female sex abusers have high levels of psychopathology, and variants of the level and type of psychopathology interact with other features (exposure to sex abuse, substance abuse) to create different types of abusers (see Miller, Turner, & Henderson, 2009; Turner, Miller, & Henderson, 2008). Significantly, none of the above-mentioned typologies or theories of causation locate the responsibility for the abuse entirely within the abuser. The fault seems to have an indirect frame of reference rather than the more direct one that is often applied to male sex abusers. FSA is likely to be justified according to a variety of aetiologies, whereas male sex abusers are often simply understood as being unable to control their apparent natural tendency to be sexually aggressive (Denov, 2003). Such heteronormative gendering is grounded in reified understandings of masculinity that provide both an explanation and a defence for apparently 'typical' male behaviours (Connell & Messerschmidt, 2005). In fact, the hegemony of masculinity supporting these gendered discourses is the very mechanism through which men and women are continuously positioned in unequal relation to one another, and thus support the constructed image of violent masculinity.

In a similar vein, a notable absence in the FSA literature is any reference to paraphilia (in relation to general FSA) and paedophilia (in relation to female-perpetrated CSA). In stark contrast to the research based on male sex abuse, there appears to be little allusion to potential sexual psychopathology as a motivating force in FSA. When there are descriptions of sexual motivation, this is never accompanied by psychological terms such as 'paedophiliac' or 'paraphiliac' urges. For example, Beech and colleagues (2009) describe female sexual abusers' distorted cognitions and only briefly touch on sexual motivation and children as sex objects, and they do so without drawing on widely circulated pathologising terms. Gannon and Rose (2008) have also noted this absence and maintain that this is because female sex abusers are less likely than their male counterparts to display paedophiliac interest and tendencies. However, as I have previously argued (Kramer & Bowman, 2011), the classification of female paedophilia would necessitate the acknowledgement that women can be sexually transgressive outside of other motivating forces such as male coercion, substance use, or mental illness. Further, paedophilia, as an attraction to prepubescent children, is so antithetical to the 'natural' maternal and caregiving functions attributed to women that 'exposing' female paedophilia would require a complete reframing of femininity. A male sex abuser motivated by sexual urges only violates the juridical law, whereas a woman acting in the same capacity violates both juridical law and the limits of heteropatriarchy and idealised motherhood. This absence of categorising women as paedophiles is evident despite CSA being the most central object of surveillance and intervention in the FSA research agenda. Thus, whilst the act of both FSA and female-perpetrated CSA may be acknowledged by the academic enterprise, the pathological sexualisation of these acts is notably absent. The invisibility of innate and uncontrollable aggression and/or sexual urges applied to aetiological explanations of FSA echoes a social fabric that cannot yet fully conceive of a woman violating heteronormative gendered and sexual norms.

While FSA typologies and theories of causation are able to demonstrate the ways in which female sex abusers are both similar and different from their male counterparts as well as provide the foundation for understanding potential aetiologies of FSA, their narrow and constrained classifications undermine the heterogeneity that other studies investigating female sex abusers have displayed (Brockman & Bluglass, 1996; Gannon et al., 2008). This is emphasised by self-reports that depict female sex abusers as exhibiting a range of different acts at different times, making it difficult to consolidate these

TABLE 1.1 Female sex offender crimes in South Africa as of 2013 (own calculations based on raw data from the Department of Correctional Services, 2013)

Crime	Frequency	Percent
Rape	53	24.65
Indecent assault	44	20.47
Illegal carnal intercourse	5	2.33
Immoral offences	30	13.95
Attempted rape	2	0.93
Unnatural sexual offences	12	5.58
Indecent exposure	24	11.16
Public pornography	13	6.05
Incest	1	0.47
Intercourse with minor	3	1.40
Living by proceeds from immorality	20	9.30
Bestiality	1	0.47
Pimping	3	1.40
Brothel keeping	4	1.86
Total	215	100.02

Note: Total will not cast due to rounding

behaviours into the above-mentioned categories. Such acts include child sex abuse, non-consensual sexual interaction with adult men, forcing both adolescent and adult men to perform cunnilingus, statutory rape, gang rape, and the raping of incapacitated or unconscious victims (Bourke, 2007). Bourke's (2007) extensive list of identified acts is based on examples from the Global North. In the South African context, the majority of incarcerated female sex offenders are convicted for rape (24.7%) and indecent assault (20.5%) (own calculations based on raw data from the Department of Correctional Services, 2013) (see Table 1.1). However, given the low reporting rate of sexual offences in general and of FSA more specifically (Freeman, 1996; Giguere & Bumby, 2007), as well as the tendency for female sex offenders to receive light sentences (if they are sentenced at all) (Denov, 2001), these data may not necessarily be reflective of all South African FSA events.

Female-perpetrated sex abuse as a category of human science knowledge: what are the implications?

The state of FSA knowledge production clearly shows that binaries such as masculine-feminine and perpetrator-victim are fictions that limit the range of subject positions people may occupy in different contexts. It also disrupts constraining gendered discourses, such as the idealisation of maternity and the sentimentality of motherhood. Bourke (2007, p. 248) emphasises this disruption with the comment that, "nurturing housewife and child abuser may be the same person". Thus, a critical exploration of FSA would expose entrenched gender ontologies which rely on modern power to remain invisible. Given the emerging counter-knowledge that has begun to challenge this invisibility of the female sexual abuser, it is likely that the emergence of an FSA victim subject position may provide an even wider and perhaps different kind of counter-knowledge on gender, power, and sexuality. However, as Weiss (2010, p. 276) reminds us, theories of sexual violence "are so well established . . . over the years that to envision men as victims (or women as aggressors) requires a conscious bracketing of preconceived notions about both sexual violence and gender".

Given that both Global North and Global South research and literature on violence is characterised by a political and academic focus on male violence (and especially male violence against women), shifting the focus to female violence "may serve to obfuscate the violence of male power and patriarchy" and "disrupt discourses that essentialize women and present women as powerless victims" (Kruger, van Straaten, Taylor, Lourens, & Dukas, 2014, p. 463). The current gendered and sexualised political landscape in South Africa, amplified by the recent surge in moral panic about rape and other forms of sexual violence (see Ambramjee, 2013; Bauer, 2013; Evans, 2013; Knoetze, 2013; Swart, 2013), provides an appropriate backdrop for the exploration of the (im)possibility of FSA victimhood. While the very current public, media, and political discursive explosions of interest surrounding sexual violence have provided the conditions of possibility for the emergence of the female sex offender, her victims continue to remain anonymous and invisible. It is therefore the objective of this text to identify the material, political, and historical conditions for the possibility of self-identifying as a victim of FSA in a country (and world) where sexual violence is consistently relayed as a ubiquitous threat to all.

Notes

1 The term 'homosexual' (along with heterosexual and hebephile) is used here to indicate categories listed by Vandiver and Kercher (2004) and Sandler and Freeman (2007). However, I do not intend to replicate the way in which these terms are offered so unproblematically. First, the use of these terms to formulate psychological categories further reifies the hetero-homosexual binary. Second, the way in which these terms are used implies that there is a particular sexual attraction inherent in the act of sexual abuse, which may not necessarily be the case. Finally, and perhaps

most significantly, the utilisation of 'homosexual' to describe a sexual abuse category is pathologising. Whilst homosexuality has not been classified as a mental illness since 1973 (Rich, 1980), this categorisation process does implicitly retain some residue of this pathologising practice.

2 The Global North refers to those countries demonstrating high human development as measured by the Human Development Index and reported in the *Human Development Report*. The Global South is used to refer to those countries and regions that are considered to be 'developing' or 'less developed' as per measures indicated by the Human Development Index and reported in the *Human Development Report* (United Nations Development Programme, 2014).

References

Abramjee, Y. (2013, February 12). Here's what we can do about rape. *Pretoria News*. Retrieved from www.iol.co.za/pretoria-news/opinion/here-s-what-we-can-do-about-rape-1.1468500.html

Ariès, P. (1973). *Centuries of childhood*. New York, NY: Jonathan Cape.

Atkinson, J. L. (1996). Female sex offenders: A literature review. *Forum on Corrections Research*, *8*(2), 39–42. Retrieved from www.cscscc.gc.ca/text/pblct/forum/e082/e082m_e.html.

Barth, J., Bermetz, L., Heim, E., Trelle, S., & Tonia, T. (2013). The current prevalence of child sexual abuse worldwide: A systematic review and meta-analysis. *International Journal of Public Health*, *58*(3), 469–483.

Bauer, N. (2013, February 12). SA: A rape crisis, but no funds or will to fight. *Mail & Guardian*. Retrieved from http://mg.co.za/article/2013–02–12-f.html

Beech, A. R., Parrett, N., Ward, T., & Fisher, D. (2009). Assessing female sexual offenders' motivations and cognitions: An exploratory study. *Psychology, Crime and Law*, *15*(2–3), 201–216.

Bhana, D. (2006). The (im)possibility of child sexual rights in South African children's account of HIV/AIDS. *IDS Bulletin*, *37*(5), 64–68.

Bourke, J. (2007). *Rape: A history from 1860 to the present*. London: Virago Press.

Bowman, B. (2010). Children, pathology and politics: A genealogy of the paedophile in South Africa between 1944 and 2004. *South African Journal of Psychology*, *40*(4), 443–464.

Brockman, B., & Bluglass, R. (1996). A general psychiatric approach to sexual deviation. In I. Rosen (Ed.), *Sexual deviation* (3rd ed.) (pp. 1–42). New York, NY: Oxford University Press.

Cahill, A. J. (2001). *Rethinking rape*. Ithaca, NY: Cornell University Press.

Carrington, K. (1991). Policing families and controlling the young. *Journal of Australian Studies*, *15*(31), 108–117.

Connell, R. W., & Messerschmidt, J. W. (2005). Hegemonic masculinity: Rethinking the concept. *Gender & Society*, *19*(6), 829–859.

Cooper, A., Swaminath, S., Baxter, D., & Poulin, C. (1990). A female sexual offender with multiple paraphilias: A psychologic, physiogic (laboratory sexual arousal) and endocrine study. *Canadian Journal of Psychiatry*, *35*(4), 334–337.

Davin, P., Hislop, J., & Dunbar, T. (1999). *Female sexual abusers*. Brandon, VT: Safer Society Press.

Denov, M. S. (2001). A culture of denial: Exploring professional perspectives on female sexual offending. *Canadian Journal of Criminology, 43*(3), 303–329.

Denov, M. S. (2003). The myth of innocence: Sexual scripts and the recognition of child sexual abuse by female perpetrators. *The Journal of Sex Research, 40*(3), 303–314.

Department of Correctional Services. (2011). *Women Per Crime Category*. Retrieved from www.dcs.gov.za/AboutUs/StatisticalInformation.aspx

Department of Correctional Services. (2013). *Women Sexual Statistics From 20010101 to 20121231*. Unpublished raw data.

Eagle, G. (2006). Masculine victims: A contradiction in terms? *The International Journal of Critical Psychology, 17*, 47–76.

Evans, J. (2013, February 8). Media united in outrage over rape. *Independent Online*. Retrieved from www.iol.co.za/news/crime-courts/media-united-in-outrage-over-rape-1.1467046#.UThgFKLviSo.html

Faller, K. C. (1987). Women who sexually abuse children. *Violence and Victims, 2*(4), 263–276.

Federal Bureau of Investigation. (2004). *Uniform crime reporting handbook*. Washington, DC: U.S. Department of Justice.

Finkelhor, D. (1979). *Sexually victimized children*. New York, NY: The Free Press.

Finkelhor, D. (1984). *Child sexual abuse: New theory and research*. New York, NY: The Free Press.

Finkelhor, D. (1994). Current information on the scope and nature of child sexual abuse. *The Future of Children, 4*(2), 31–53.

Finkelhor, D., & Russell, D. (1984). Women as perpetrators. In D. Finkelhor (Ed.), *Child sexual abuse: New theory and research* (pp. 171–187). New York, NY: The Free Press.

Fisher, B. S., & Cullen, F. T. (2000). Measuring the sexual victimization of women: Evolution, current controversies and future research. *Criminal Justice, 4*, 317–390.

Freeman, M. (1996). Sexual deviance and the law. In I. Rosen (Ed.), *Sexual deviation* (3rd ed.) (pp. 399–451). New York, NY: Oxford University Press.

Furedi, F. (1998). New Britain – A nation of victims. *Society, 35*(3), 80–84.

Gannon, T. A., & Rose, M. R. (2008). Female child sexual offenders: Towards integrating theory and practice. *Aggression and Violent Behaviour, 13*(6), 442–461.

Gannon, T. A., Rose, M. R., & Ward, T. (2008). A descriptive model of the offense process for female sexual offenders. *Sexual Abuse: A Journal of Research and Treatment, 20*(3), 352–374.

Gavey, N. (2013). *Just sex? The cultural scaffolding of rape*. New York, NY: Routledge.

Gidycz, C. A. (2011). Sexual revictimization revisited: A commentary. *Psychology of Women Quarterly, 35*(2), 355–361.

Giguere, R., & Bumby, K. (2007). *Female sexual offenders*. Silver Spring, MD: Center for Sex Offender Management.

Girshik, L. B. (2002) No sugar, no spice: Reflections on research on woman-to-woman sexual violence. *Violence Against Women, 8*(12), 1500–1520.

Higgs, D. C., Canavan, M. M., & Meyer, W. J. (1992). Moving from defense to offense: The development of an adolescent female sexual offender. *The Journal of Sex Research, 29*(1), 131–139.

Hook, D. (2001). Discourse, knowledge, materiality, history. *Theory & Psychology, 11*(4), 521–547.

Institute for Security Studies. (2015). *Africa Check. Factsheet: South Africa's 2014/15 Assault and Sexual Crime Statistics*. Retrieved from https://africacheck.org/factsheets/factsheet-south-africas-201415-assault-and-sexual-crime-statistics/

Jewkes, R. K., Levin, J. B., & Loveday, A. P. (2003). Gender inequalities, intimate partner violence and HIV preventative practices: Findings of a South African cross-sectional study. *Social Science & Medicine, 56*(1), 125–134.

Knoetze, D. (2013, February 8). 150 rapes an hour. *The Star*. Retrieved from www.iol.co.za/the-star/150-rapes-an-hour-1.1466999#.UThg9qLviSo.html

Koss, M. P. (1985). The hidden rape victim: Personality, attitudinal, and situational characteristics. *Psychology of Women Quarterly, 9*(2), 193–212.

Koss, M. P. (1992). The underdetection of rape: Methodological choices influence incidence estimates. *Journal of Social Issues, 48*(1), 61–75.

Koss, M. P. (2011). Hidden, unacknowledged, acquaintance, and date rape: Looking back, looking forward. *Psychology of Women Quarterly, 35*(2), 348–354.

Koss, M. P., Gidycz, C. A., & Wisniewski, N. (1987). The scope of rape: Incidence and prevalence of sexual aggression and victimization in a national sample of higher education students. *Journal of Consulting and Clinical Psychology, 55*(2), 162–170.

Koss, M. P., Heise, L., & Russo, N. P. (1994). The global health burden of rape. *Psychology of Women Quarterly, 18*(4), 509–537.

Kramer, S. (2010). *Discourse and power in the self-perceptions of incarcerated South African female sex offenders*. Unpublished Masters thesis. University of the Witwatersrand, Johannesburg.

Kramer, S. (2011). "Truth", gender and the female psyche: Confessions from female sexual offenders. *Psychology of Women Section Review, 13*(1), 2–8.

Kramer, S., & Bowman, B. (2011). Accounting for the "invisibility" of the female paedophile: An expert-based perspective from South Africa. *Psychology and Sexuality, 2*(3), 1–15.

Kramer, S., & Ratele, K. (2012). Young black men's risk to firearm homicide in night time Johannesburg, South Africa: A retrospective analysis based on the National Injury Mortality Surveillance System. *African Safety Promotion: A Journal of Injury and Violence Prevention, 10*(1), 16–28.

Kruger, L. M., van Straaten, K., Taylor, L., Lourens, M., & Dukas, C. (2014). The melancholy of murderous mothers: Depression and the medicalization of women's anger. *Feminism & Psychology, 24*(4), 461–478.

Lawson, L. (2008). Female sexual offenders' relationship experiences. *Violence and Victims, 23*(3), 331–343.

Levett, A. (1990). Childhood sexual abuse and problems in conceptualisation. *Agenda, 6*(7), 38–47.

Martin, S. E. (2002). Book Review: Rethinking Rape. *Violence Against Women, 8*(7), 901–907.

Mathews, R., Matthews, J. K., & Speltz, K. (1989). *Female sexual offenders: An exploratory study*. Brandon, VT: Safer Society Press.

McMahon, S. (2011). *Changing perceptions of sexual violence over time*. Harrisburg, PA: VAWnet. Retrieved from www.vawnet.org/applied-research-papers.html

Mendel, M. P. (1995). *Male survivor: The impact of sexual abuse.* Thousand Oaks, CA: Sage Publications.

Miller, H. A., Turner, K., & Henderson, C. E. (2009). Psychopathology of sex offenders: A comparison of males and females using latent profile analysis. *Criminal Justice and Behaviour, 36*(8), 778–792.

Minister for Justice and Constitutional Development. (2007). *Criminal law (Sexual offences and related matters) amendment bill.* Republic of South Africa: Creda Communications.

Muehlenhard, C. L., & Kimes, L. A. (1999). The social construction of violence: The case of sexual and domestic violence. *Personality and Social Psychology Review, 3*(3), 234–245.

Murnen, S. K., Wright, C., & Kaluzny, G. (2002). If "boys will be boys," then girls will be victims? A meta-analytic review of the research that relates masculine ideology to sexual aggression. *Sex Roles, 46*(11/12), 359–375.

Nathan, P., & Ward, T. (2002). Female sex offenders: Clinical and demographic features. *The Journal of Sex Aggression, 8*(1), 5–21.

Neser, J. J. (2001). Mandatory minimum sentences in the South African context. *Crime Research in South Africa, 3*(3). Retrieved from www.crisa.org.za/volume3/vvs.html

Renzetti, C. M. (1992). *Violent betrayal: Partner abuse in lesbian relationships.* Thousand Oaks, CA: Sage Publications.

Rich, A. (1980). Compulsory heterosexuality and lesbian existence. *Women, Sex and Sexuality, 5*(4), 631–660.

Ristock, J. L. (2003). Exploring dynamics of abusive lesbian relationships: Preliminary analysis of a multisite, qualitative study. *American Journal of Community Psychology, 31*(3–4), 329–341.

Rosencrans, B. (1997). *Last secret: Daughters sexually abused by mothers.* Brandon, VT: Safer Society Press.

Russell, D. E. H. (1983). The incidence and prevalence of intrafamial and extrafamilial sexual abuse of female children. *Child Abuse & Neglect, 7*(2), 133–146.

Rutherford, A. (2011). Sexual violence against women: Putting rape research into context. *Psychology of Women Quarterly, 35*(2), 342–347.

Sandler, J. C., & Freeman, N. J. (2007). Typology of female sex offenders: A test of Vandiver and Kercher. *Sexual Abuse: A Journal of Research and Treatment, 19*(2), 73–89.

Schaeffer, P., Leventhal, J. M., & Asnes, A. G. (2011). Children's disclosures of sexual abuse: Learning from direct inquiry. *Child Abuse & Neglect, 35*(5), 343–352.

Shumba, A. (2001). "Who guards the schools?" A study of reported cases of child abuse by teachers in Zimbabwean secondary schools. *Sex Education, 1*(1), 77–86.

Shumba, A. (2004). Male sexual abuse by female and male perpetrators in Zimbabwean schools. *Child Abuse Review, 13*(5), 353–359.

South African Police Services. (2012). *Crime Statistics Overview RSA 2011/2012.* Retrieved from www.info.gov.za/view/DownloadFileAction?id=150105.html

Statistics South Africa. (2011). *Mid-Year Population Estimates, 2011.* Retrieved from www.statssa.gov.za/publications/P0302/P03022011.pdf.html

Statistics South Africa. (2016). *Crime Statistics Series Volume III: Exploration of Selected Contact Crimes in South Africa. In-Depth Analysis of Victims of Crime Survey Data 2011–2014/2015.* Retrieved from www.statssa.gov.za/publications/Report-03-40-01/Report-03-40-012015.pdf

Swart, H. (2013, February 15). Will Anene Booysen's brutal rape and murder shake the nation into action? *Mail & Guardian*. Retrieved from http://mg.co.za/article/2013-02-15-00-will-anene-booysens-brutal-rape-and-murder-shake-the-nation-into-action.html

Tjaden, P., & Thoennes, N. (2000). Prevalence and consequences of male-to-female and female-to-male intimate partner violence as measured by the National Violence against Women Survey. *Violence Against Women, 6*(2), 142–161.

Travers, O. (1999). *Behind the silhouettes: Exploring the myths of child sexual abuse.* Belfast, CA: The Blackstaff Press Limited.

Turner, K., Miller, H. A., & Henderson, C. E. (2008). Latent profile analyses of offense and personality characteristics in a sample of incarcerated female sexual offenders. *Criminal Justice and Behaviour, 35*(7), 879–894.

United Nations Development Programme. (2014). *Human Development Report 2014. Sustaining Human Progress: Reducing Vulnerabilities and Building Resilience.* New York, NY: United Nations Development Programme.

U.S. Census Bureau. (n.d.). *Michigan Population Estimate by Age Sex, Race and Hispanic Origin: 1981–1989* [Data File]. Retrieved from www.michigan.gov/documents/8015_26025_7.400(80-89).pdf?20140422014820

Vandiver, D. M. (2006). Female sex offenders: A comparison of solo offenders and co-offenders. *Violence and Victims, 21*(3), 339–354.

Vandiver, D. M., & Kercher, G. (2004). Offender and victim characteristics of registered female sexual offenders in Texas: A proposed typology of female sexual offenders. *Sexual Abuse: A Journal of Research and Treatment, 16*(2), 121–137.

Vandiver, D. M., & Walker, J. T. (2002). Female sex offenders: An overview and analysis of 40 cases. *Criminal Justice Review, 27*(2), 284–300.

Waterman, C. K., Dawson, L. J., & Bolagna, M. J. (1989). Sexual coercion in gay male and lesbian relationship: Predictors and implications for support services. *Journal of Sex Research, 26*(1), 118–124.

Weiss, K. G. (2010). Male sexual victimization: Examining men's experiences of rape and sexual assault. *Men and Masculinities, 12*(3), 275–298.

Wijkman, M., Bijleveld, C., & Hendriks, J. (2010). Women don't do such things! Characteristics of female sex offenders and offender types. *Sexual Abuse: A Journal of Research and Treatment, 22*(2), 135–156.

Worrell, J., & Etaugh, C. (1994). Transforming theory and research with women. *Psychology of Women Quarterly, 18*(4), 443–450.

Wyatt, G. E., & Peters, S. D. (1986). Issues in the definition of child sexual abuse in prevalence research. *Child Abuse & Neglect, 10*(2), 231–240.

PART II

Female-perpetrated sex abuse victimisation

Conditions of (im)possibility

2

MATERIAL, POLITICAL, AND HISTORICAL CONDITIONS FOR GENDER AND SEXUALITY

This chapter begins the work of demonstrating the conditions of possibility for FSA victimhood. In order to achieve this, Foucault's (1978) seminal work, *The History of Sexuality*, is used to structure an argument on how sexuality is subject to particular material, political, and historical conditions. The argument follows Foucault's (1978) formulation of biopower[1] in order to reveal the ways that gender and sexuality are products of the technologies of modern power. This is further supported by Butler's (1989, 1999, 2004) theoretical postulations on gender identity formation and understood in terms of the range of theorised meanings of the hegemony of masculinity (Bartky, 1988; Connell, 1993; Hearn, 2004) in the social determination of gender and sexuality. This framework for exploring the historical and social construction of gender and sexuality exposes the role of the power/knowledge coupling in the making of possible, conceivable, and 'real' subject positions. In addition, the use of Butler's (1989, 1999, 2004) theory on performativity to support this framework provides a clear portrayal of how these subject positions are products of the modern constructions of gender and sexuality and, more significantly, how these positions are reproduced and sustained. The implications of these arguments are presented through the particular examples of sexual 'deviance', female criminality, and male victimhood. These examples underpin the importance of the role of gender and sexuality constructions for the critical analysis of FSA victimhood.

The history of sexuality, gender, and power

This section intends to trace the historical production of gender and sexuality in order to demonstrate how these products are an outcome of the power/knowledge coupling, and the implications thereof. The fundamental assumption of this text rests on Foucault's (1978) conceptualisation of sexuality and, by extension, gender as discursive constructs arising out of historical and institutionalised practices that are both instruments and effects of modern power. Power materialises in the apparatuses of knowledge entrenched in religious, political, economic and legal practices and the organised hierarchical network of interactions between them such that subjects and social practices are both the channels for and the products of power (Digeser, 1992). Discourses emanating from these apparatuses inscribe themselves onto the site of the body, which in turn becomes "a nodal point or nexus for relations of juridical and productive power" (Butler, 1989, p. 601). Foucault (1978) uses the term 'biopower' to indicate that the anchor points for forms, exercises, and strategies of power are populations, or the social body (Genel, 2006). Biopower is thus comprised of "numerous and diverse techniques for achieving the subjugation of bodies and the control of populations" (Foucault, 1978, p. 140). This form of power, emerging at the threshold of modernity, moves through a capillary of networks and relations, and is thus distinct from sovereign power, which is characterised by a monarchy that exerts legal and political influence in a top-down fashion. For Foucault (1980), biopower comprises diffuse points that exist everywhere. Biopower both regulates the social body and is practiced and reproduced by the individual body. There are therefore two poles along which biopower operates, linked together by a network of relations. The first is anamatopolitics, which is centred on the disciplining of the individual body. The second is focused on the monitoring, surveillance, and regulation of the social body or a biopolitics of the population (Foucault, 1978).

The calculus of populations is reducible to the sex of its constituents, and therefore biopower targets sexuality as the lynchpin around which subjectivity and identity are clustered (Cahill, 2000). For Posel (2005), this sexuality within modern society is a political site for the operation of multiple and contesting regulatory and disciplinary effects. Sexuality and gender (which are informed by 'truths' about sexuality) can therefore be more critically appreciated through the understanding of the historical, political, and material conditions that constitute them, and through exploring how sexuality and gender interact with modern power to produce subject positions that have a regulatory function. In line with a Foucauldian understanding of power, both gender and sexuality should be understood as historical and malleable products that have been moulded and continue to be remoulded by biopower. Weeks (1981, p. 288) thus emphasises that the meanings applied to gender and sexuality "are not eternal givens, are not simple products of objective forces outside human control, but are products of human endeavour in the context of given historical circumstances".

Whilst Foucault's (1978) account of the history of sexuality provides an entry point into understanding sexuality, his major blind spot is arguably the differential power/knowledge effects on and of the female and male bodies (Bartky, 1988). Because this text is centred on femaleness in sex abuse, it is important to identify and examine those discursive strategies that produce the female sexual perpetrator and her victims, be they male or female. Thus, whilst a Foucauldian theoretical framework with which to examine sexuality is critical to this text, the application of this framework to the differential effects of modern power upon the gendered body is also important. Butler's (1989, 1999, 2004) gender theory is therefore used to support this. Likewise, given the use of specific examples from the postcolonial context of South Africa in this text, it is equally significant to acknowledge that Foucault rarely engages with how colonialism and imperialism use the site of the colonised body as a means to construct sexuality in colonised contexts (Stoler, 1995). The employment of Foucault's (1978) analysis of the emergence of sexuality as discourse for understanding South African sexuality is therefore problematic, because it runs the risk of reproducing and thus reinforcing the very colonial discourse that reifies nineteenth-century European sexuality and marginalises the effects of colonial discourse on the colonial context and the colonised body. This is not to suggest that Foucault ignores colonialism and racism. In fact, Foucault (1977b) argues that evocations of race and racism have surfaced at different historical periods as social technologies underwritten largely by a biopower that defines who can or cannot be 'human'. Stoler (1995) proposes that Foucault's (1978) appreciation of the incitement of sexuality discourse as both an instrument and effect of modern power is mainly centred on the production of *particular* objects of knowledge, such as the perverse adult, the hysterical woman, and the bourgeois family. Stoler (1995, p. 6–7) argues that these nineteenth-century objects of knowledge could not exist without "a racially erotic counterpoint, without reference to the libidinal energies of the savage, the primitive, the colonized" and that the invention of these particular subjects and objects occurs at the intersection of racial and sexual discourses. Stoler's (1995) recognition that the sexual discourse of the European bourgeois society and the colonised empire were mutually constitutive is important for this text, given the backdrop of postcolonial South African examples and the conditions for sexuality that it implies. Thus, whilst

Foucault's central concerns are privileged throughout the following chapters, they are continuously interrogated by, supplemented with, and juxtaposed against theories that may more fully appreciate the complex intersections of race, power, gender, and sexuality, especially as they emerge in an African and Global South context.

This text thus attempts to follow Terre Blanche's (2002) suggestion that when using Foucauldian frameworks to understand African subject positions, it is important to resist treating the African body as solely a product of European colonisation and rather understand it as performative and productive in its own right. While the sexual discourse of the coloniser and the colonised are mutually constitutive, the African body is constructed by different kinds of gender–sexuality–race intersections that result in a unique object, distinctive from its European counterparts. The objective of this text is therefore to go beyond the limits of Foucault's (1978) work and identify particular articulations of race, sexuality, class, and gender, and their multidirectional and intersecting capacities, to co-construct identity. This objective echoes Collins' (1998) call for the use of intersectionality in the understanding of African identities through the treatment of social class, gender, race, and sexuality as mutually constructing and intersecting systems.

In this text, I also support Butler's (2004) argument that gender and sexuality cannot be defined in binary and rigid terms. Narrow definitions of gender or sexuality that are based on masculine-feminine or hetero-homosexual dichotomies ignore the multiple productive possibilities for gender and sexuality, and foreclose the possibility of interrogating how they have been produced by material, historical, and institutionalised conditions. Moreover, given that productions of (hetero)sexuality inform the very meanings of being male or female, and vice versa, gender and sexuality are often mutually constitutive. Furthermore, the way gender and sexuality are mapped onto the individual body and taken up by the subject has profound macro-level political as well as micro-level relational and subjective effects. Widely circulated discourses on gender and sexuality presented as 'truths' about the social body are imprinted onto individuals such that their identities become instantiations of these truths. Consequently, individuals reproduce and thus maintain these by (re)performing them in social contexts. However, where there is power, there is resistance; and this makes possible the emergence of alternative discourses and a consequential reframing of the overriding apparatus of knowledge into a counter-knowledge. Gender and sexuality are produced through heteronormative constructions, and this has obvious implications for the way that FSA victims are excluded from discourse and the way that these victims frame their experiences, if they are able to frame them at all. The historical and social constitution of gender and sexuality are thus integral to the identification of the current material and cultural conditions that may or may not give rise to FSA victimhood.

The production of gender and sexuality

Foucault's (1978) analysis of sexuality "calls into question classical notions of the universality of truth by establishing the historicity of knowledge" (Rawlinson, 1987, p. 374), thus undermining and disrupting scientific 'fact', 'neutrality', and 'objectivity'. This process produces an alternative language that resists normalising and naturalising systems of 'truth'. By investigating the historical production of sexuality, we demonstrate how and why it is that modern society has understood sexuality as ahistorical, primordial, and natural (Bem, 1993). In light of this, a postmodernist framework is useful as a means to impugn the more radical essentialist conceptualisation of sexuality as an inexorable biological instinct. That is not to say that biological sexuality does not exist, but rather that it "is only a precondition, a set of potentialities, which is never unmediated by human reality" (Weeks, 1981, p. 11). For Foucault (1978), this precondition is bodies and populations.

The widespread belief in modern society has long been that heterosexuality is an ahistorical and biological fact (Bem, 1993), and thus, given its biological nature, it is additionally immutable. In his seminal work, *The History of Sexuality*, Foucault (1978, p. 105) challenges this assumption with the assertion that "sexuality . . . is the name that can be given to a historical construct", a production of modernity, and he therefore tracks the production of sexuality from its roots in the seventeenth century. During this period, sexual discourses and practices were not governed by set laws and regulations produced by a legal system that acted in the name of some natural order. There were also no medical categories available to describe and classify instances of sexual deviancy. Even sexual interaction between adults and children occurred with little consequence (Ariès, 1973). As the institutional character of modern society gradually developed, previous permissive discourses around sex and sexuality appeared to shut down at the level of everyday interaction, and this seemed to be replaced with silence, shame, and taboo. In the eighteenth and nineteenth centuries, a large-scale transformation of what is now the Global North occurred with the shift from a traditional and hierarchical social system to a more individualistic and modern one characterised by industrialisation and capitalism. Power, traditionally embodied in the figure of a monarch, gradually transformed from state-sanctioned sovereign power into disciplinary power, so that it became anonymous and moved through diffuse capillaries and networks that relay the structure of power onto the sites of bodies and populations (Bartky, 1988). Power no longer operated from a singular and identifiable authoritative source, but rather power was everywhere and operated through surveillance, objectification, and subjectification. This rearrangement of power created the conditions of possibility for the emergence of disciplines such as the social sciences and clinical medicine, which in turn provided the conditions for these institutions to invent the modern subject as the target of modern power (Butchart, 1997). Alongside this shift, sexuality took on a new function in "defining and normalizing the modern self" (Halperin, 1998, p. 96), and the human body became rearranged through machineries of power (Foucault, 1978). This occurred particularly through the realms of science, medicine, and the law, which analysed, documented, classified, and diagnosed apparently different forms of sexuality. Foucault (1978, p. 35) thus argues that although sex was exploited "as *the* secret", and the silence and taboo circulating the topic could be interpreted as a repression of sexuality, science was in fact carefully surveilling, documenting, and categorising different forms of hitherto 'corporeal desire' into new coded types of 'sexuality'.

Discourses on sexuality have been reinforced as 'truth' across the last three centuries, making heteronormative monogamy appear a biological reality (Phelan, 1990). Hence, through legal, medical, and scientific discourses, apparently 'normal' standards of sexuality and sexual development came to exist. In this way, the very perversions and abnormalities that were deemed taboo were in fact simultaneously produced and sustained by the discourses on normative sex (Weeks, 1995). The 'truth' about sexuality is therefore produced rather than discovered, and discourse "participates in normalization even as it claims to challenge it" (Phelan, 1990, p. 432). More significantly, the production of this knowledge, and the promotion of it as legal or scientific 'fact', resulted in classification schemes that, when taken up by subjects, ensured the social regulation, and consequently self-regulation, of individuals. The availability of a new and vast scientific discourse allowed for a subjectification of both the human 'mind' and the body which could now be documented, analysed, corrected, and thus regulated (Rawlinson, 1987). Accordingly, Weeks (1981, p. 5) highlights that "sexual behaviour is organised not through mechanisms of 'repression' but through powers of 'incitement', definition and regulation", and it is in this way that discourses contribute to the reproduction of sexuality (Phillips & Jørgenson, 2002).

An apt example is the various revisions attached to the term 'rape' since the early 1970s, and the consequent reactions from critics arguing that these revisions have resulted in the false impression that a rape epidemic exists (Koss, 1992).

However, whilst these counterclaims appear to limit the frame of reference for rape victims, it is their very accusations that ensured the consistent revisions to the term, allowing for additional bodies and subjects to be exposed to analysis, surveillance, and regulation. In fact, Koss (2011), a key figure in the defining and redefining of the theoretical framework for rape and an advocate for definitions that implicate male aggressors and female victims, recently stated,

> I deeply regret that … I thought it was appropriate to defend a research initiative that prevented LGBT[2] people from reporting their experiences of same-sex victimisation and precluded inquiry into sexual aggression perpetration by women and men's sexual victimization.
>
> *(p. 350)*

Koss' (2011) statement thus forms part of the scientific discourse currently in circulation that begins to surface conditions for the redefinition of 'rape'.

Sexual discourse has provided modern power with the means to police and regulate society, and the façade of silence was merely a means of censorship, restriction, and prohibition that formed part of the mechanisms driving the discursive explosion on sexuality through science. Foucault's (1978) conception of 'the perverse implantation' describes the explosion of multiple and unorthodox sexualities, and argues that the production of a variety of abnormal sexualities justifies the use of regulatory measures to document and regulate them. The perverse implantation was thus a key driver of disciplinary power in the eighteenth and nineteenth centuries, particularly given its capacity to compel "figures, scarcely noticed in the past, to step forward and speak, to make the difficult confession of what they were" (Foucault, 1978, p. 39). Thus, rather than treating sexuality as a fixed, stable, natural, or immovable somatic fact, a postmodern framework begins with the assumption that sexuality is a "uniquely modern production" (Halperin, 1989, p. 258). Foucault (1978, pp. 105–106) summarises these points in the following way:

> Sexuality must not be thought of as a kind of natural given which power tries to hold in check, or as an obscure domain which knowledge tries gradually to uncover. It is the name which can be given to a historical construct: not a furtive reality that is difficult to grasp, but a great surface network in which the stimulation of bodies, the intensification of pleasures, the incitement to discourse, the formation of special knowledges, the strengthening of controls and resistances, are linked to one another, in accordance with a few major strategies of knowledge and power.

Sex and sexuality are vehicles for the transmission of modern power, and in this way, sex became the centre of both subjectivity and 'truth'. Sexuality takes on a normalising, productive, and regulatory function – it both produces the subject and ensures that the subject is disciplined, productive, and reproductive (Phelan, 1990). The demands of capitalism necessitate certain healthy and productive subjects (although other subjects must be sick and poor); thus, sexual norms and standards developed through legal and medical technologies are utilised as discursive strategies to ensure a disciplined populace (Dean, 1994). Specifically, exclusive heterosexuality has historically been constructed as that which is both privileged and desired, thus the institutionalised requirement that the biological sex of the body match the gender of one's identity (Bem, 1993). By resisting conformity to the heterosexual imperative, one risks the consequence of being categorised as 'abnormal'. In this way, the heterosexual and procreative couple is constituted as the biological and natural 'norm', and the modern subject is read through the very concept that society appears to repress – sexuality (Winnubst, 1999). Sexuality is therefore a cultural and social product mapped onto the body as a means of social regulation and control (McNay, 1991). The cultural and historical character of the sexualisation of the body is easily demonstrated by turning to examples of the various constructions and codes recorded on the body across cultures and time (Cahill, 2000). For instance, while sexuality in modernity is grounded in the anatomical differences between men and women, or the binary between heterosexuality and homosexuality, sexuality in classical Athens was regulated according to power differentials. In this particular historical period and context, sexual object choices were based on superordinate-subordinate relationships, regardless of gender (Halperin, 1989).

Social regulation occurs through productive rather than through prohibitory power by "imposing a grid of definition on the possibilities of the body" (Weeks, 1981, p. 7). Power is thus relayed in the forms of discipline and surveillance through "examination and insistent observation . . . [and] the medicalization of the sexually peculiar" (Foucault, 1978, p. 44). Power, then, is bound to knowledge and "functions through it and the systems of meaning upon which it rests" (Phelan, 1990, p. 424). However, because modernity is constructed as the age of liberation that provides freedom for the subject, modern power and its objective to control and discipline the body must remain invisible, as taken-for-granted knowledge that we own, as evidence of a sexual selfhood or self-knowledge. This occurs through the individual subject internalising institutionalised disciplinary power and experiencing it as self, rather than social regulation. It is through the masking of modern power as self-knowledge that a permanent state of self-regulation is produced in the individual and, in turn, this self-regulation is celebrated as individualism, the hallmark of modernity and capitalism (Bartky, 1988).

Foucault (1978) argues that sexuality occupies a critical symbolic function rather than represents a biological reality, and these constructions, masked as scientific 'truths', allow institutions such as science, medicine, and psychology a privileged position in the constitution of the modern subject (Miller, 1998). For Foucault (1978), this is particularly with reference to the way language has structured and shaped scientific discourse on biology and sexuality. These objects of study have been constructed as 'fact' by the human sciences, which has implications for the way discourse on sexuality is then taken up and used to structure individual bodies and subjectivities. Values and meanings are constructed by culture and history, and the subjection of the body to these produces the speaking and 'self-identifying' subject (Butler, 1989). In this way, scientific discourse is mapped onto human individuals and thereafter produced and reproduced as self-knowledge through the subject in the act of speaking and performing these 'truths'. Thus, studies in human sciences that purport the unlikelihood of FSA and are supported by institutionalised social-science discourses that circulate constructions of the male aggressor and female victim exclude discourses that would provide at least the coordinates by which a subject could self-identify as an FSA victim. Consequently, individuals that may have been involved in sexual 'transgressions' with a female are unlikely to speak, perform, or self-identify as a victim.

Language has productive power and is thus "the field out of which the figure of 'man' emerges" (Winnubst, 1999, p. 17). The structure of language provides man[3] with his material existence and the subject emerges through the effects of language, which ground individual subjectivity. All individual and social ontologies are therefore effects of signifiers rooted in language systems. Language becomes a site of power through its ability to constitute meaning. For example, gender is "a position constructed in language", and thus femininity, for example, is "a position that can be taken up by men as well as women" (Moi, 2004, p. 842). An understanding of gender as a position in language implies that subjects are free to take up certain positions. However, this apparent freedom is constrained by the materiality of biopower and the discursive limits on gendered and sexualised possibilities for being human therein. Donaldson (1993, p. 651) thus argues that "there is nothing outside gender . . . to be involved in social relations is to be inextricably 'inside' gender". This is made possible by the relay of institutionalised norms onto the individual through disciplinary and pastoral technologies such as the family, the school, and the church.

Gender, families, and patriarchy

For Collins (1998), the family is the primary space where gender hierarchies and heterosexuality are reinforced, and other sexualities are made invisible. It is in this way that the individual replicates institutionalised, gendered discursive practices and thus becomes "a deeply implicated . . . collaborator in the social reproduction of male power" (Bem, 1993, p. 139). Sexuality tends to be organised within the framework of the family particularly because it is through the family that the survival of heteronormativity can be leveraged. As a product of widely circulated domestic discourses, heterosexual marriage becomes "deeply engrained in the social consciousness" (Weeks, 1981, p. 214) and "the heterosexually constituted family . . . [thus becomes] the basic social unit" (Rich, 1980, p. 657). This is made possible through what Foucault (1978) calls the Malthusian unit or the Malthusian couple, whereby prevailing legal, medical, and educational discourses have normalised the child-centred nuclear family as the natural mode for the modern family, thus ensuring the family's adherence to social norms. This adherence guarantees that modern power is able to regulate or police individual bodies through the apparatus of the family (Donzelot, 1979). Family policing is made possible through normative practices whereby larger institutions such as the hospital, school, and legal system make intimate details of family life available for public use, recording, and documentation (Gubrium & Holstein, 1994). Given that "politics, economics, technology are gendered" (Donaldson, 1993, p. 651), availing the details of the family to these institutions, genders the family unit.

Butler (2004) argues that gender regulation in modernity is a function of heterosexist normativity, and that gendered subject positions imply sexual subject positions. Sexual and gender constructions inform one another because heteronormative sexual constructions produce and reinforce gender binaries (Butler, 1999). Butler (2004, p. 13) further argues that "norms encode operations of power" and thus "power emerges in language". Sexual and gendered norms, although sometimes explicit, are, for the most part, implicitly embedded in language such that they are only clearly decipherable in the consequences that they produce. To further develop this argument, gender and sexual assumptions are so entrenched in social discourses, institutions, and individual psychologies that they are able to invisibly reproduce the effects of modern power across generations (Bem, 1993). These norms operate at the nexus of power and knowledge, and thus the organisation of gender and sexuality in turn organise understandings of the social world (Foucault, 1978). Specifically, the organisation of these norms is restricted to dichotomous definitions emphasising the masculine-feminine and hetero-homosexual binaries as the exclusive means of understanding gender

and sexuality. These binaries serve a regulatory function of power that naturalises the hegemony of heteronormativity and forecloses the possibility of
its resistance (Butler, 2004). Given that heteronormative assumptions are key
constructs to the production of the gender hegemony of masculinity, this
dichotomising process thus also sustains patriarchal norms and practices.

The masculine-feminine binary is particularly and strongly consolidated
in social discourse, and thus has the tendency to erode other possibilities in
discursive constructions of gender. The undue focus on feminine versus masculine behaviours in both the public imagination as well as within academia
itself often results in the exclusion of alternative conceptualisations of gender
as fluid and diverse. For example, discussions on femininity are often based
on white Eurocentric, and thus dominant, constructions of the female body.
However, the constituents of femininity and masculinity will vary as they
intersect with other social constructions such as culture, race, and ethnicity
(Shefer, 2010). While some of these racialised or social discourses may be subordinate to the discourse on femaleness, they may be dominant enough in a
given culture such that they have the effect of constituting the female body. In
addition, fundamental sexuality discourses in sub-Saharan Africa do not necessarily have the same contours and effects as those in the Global North, despite
being framed in relation to them. Whilst some South African women may be
excluded from the dominant discourse that relates to the white or colonial
female, they are still measured against this standard (Mohanty, 1988). Woman-
ness (and gender in general) is raced, ethnicised, and cultured through the
power of discourse; however, each articulation of femininity will have varying
degrees of productive power in the social structure (Cahill, 2000). In the context of this text, I follow suggestions proposed by Winnubst (1999) – whilst
Foucault's (1978) analysis of history does not regard the subject through the
lens of sexual difference, it is still possible to use a Foucauldian understanding of the cultural constitution of the social body as a means to understand
gender and other cultural (racial, ethnic, economic) differences by invoking
and accentuating these constructions throughout the text. In light of this, a
Foucauldian understanding of FSA victimhood in both a South African and
a global context requires an appreciation of the forms and effects of various
intersecting discourses that bind gender, sexuality, and power across diverse
and unequal contexts. For South Africa, a country still characterised by the
racialised legacies of colonialism and Apartheid, this is important because the
ability to self-identify as an FSA victim may be conditional on the possibilities that emerge through various cultural domains. For example, under the
Apartheid regime, white children were constructed as vulnerable and thus
subjected to constant surveillance, monitoring, regulation, and intervention

(Bowman, 2010). These practices provided the conditions of possibility necessary for these subjects to assume victimhood. In contrast, black children were treated as threats to the hegemonic Apartheid system and thus were unable to access the same conditions of possibility. Similarly, young black men in urban areas of South Africa are more likely than any other demographic population to be victims of interpersonal violence. Here, the intersectionality of race, socioeconomic status, and gender are central to victimhood. The imagined set of rules that govern manhood (aggression, alcohol consumption, gangsterism), combined with the impoverished infrastructure of many South African environments, results in young black South African men defining and identifying with a particular (and usually violent) masculinity that will ensure their survival. However, it is this same masculinity that renders them vulnerable to other men faced with similar conditions (Ratele, 2009). In the case of South African FSA victims, it will later be demonstrated how similar conditions of (im)possibility emerging at the intersection of economic status, race, gender, and sexuality have filtered into constructions of post-Apartheid victimhood.

The hegemony of masculinity, power, and the disciplined body

For Foucault (1978), biopower is ubiquitous and all social subjects are participants in its exercises and relations. That is, there is an "event of power struggle with everybody attempting to affect the others and everybody resisting the effect of others" (McWhorter, 2004, p. 42). This understanding underlines how social subjects are all relays in the operations of biopower. It also reveals how no individual dominant system can operate as a singular source of power. Rather, different systems of power, such as the legal system or medical knowledge, are each "but one node in a complex matrix of relationships and institutions" that renders each dominant system as both able to express and relay discourses and as subject to other dominant discourses (Cahill, 2000, p. 57). Thus, the authors or 'knowers' of a particular discourse – be they scientists, lawyers, doctors, psychologists, or politicians – are also a function of that discourse (Phelan, 1990). In contrast to traditional monarchies, there is no individual who is formally empowered to exercise social control in modernity. Rather, the gender hegemony of masculinity operates through and as a function of modern power (Bartky, 1988). The hegemony of masculinity is a historical effect of various institutionalised practices that have emerged across time and space, and have been produced and reproduced by and through networks within widely circulated apparatuses of knowledge. Connell (1993, p. 602) lists examples of these apparatuses:

Thus we cannot begin to talk intelligibly about "masculinity and power" without addressing the institutionalized masculinization of state elites, the gender differentiation of parts of the state apparatus (consider the military in the Gulf deployment), the history of state strategies for the control of populations via women's fertility. The sexual division of labor in production, the masculinized character of the very concept of "the economic," the levels of income and asset inequality between men and women, make it impossible to speak about "masculinity and work" as if they were somehow separate entities being brought into relation.

Connell (1993) further adds that beyond this institutionalisation through systems of knowledge, two other factors have ensured the construction and maintenance of some forms of masculinity as hegemonic. First, modern sexuality is fundamental to the construction of gender difference, and thus gender and sexuality must be understood as mutually constitutive components of masculine social practices that constitute the hegemony of masculinity. Second, these masculine social practices have further reified the masculine character of Connell's (1993) above-mentioned institutionalised conditions in which the gender hegemony of masculinity originally arose. This reification reproduces and intensifies these institutions and their adjunct masculine practices. The gender hegemony of masculinity therefore exists primarily within institutions, structures, relationships, and discourses rather than within individual masculine figures. As such, masculine discourses, rather than masculine individuals or groups, practice their own control and restrict themselves (Foucault, 1981). As Hearn (2004, p. 51) has argued,

> To say that all men are (all) powerful or men are all powerful: that is not so: this is especially clear from a global perspective on men. Rather it is that power is a very significant, pervasive aspect of men's social relations, actions and experiences.

Classical social theory views power as operating top-down and argues that dominant groups relay hegemonic masculine discourses onto social structures and individual bodies of subordinate groups. However, a Foucauldian viewpoint suggests that the hegemony of masculinity operates bottom-up, in a capillary-like fashion, through nodal points of modern power that exist everywhere between people within the social body (Hearn, 2004). As society, culture, and power relations are all constituted by discourse, "it is in discourse that power and knowledge are joined together" (Foucault, 1978, p. 100). Power, domination, and the hegemony of masculinity are therefore made legitimate through discursive practices (van Dijk, 2001). These discourses are hegemonic in that they remain dominant in our understandings of reality and are sustained through various modes, such as the media and social institutions that continue to assert their normality and naturalness (Donaldson, 1993). These normative discourses have a regulatory function and operate as technologies of discipline and surveillance (Foucault, 1978). This is possible because "relations of power . . . circumscribe in advance what will and will not count as truth, which order[s] the world in certain regular and regulatable ways, and which we come to accept as the given field of knowledge" (Butler, 2004, pp. 57–58). As such, sexual and gender regulations make gendered and sexual agency difficult. Additionally, pathologising sexual and gendered discourses that map out the normal-abnormal binary allow subject positions to be taken up that either restrict or enable 'freedom'. By submitting to these discourses, one can seemingly gain such freedom. However, in light of this pattern, freedom is really what Butler (2004, p. 101) calls "unfreedom", as it is heavily policed, surveilled, and regulated through modern power. In summary then, "we live, more or less implicitly, with received notions of reality, implicit accounts of ontology, which determine what kinds of bodies and sexualities will be considered real and true, and which kind will not" (Butler, 2004, p. 214). It is in this way that hegemonic masculinity is an important social construction (that implicates sex and gender) against which subjects normalise and therefore regulate themselves (Bartky, 1988).

Power/knowledge and patriarchy

A Foucauldian analysis of power and knowledge illustrates how the material body is made visible through technologies of modern power. Rather than being a unitary and single force, power is created by the relationships that sustain it. Moreover, power operates in relation to knowledge production (Weeks, 1981) because authoritative, scientific, or religious discourse implies that these productions represent sound and rational 'truth'. Power does not only produce knowledge, but

> power and knowledge directly imply one another . . . [and thus] there is no power relation without the correlative constitution of a field of knowledge, nor any knowledge that does not presuppose and constitute . . . power relations.
>
> *(Foucault, 1977a, p. 27)*

Regardless of status, profession, or social presence, individual men are not powerful in society. Rather, because the body is a fundamental site onto which sexual and gender constructions are mapped (McNay, 1991), male bodies are inscribed with a dominant status and female bodies with an inferior status. Thus, "the disciplinary power that inscribes femininity in the female body [and masculinity in the male body] is everywhere and is nowhere; the disciplinarian is everyone and yet no one in particular" (Bartky, 1988, p. 103). Foucault (1977a, p. 28) uses the term 'body politic' to describe the discourses and practices "that serve as weapons, relays, communication routes and supports for the power and knowledge relations that invest human bodies and subjugate them by turning them into objects of knowledge". Because the material body is the privileged site upon which power and knowledge come to rest, power exists in the dynamics, relations, and structures of social systems, and creates conditions of possibility for the subject.

Given that discourse represents a vehicle for power/knowledge and the gender hegemony of masculinity is a dominant discourse, gendered codes are continuously mapped onto the modern grid of the body. These codes have traditionally upheld masculinity as the dominant gender pole. However, as modern society changes, in part through resistant discourses, gendered bodies transform. In the current context, older forms of gendering are being eroded and replaced with new versions. Bartky (1988, p. 107) identifies these changes:

> Women are no longer required to be chaste or modest, to restrict their sphere of activity to the home, or even to realize their properly feminine destiny in maternity. Normative femininity is coming more and more to be centred on woman's body – not its duties or obligations or even capacity to bear children, but its sexuality, more precisely, its presumed heterosexuality and its appearance.

While these increased provisions for female economic, sexual, and political empowerment currently circulate as possibilities for the female or 'feminine' subject, the gender hegemony of masculinity remains recalcitrant. Evidence for this can be found in both the implicit and explicit restrictions placed on women's salaries and/or professional positions, by the continued employment of pejorative terms such as 'whore' or 'slut' to describe sexually promiscuous women, and in the ongoing assumption that women will be the primary caregivers regardless of professional status (Shaw, 2010). These embedded aspects of discourse result in women either being forced to occupy a masculine position and risk vilification, or to remain constrained by traditional female roles that are not necessarily professionally, economically, or sexually conducive to modernity. Hegemony is also maintained through variously circulated images and messages that produce the empowered female as necessarily white, heterosexual, and middle-income (Gill, 2012). Women operating outside of these categories are therefore forced either to occupy typical positions reserved for the 'marginalised' (Shaw, 2010), or alternatively, to assume a hegemonic position through the replication of valued heteronormative, middle-class, and Anglo-Saxon preoccupations, behaviours, and viewpoints. Apparent female sexual empowerment thus serves as a useful example of how hegemony can be sustained despite apparent shifts towards non-hegemonic values (the virginal and virtuous female is now constructed as sexually confident), which are then themselves incorporated within heteronormative codes of living. At least in middle- and high-income contexts, sexual confidence is now regarded as part of compulsory heterosexual behaviour (albeit the social valuations of this behaviour, evident in pejorative terms such as 'whore' or 'slut', have not necessarily been replaced), and so apparent sexual freedom is simply another form of hegemonic regulation of social bodies.

Nonetheless, with the more recent focus on female sexuality and shifting hegemonic masculine values, women's bodies become the sites of increased surveillance and women begin to operate within the incitement to new and alternative discourses. Whilst women have always participated in the incitement to discourse, particularly with regards to the hysterisation of female sexuality and bodies (Foucault, 1978) and in terms of reproductive capacities, women have, up until recently, been able to operate outside of particular sexual abuse surveillance machineries. Women's bodies were previously monitored primarily to demonstrate the intrinsic pathological hysteria apparently present in female sexuality (Gilman, King, Porter, Rousseau, & Showalter, 1993), yet they were rarely surveilled as agents of sexual violence. However, women's sexual behaviours are now being organised through alternative definitions, regulations, and knowledge formations. This has profound implications for the recent emergence of the female sexual offender and the coterminous surfacing of her victims. Nonetheless, it must also be noted that given the particular rooting of this text in a South African context, gendered bodies cannot be understood as clones of their European and American variants. Gender always intersects with other aspects of identity, such as race and socioeconomic status (Shefer, 2010), and different social systems will have different dominant gender discourses. Thus, even if two given societies are both configured by and through hegemonic masculinity, those masculine hegemonies may have very different meanings, values, and implications. Furthermore, there is a complex interplay of subordination, marginalisation, and domination in the discursive relay of the hegemony of masculinity, which often results in the same body being produced as dominant in one instance and subordinate in another. This most typically occurs at the intersection of race, ethnicity, and economic status (Hearn, 2004). For example, some black men in rural parts of South Africa may accept and practice aspects of hegemonic masculinity; however, these men may remain marginalised in their relationship to the hegemony of whiteness implicated in urban masculinities (Morrell, Jewkes, & Lindegger, 2012).

Hegemonic masculinity, at least in its older, more traditional sense, represents an ideal masculinity. Whilst it is normative, it is by no means "normal in a statistical sense; only a minority of men might enact it", thus serving to position other men, women, and children against it (Connell & Messerschmidt, 2005, p. 832). Traditionally, hegemonic masculinity has been relayed through rigid images of the ideal man – physically strong, sexually assertive, intellectually powerful, and heterosexual. However, with context and temporal changes across history, counter-hegemonies have surfaced whereby alternative permissible discourses about men and masculinity (and consequently women and femininity) have been produced and included in the repertoire of dominant discourses (Donaldson, 1993; Shefer, Stevens, & Clowes, 2010). For example, before the 1970s, hegemonic masculinity required heterosexuality which was enforced through legal systems and the pathologisation of homosexuality (Weeks, 1981). This was particularly due to prevailing discourses that implied the association between homosexuality and femininity. Thus, historically, homophobia was discursively linked to hegemonic masculinity (Donaldson, 1993). However, today there are contexts where homosexuality and other 'different' forms of masculinity, such as the metrosexual man and the 'stay at home father', are constructed as appropriate and acceptable masculinities, and thus fit neatly into some (most often Global North) versions of hegemonic masculinity. Additionally, it has become obvious that many men who hold social power cannot comfortably be classified into the masculine categories aligned with hegemonic discourse. Thus, even men with power do not necessarily occupy a traditional masculine position characterised by typical male traits such as physical strength, aggression, and economic success. It thus seems that whilst this normative discourse on masculinity may be constitutive of the 'ideal man' that represents that to which men 'should' aspire, it is possible that "hegemonic masculinities . . . do not correspond closely to the lives of any actual men" (Connell & Messerschmidt, 2005, p. 838), regardless of the status, position, and power of these men. This is significant, as the image of the strong and sexually assertive 'ideal man' is potentially incompatible with discourses that may accommodate a male victim of FSA.

Although the hegemony of masculinity has been sustained across space and time, it has temporal and contextual qualities that can change and therefore create new conditions of possibility for masculinity – and thus for femininity and gender and sexuality more generally. Furthermore, hegemonic masculinity is a representation of a set of discursive positions available for adoption or resistance by subjects. Thus, even hegemonic masculinity cannot be understood monoculturally, but should rather be understood as a diffuse and diverse representation of gender within the context of multiculturalism and political and social pluralities (Hearn, 2004; Connell & Messerschmidt, 2005). Demetriou (2001, p. 340) highlights this point by arguing that "since gender practice takes place within different historic-cultural contexts and since it is also performed by agents of different race, class, or generation, we need to talk about masculinities/femininities, not masculinity/femininity". Thus, even though the same hegemonic, gendered representations of masculinity and femininity may be relayed across different contexts, these representations meet at the intersection of various other social constructions, including race, culture, and ethnicity. This intersection results in the gender hegemony being re-articulated and, in turn, translated, transformed, and re-contextualised.

This is significant, as certain parts of South Africa are rooted in a hegemonic system that is quite different from Global North expressions of masculine power (although other parts are perfectly in concert with these expressions). During Apartheid, sexuality in South Africa was subject to censorship, prohibition, and policing, particularly driven by attempts to police sexual boundaries between the 'races' and the control of black fertility. Sex was predominantly a private issue; however, sexual violence was targeted publicly if it involved a black perpetrator and a white victim. The prohibition of sexual images, messages, and practices was very quickly replaced by a proliferation of sexual representations in post-Apartheid South Africa. Whilst gender and racial inequalities, along with issues concerning economic and educational transformations, were foregrounded as key post-Apartheid priorities, sex and sexuality were not. The centrality of sex and sexuality and its resultant politicisation was thus unexpected, but, as argued by Posel (2005, p. 127), it was both inevitable and "perhaps the most revealing marker of the complexities and vulnerabilities of the drive to produce a newly democratic, unified nation". Posel (2005, p. 127) develops this further by showing that:

> Modern sexuality is always, therefore, a political phenomenon: entangled in relations of power, and fashioned in ways which bear the imprints of other vectors of inequality and difference, such as race, class, status and generation. Meanings and materialities of desire, forms and technologies of pleasure, ways of practising sex, and the sexual identities which attach to all of these, form and re-form within other

hierarchies of dominance and the contestations they provoke. And, of course, sexuality is always the site of multiple and contending regimes of moral regulation.

Shaped by particular axes, nodes, and channels of power, sexual discourse and the silences that structure it are now central sites of regulation, mobilisation, conflict, and contest, and thus key to the politicisation of South Africa. This discourse is relayed through particular cultural strategies, moments, and sites, such as the rise of the consumer black elite, social movements promoting and supporting alternative sexualities, sexual violence as a mounting platform for public outrage, and the HIV/AIDS pandemic. Framing these sites is the continued representation of male heterosexuality as threatening, dangerous, and predatory (Posel, 2005). By bringing sexuality into public discourse, South Africa has sustained the image of traditional masculine power and gendered relationships. This is particularly in rural areas, where traditional 'African' authority is based on a patriarchal masculinity defined through strength, chiefship, and sexual and economic entitlement (O'Sullivan, Harrison, Morrell, Monroe-Wise, & Kubeka, 2006). In many South African contexts, traditional values and codes maintain older hegemonic masculinity discourses. These codes are both instruments and effects of the high prevalence of the rape of women; of women being dependent on their husbands for food, shelter, and their children's education; and of high levels of male-perpetrated intimate partner violence (Jewkes, Penn-Kekana, Levin, Ratsaka, & Schreiber, 1999). Therefore, in this context, it is through this particular instantiation of power/knowledge that victimhood is tied to womanhood and perpetration to men within conventional constructions of sexual violence. These constantly circulating constructions ensure that FSA remains unlikely in the network of discourses; and in turn, the identity coordinates for victimhood, especially amongst males, remain excluded from South African discourse. These particularly South African race-gender intersections impede on the conditions of possibility for FSA victimhood, thus the significance of this context (and its comparison to other contexts).

Bem (1993) notes that the hegemony of masculinity that sustains cultural discourses and social institutions does not only disadvantage women, but also minority races, classes, and sexualities. Additionally, even postmodern feminists fail to acknowledge the full range of available genders and sexualities, and thus restrict the diversity and variety that exists in human identity (Petchesky, 2008). For example, women are often framed as a single and united category rather than as identifying with a range of classes, races, nationalities, economic statuses, and educational backgrounds. The assumption is thus made that all women are subject to the same level of oppression, which fails to acknowledge the specificity and complexity of each individual woman's particular identity and experience (Fuss, 1989). This assumption also fails to acknowledge that some women benefit from hegemonic values, and some men do not (Hearn, 2004). For example, when a woman belonging to a marginalised group reports sexual violence involving a white male perpetrator, she is less likely to be believed than a white woman reporting sexual assault involving a black male perpetrator (Alcoff & Gray, 1993).

Whilst the gender hegemony of masculinity may have traditionally been based on a masculine-dominated and female-subordinated social structure, contemporary hegemony is concerned with representations of complex gender relations that intersect across culture, economy, age, and race, resulting in a variety of multiple and hybridised masculinities and femininities (Demetriou, 2001). For example, whereas female sexuality is characteristically constructed around purity and innocence in the Global North, the sexuality of African women is often constructed as morally corrupting and 'dirty' (McFadden, 2003). The implication here is that when FSA emerges in South Africa, it may have a completely different configuration to counterparts in the Global North. Given the racial, class, and economic diversity that characterises South Africa, the hegemony of masculinity tends to relay itself in different ways and modes across the social body (in part through influences of globalisation), and so gender discourses and constructions bear the marks of 'glocalisation'. For instance, there are contexts where the hegemony of masculinity is maintained only as a silent and implicit underlying current, and women are given opportunities to be sexually, physically, and intellectually assertive, albeit within boundaries. In other words, much like in the Global North, there are some South African contexts where the male-female binary is currently being discernibly eroded. This may be due to the fact that, in line with Hopper's (2007) argument, previously acceptable behaviour is becoming more heavily criticised, resulting in increased surveillance and the tightening of social standards. Formerly, women, by virtue of their gender, were able to operate outside of the incitement to particular sexual discourses, specifically those that imply sexual agency. However, with shifting regulations, knowledge formations, and boundaries around sexuality, there is a resultant increase in disciplinary surveillance, and women's ability to remain outside of this surveillance is reduced. This reconfiguration of sexuality is evident in contemporary fertility technologies, such as contraceptive pills that regulate and monitor the female body. This is only a suggestion, and there may be a number of other reasons for the erosion of these binaries, including modern practices such as women's entry into the economic domain (Collins, Saltzman Chafetz, Lesser Blumberg, Coltrane, & Turner, 1993).

It is also important to acknowledge that despite the current modern tendency to assert female economic power, sexuality, and desire, this tendency is still immersed in the implicit assumption that such desire and its accompanying behaviour should take place in a heterosexual context with the long-term ambition of cohabitation reproduction. This is evidenced by media images that promote female sexual power so long as these are read through a desiring heterosexual male gaze or as a point of heterosexual identification for the female gaze (Gill, 2008). This again illustrates the way sexual 'liberation' continues to be confined to a heteronormativity that is always organised around female subordination (Lorber, 2000). Moreover, various mechanisms, such as reproductive techniques that appear to liberate women, can be understood as, in effect, surveillance technologies that aim to monitor, control, and regulate female bodies with the medical and scientific objective of ensuring the continued invention of the female body as reproductive and childbearing (Shaw, 2010). As such, biopower is indispensable to the gender hegemony of masculinity "insofar as it provides instruments for the insertion of women's bodies into the machinery of reproduction" (Sawicki, 1999, p. 91). It is perhaps for these reasons that there continues to be public disbelief and shock in circumstances of gender nonconformity, such as female crime, despite the commonly held belief that women's social roles and statuses have fundamentally changed in modernity (Kruttschnitt, Gartner, & Husseman, 2008). Whilst current hegemonic representations have made way for an increased gender plurality, these representations are still constrained by implicit gender boundaries that impose limits on the subject (Connell & Messerschmidt, 2005). Such discursive limits are based on the centrality of sexuality in modernity and the implicit discourses that continue to privilege those sexualities and genders that, in some way, ensure both the production and the reproduction of humanity. These discursive limits have implications for the kinds of subject positions that are made possible by the power/knowledge coupling, and the ways that these positions are maintained at the level of populations and inform the subjection of individuals.

Subjection and performativity as instruments and effects of modern power: implications for gender and sexuality

Poststructuralist theories view the subject as a cultural construction that should always be regarded as "a condition of knowledge" (Gubrium & Holstein, 1994, p. 687) rather than as a natural or essential consequence of human sentience. Accordingly, personhood and individuality are not born from pre-given biological roots, but are rather the social (re)productions of ongoing cultural and interpersonal relations that have the power to invent and reinvent the subject (Richardson & May, 1999). Therefore, the subject can be understood as located at the intersection of a variety of discursive nodal points that make subject positions available. When a person takes up a subject position made available in discourse, the individual in question is producing his/her subjectivity (Staunæs, 2003). In this way, that which the individual believes is subjectivity, is actually the process of becoming "subjected to the power and regulation of the discourse" and thus an instrument and effect of biopower (Weedon, 1987, p. 119). At the micro-level of the individual, discourses remain invisible as 'taken-for-granted' knowledge. Thus, the occupation of a discursively relayed subject position is understood by the individual as self-knowledge (Wilbraham, 2004). However, people are not powerless in the face of discursive regulation. While discourses may be finite and thus constraining, people are able to "take up, ignore or resist accessible discourses" (Staunæs, 2003, p. 103). Furthermore, new conditions of possibility generate new counter-knowledge, which in turn generates potentially new subject positions (Weedon, 1987). It is for this reason that, through the exploration of discourses in a particular context, individuals can come to occupy new subject positions that will inform their recursive processes of subjection.

Subjection is thus the process (and the personal experience of this process) of the subject being positioned by and within various discursive nodes available in circulated discourse at a particular historical moment in a specific cultural context. One of the outcomes of this process is the production of sexual subjectivity, thus ensuring that individual experiences of sexual subjectivity are personalised, individuated, and considered different to the sexuality of others. It further allows for the internalisation of widely circulated sexual regulations, which are thereafter imagined by the subject to be self-generating (Posel, 2005). So, while "the social body precedes the sexual body", the cultural implication that sexuality is a biologically determined and individual aspect of a particular person ensures that sexuality discourse is able to invisibly construct the individual at the level of subjectivity (Halperin, 1989, p. 263). This is particularly powerful because sexuality has been constructed as part of human 'nature', so long as it is heteronormative. Thus, whilst sexuality discourse constructs one individual, it simultaneously excludes another. This discursive exclusion has profound effects for sexual violence and victimisation, as it determines who can and cannot be considered a victim, and what does and does not constitute sexual violence. An appropriate example of differential treatment of sexual victimisation as a consequence of sexual subjectification is the 'normalisation' of male-to-female rape and the pathologising of homosexual rape, even at the level of the victim (Richardson & May, 1999).

For Butler (1999, p. 7), gender as a subject position is a performance, a social expectation "that ends up producing the very phenomenon that it anticipates". Butler's (1999) concept of performativity refers to the ritualised and repeated acts that serve to naturalise gender onto the body. Gender, sexuality, and in fact all aspects of identity are performed, acted out, and in this way, reinforced. Norms therefore persist "to the extent that ... [they are] acted out in social practice and reidealized and reinstituted in and through the daily social rituals of bodily life" (Butler, 2004, p. 48). In this sense, gender is not a fixed and rigid set of social codes that are passively inscribed onto bodies and thereafter internalised. Rather, gender is selected, produced, reproduced, and dynamically performed through various social practices (Demetriou, 2001). For example, femininity has no essential meaning outside of the institutions (such as marriage and the nuclear family) that it operates within. However, gender, sexuality, and other identity elements must also be understood in the Foucauldian sense, as part of a technology of self, as an organisation of relations within the subject.

The concept of performativity necessitates an understanding of the body as malleable. Whilst this text rests on the assumption that subjects are constituted by modern power, this constitution is not monolithic. In fact, although Foucault (1980) regards the body as a 'docile' site in reference to its constitution, production, and reproduction of dominant discourses, he simultaneously argues that the body is also a site for resistance. Foucault (1980) explains that the body's ability to defy the constraints of discourse is an effect of the nature of power as "diffuse, lacking a single source as well as a single object" and effecting multiple sites unevenly (Cahill, 2000, p. 47). Thus, resistance as an attempt to avoid objectification and surveillance is evidence of modern power's success in the invention of the 'autonomous' self-regulating subject (Butchart, 1997). However, a subjective sense of resistance does not necessarily mean that oppressing discursive frameworks are being disrupted. As an instantiation of this important caveat, Lamb and Peterson (2012) give the example of the current promotion of female sexual empowerment and warn that whilst women may subjectively feel empowered, this is really only a 'false consciousness'. Gill (2012, p. 743) concurs by suggesting that 'fake' female sexual empowerment is ubiquitous and comprises feminist concepts that "have been taken up and sold back to us emptied of their political force". While women may feel empowered by images and messages that celebrate female sexuality, the actual power in this subjective experience is the way that these messages sustain a heteronormative society. In particular, the commodification of *heterosexual* female sexuality serves a regulating function that ensures women remain tied to capital and heteronormativity, despite the implicit messages that recent female sexual 'liberation' serves to free femininity. This is clear in the case of FSA, because despite the apparent acceptance of female sexuality and prowess, the female sexual offender remains effete and her victims invisible to public consciousness.

Whilst resistance is possible, the Foucauldian project would assert that absolute bodily liberation from discourse is impossible given that the 'natural' body does not exist other than within and through the discourses that constitute it. As Foucault (1978, p. 95) reminds us, "where there is power, there is resistance, and yet, or rather consequently, this resistance is never in a position of exteriority in relation to power". Performativity and resistance offer subjects the opportunity to both align with and/or contest dominant discourses; however, absolute resistance is never achievable outside or against power, because the body is always already inscribed within and by power and discourse. Sensations may pre-exist culture; however, body-consciousness is a cultural production, and thus the body is culturally constituted from conception (Foucault, 1978). The body therefore serves as a text for both explicit and implicit dominant discourses, and the reading of the body makes both the recognition and the resistance of sexual and gendered constructions possible. While the body is therefore broadly always implicated in networks of power, the local conditions in which it is situated will also obviously delimit these networks and their meanings. This allows for an explanation of context and temporal differences across bodies and subjects (Butler, 1989). This is a significant point given that local conditions are important in as far as they are able to illuminate the way that FSA may, in some ways, be related to the specificities of context.

Gendered and sexualised constructions and consequences

Gender and sexuality are mapped onto the body through subjectification, and so even self-knowledge and subjectivity are socially constructed. It is in this way that "the conditions within which those defined can begin to develop their own consciousness and identity" (Weeks, 1981, p. 108). Whilst dominant gender discourses are primarily well established and stable, the conditions under which these are constructed vary (Kruttschnitt et al., 2008), resulting in varying expressions of gender and sexuality across contexts. Additionally, because sexuality has been constructed as an innate and intrinsic aspect of the self that is central to understandings of human psychology, sexuality (along with gender and other derivatives of sexual selfhood) has come to occupy a particularly powerful discursive position in the modern world (Halperin,

1989). This has the effect of ensuring that modern sexuality itself becomes a political project, and consequently the site for multiple technologies of power and regulation. Posel (2005) develops this argument by explaining that modern sexuality is always interweaved in relations of power and always intersects with other constructions of difference and inequality, such as race and class. Thus, sexual identities are constantly produced and reproduced within structures of dominance and the resistances that these incite.

This political quality of modern sexuality, as well as its complex (self)-regulatory functions embedded in individual expressions of sexuality, is nonetheless always governed through biopower. This has profound implications for the types of sexual behaviours that are considered acceptable and normative, as well as for who is able to perform these.

The historical and cultural constitution of sexual 'deviance' and other sexual 'abnormalities'

Psychology, biomedicine, and the social sciences assume that the human exists as a body and mind to be discovered, mapped, and studied. However, according to Armstrong (1986), the body, and all of its physical, psychological, and emotional components, have been constructed by the very disciplines that claim to have discovered them. Thus, the human as an object of knowledge only exists in so far as it is produced, reproduced, and sustained through methods of modern disciplines. In this way, scientific observation and analysis are procedures through which the body, the mind, and the social are created (Butchart, 1997). This process of analysis is itself framed by disciplinary history; thus, contemporary understandings of sex, sexuality, sexual practices, and sexual deviance are constructed consequences of the material and historical circumstances that gave rise to the conditions that made them possible, fathomable, conceivable, and historical.

Scientific discourse not only draws the boundaries for what is thinkable, but it also produces a normative standard against which sex and sexuality are policed and regulated (Rawlinson, 1987). The current classification schemes that delimit sexual deviancy did not exist until the eighteenth and nineteenth centuries, which were characterised by the consolidation of medico-legal discourses and institutions. Through operations of power expressed through vehicles such as clinical technologies and the establishment of the hospital as a site of discipline, human anatomy became an atlas for producing new knowledge on disease and pathology (Pryce, 2000). During the course of this history, the production of standardised norms and multiple types of 'pathological' sexual deviations came to be produced, defined, and accepted as 'truth' through discursive practices that implied that these 'abnormalities'"are unnatural or immoral from a religious perspective or . . . biologically anomalous or psychologically pathological from a scientific perspective" (Bem, 1993, p. 81). Categorisation and classification of sexuality and gender allowed for the unexplainable to be explained and the not-so-obviously sexual to become sexualised (Lützen, 1995). This produced the sexually abnormal in what had, up until then, appeared to be acceptable (Weeks, 1981), or at worst defined as sin (Pryce, 2000). It also resulted in the division of sexualities so that any behaviour that did not fit neatly into these categories, or into the heterosexual and reproductive requirement more generally, became marked as a deviation from the norm (Weeks, 1995). For example, whilst the act of sodomy may have occurred and may have even been viewed as immoral, it is only with the construction of rigid classification schemes that such an act constituted a particular type of abnormality attached to a homosexual subjectivity which then came to be both pathologised and illegal (Halperin, 1998). Thus, 'perversions' and 'pathologies' are not natural biological, genetic, or psychological phenomena, but are rather historical products.

The production of institutionalised discourse provided the foundation for the development of categories of sexual deviancy that could be endorsed as 'fact' and 'truth' as a result of their being embedded in a specific type of discourse (Foucault, 1978). The construction of these so-called abnormalities, perversions, and pathologies, masked as a scientific and medical discovery, provide the means to consistently surveil and regulate human sexuality (Halperin, 1998). Moreover, this practice of presenting sexuality as fact is recursive, so that apparently 'new' knowledge and insight can further direct social and individual freedom. It is in this way that the body politic is treated as a cohort to be either 'cured' or controlled (Swartz & Levett, 1989). Research and empirical evidence demonstrating the existence of pathology thus serve to reify and reinforce pathologising discourses (Levett, 1992), and in this manner, science itself is a particularly productive relay of biopower.

Sexual deviation is therefore produced as an instrument and effect of biopower which (at least in the case of eighteenth-century biopower) was key to ordering the social imperatives of the time (Foucault, 1978). By extension then, "it is through 'discourses' . . . that our relation to reality is organised" (Weeks, 1981, p. 5). Therefore, an understanding of the history of sexual deviancy takes seriously the argument that there is no 'natural' or 'normal' type of sexuality, but rather there are *normalised* sexualities that have constituted the abnormal frontiers of human sexuality. So entrenched is this normalisation that the individual now scans the surface of his/her desire and body in an attempt to define his/her sexual self. This process of self-regulation through self-examination ensures the continued organisation and government of sexuality (Pryce, 2000).

Whilst medical and/or scientific discourse does operate as a privileged source of 'fact', other widely circulated dominant discourses can and do result in a complex matrix of competing knowledge systems. The recent surfacing of female sex crime is a powerful example of how the emergence of new discourses and concepts "marks the site of struggle between competing discourses" (Winnubst, 1999, p. 23). In cases of male-perpetrated sex offences, "the penalties are . . . more severe [for other sexualities] than those for equivalent heterosexual offences" (Freeman, 1996, p. 430). In modern society, constructions of sexual perversions continue to result in harsher sentencing for male sexual offenders and disproportionate interest and prejudice from the realm of psychiatry compared to other offenders (Brockman & Bluglass, 1996). So entrenched are these constructions of pathology that they are even able to supersede certain scientific 'facts'. For example, harsher sentencing and psychiatric prejudice persist, despite scientific 'evidence' that demonstrates medical and legal intervention to be ineffective, as indicated by high recidivism rates in spite of psychiatric treatment (Freeman, 1996). However, in the case of female sexual offenders, gender constructions tend to override these prevailing discourses concerning sexual offenders because "sexual abuse perpetrated by women is perceived in a gendered context" (Denov, 2003, p. 312). Consequently, gender differences "play a role in the willingness of various criminal justice and treatment professionals to acknowledge female sexual offending" (Giguere & Bumby, 2007, p. 3). As Denov (2003, p. 311) illustrates, "both psychiatrists and police officers . . . [make] efforts, either consciously or unconsciously, to transform the female sex offender and her offence to realign them with more culturally acceptable notions of female behaviour". This leads to the denial of the existence of female sexual perpetration and consequently the continued invisibility of her victims. This is exacerbated by an adherence to apparent scientific representations of stereotyped and pathologised groups of violent individuals in the identification of sex abusers, which results in limited definitions for what can and cannot be demarcated as a sex crime or indeed sexual violence (Richardson & May, 1999). However, it also illustrates that behaviours constructed as deviant by science can be reformulated should they be pitted against more embedded constructions of gender. Notwithstanding these competing discourses, ChildLine in Britain has recently begun to take female child sexual perpetration more seriously, which has resulted in the deconstruction of the previously taken-for-granted assumptions about males as sexual perpetrators (Holden, 2009). This has visibilised female CSA and, as such, the increasing 'acknowledgement' of women as possible perpetrators of child sex crimes that were historically the preserve of men. However, the same cannot be said for other types of female sex offences.

Through the construction of sexual deviance as that which falls beyond the boundaries of our 'normal' social ontology, particular behaviours such as female sex crimes cannot be assimilated into the daily structure of social life. This results in reactions to these crimes that often include either minimisation, revulsion, shock, or moral panic, which in turn drives the increasing scrutiny and regulation of female sex offenders (Bartky, 1988). In fact, moral panic has played a particularly powerful role in the social regulation of sexual behaviour across the course of history. For instance, until the 1970s, rape was rarely an object of study. However, as research interest in the area grew, so too a scientific language developed for the sexual victimisation of women "that prompted claims that rape and sexual assault . . . heretofore rendered invisible, were rampant" (Fisher & Cullen, 2000, p. 317), and this in turn drove further research in a mutually constitutive cycle. This 'discovery' of modern rape in the 1970s spurred a rapid interest in the area so that by the 1980s, multiple assessments, measures, and legal documents devoted to understanding sexual victimisation were established (Fisher & Cullen, 2000). This was further propelled by research demonstrating that the effects of sex abuse included a range of psychological symptoms, disorders, and syndromes such as depression, post-traumatic stress disorder, anxiety disorders, and alcohol and substance abuse (see Koss, Heise, & Russo, 1994), thus further pathologising both the perpetrator and the victim. As a consequence, more stringent surveillance systems in the home, school, and clinic were installed to further document this prevalence. Similarly, it was only in the 1960s that CSA was even considered a possibility. However, by the 1990s, the sexual victimisation of children (albeit mostly female children) was firmly located in the public consciousness as a very real and serious social issue. This resulted in widespread social hysteria concerning the prevalence and manifestations of CSA, which had the effect of pressurising legal, medical, and police systems to become more sensitised to its possibilities (Finkelhor, 1994) – which in turn catalysed further moral panic. It is thus likely that the recent FSA emergence will be coupled with a growth of scientific investigation in the area that will undoubtedly stimulate further research, legal and medical FSA initiatives, and widespread moral panic. This possibility will be an outcome of the capacity for science to construct, normalise, and thereafter reify particular categories of existence through the noble ruse of 'medical discovery'.

This practice of naturalising pathology through science is thus admittedly also the very practice that will ensure the emergence of FSA victims.

Much like the popular adherence to traditional gender roles of the masculine aggressor and female victim has made male-to-female sexual assault both possible and 'real' (Murnen, Wright, & Kaluzny, 2002), so too will a reconfiguration of this traditional gendering language, through the act of scientific research, provide the conditions of possibility for the emergence of the FSA victim.

The rise of female criminality

Historically, women, by virtue of their gender, have been able to operate outside of the incitement to criminal discourse and thus escape particular forms of confessionals. Due to gendered social practices that exclude certain behaviours, such as criminal acts, from the circulated framework for femininity, female criminals have traditionally been 'unthinkably rare' (Dean, 1994). However, within modern technologies of power, the entry of women into the economic domain and the increased surveillance of women through clinical mechanisms, such as the contraceptive pill and fertility treatments, the number of spaces that enable women to remain outside of new kinds of surveillance is rapidly decreasing, resulting in the appearance that women are suddenly occupying gender-conflicting roles and behaviours. One example of this is the apparent rise of female crime.

There is widespread belief that, unlike male children, female children are not socialised into acting violently or sexually as a primary means of expression, and thus males are more likely to become offenders (Bourke, 2007). In fact, Higgs and colleagues (1992, pp. 137–138) go so far as to assert that "males of most species appear to possess a biologically based drive which renders them more sexually aggressive than females". Denov (2003) argues that such ideas are built on widely circulated impressions that men are unable to control their aggressive and sexual drives and urges. These gendered constructions have inadvertently provided men with more freedom to deviate from the norm, as their deviance is paradoxically normalised by the constructed intractability of their aggressive (sex) drives (Naffine, 1987). Gendered constructions of apparently 'natural' masculine aggressive tendencies, often targeted at a female victim, in combination with very particular definitions of what does and does not constitute violence (Muehlenhard & Kimes, 1999), have ensured the continued denial of female crime. This is further evidenced by the circumstances typically surrounding a female-perpetrated crime – the offender is usually not arrested, and if she is, she tends to evade being formally charged (Cauffman, 2008) and is likely to be treated more leniently than her male counterpart by correctional officials (Kramer, 2010;

White & Kowalski, 1994). In addition, female offenders recognised by the system have been accused of deviating from their feminine roles, and treatment suggestions have focused on a readjustment to feminine norms (Klein, 1976). The justification here is often based on the assumption that female offenders had poor maternal childhood relationships and have subsequently failed to internalise nurturing and maternal characteristics that define femininity (Higgs et al., 1992). However, women, both masculine and feminine, can and do behave in ways that challenge these definitions (Travers, 1999; White & Kowalski, 1994). Notwithstanding this comment, the arrest, charging, and treatment patterns (or lack thereof) typified in female crime events have demonstrated the emergence of the barely discernible, but nonetheless emerging, female criminal.

Female crime has gradually been targeted by criminology and sociology as a legitimate object of research, with the consequence of both a surge in theories relating to female offending and an increased visibilisation of women that commit crimes. One notable early theory is the gender equality hypothesis which suggests that the increased prevalence of female crime is directly associated with modernisation, feminist movements, and women's increasing access to gender equality (see Adler, 1975; Simon, 1975; Sutherland, 1924). In fact, Adler (1975) argues that it is the very emancipation of women that has ironically resulted in the rise of female crime, or what she calls the 'darker side of liberation', whereby women, now given the same opportunities as men, become and act like men. However, by the 1980s, the gender equality and masculinisation hypotheses were refuted by feminists, who argued for a gender inequality hypothesis that located the aetiology of female crime in the continued pattern of global gender discriminatory practices. These theories contend that sustained inequality results in female victimisation and economic marginality, and consequently criminal offences by women (see Chesney-Lind, 1989; Miller, 1986), thus linking female crime to economic motive. Still later, Steffensmeier and Allan (1996) argue that whilst gender inequality is an important consideration, it is the organisation of gender that is paramount to elucidating patterns of female crime. Thus, female subordination as a primary explanation is replaced with an understanding of the way particular gender roles that govern female behaviour present the conditions of possibility for a female crime event. Specifically, Steffensmeier and Allan (1996) highlight that five areas of social life govern crime in general, and these areas result in the facilitation of male crime and the constraints on female crime. These areas include gender norms, moral development and relationships, social control, physical strength, and aggression and sexuality. The fundamental assumption of this theory is that types of crimes are dictated by normative social standards, and thus females only have the opportunity to commit crimes that resonate with traditional female roles – fraud, shoplifting, embezzlement, prostitution, and possibly homicide in the context of battered woman's syndrome. Where there are examples of female-perpetrated crimes at odds with gender norms, Steffensmeier and Allan (1996, p. 480) have argued that "for women to kill, they generally must see their situation as life-threatening, as affecting the physical or emotional well-being of themselves or their children". In offering this argument, they reassert that which the act of homicide had seemingly eroded – the traditional female role as nurturer. In a similar way, they explain female substance abuse by emphasising its routes as based on emotional or relationship difficulties or as a result of introduction to drugs by a male figure.

The aforementioned theories all attempt to explain female crime by showing how particular offences are enabled by an inherently pathological relationship to gender. However, these hypotheses could not be sustained in the context of the ever-increasing presence of nontraditional gender behaviours in female offences, such as the escalating 'recognition' of female-perpetrated violence. With reported rates of female-perpetrated violence rising to comparability with those of males (Cauffman, 2008; Graves, 2007; Kruttschnitt et al., 2008), it becomes impossible to ignore the potential for the female aggressor, regardless of circumstance. Furthermore, there are many recent examples of female-perpetrated violence in intimate partner contexts that are so obviously aggressive that they can no longer be rationalised as defensive (Muftić, Bouffard, & Bouffard, 2007). In response, a number of different theories have been offered, such as Graves' (2007) proposal that female crime is based on a gender paradox whereby some individuals develop strong gender-atypical disorders (such as aggressive tendencies in females) and consequently behave atypically (violently). Other theories are based on sex-specific aetiologies locating the cause within the biology, hormones, or personalities of women (White & Kowalski, 1994). Whilst theories such as these do ensure the longevity of constraining gender frameworks for offenders, there is simultaneously a growing recognition that gender differences account for less variation between female and male offenders than previously acknowledged. This is reflected in the recent call for the treatment of female offenders as a heterogeneous group as well as recommendations for individually tailored rather than gender-specific interventions in correctional settings (see Cauffman, 2008). This recognition, however, comes with a cost – the acknowledgement that gendered social boundaries can and do shift, as well as the appreciation that traditional mechanisms of informal control over women's lives have weakened. The perception that women are no longer informally controlled and regulated through their expectations to remain limited to particular roles (housewife, mother) further results in the sense that there is a general decline in the regulation and discipline of the nuclear family unit (Kruttschnitt et al., 2008) – a key area for the reproduction and maintenance of gendered discourses. This decline thus sets off additional shifts in normative gender discourse, which consequently allows for a further emergence of non-gendered behaviour such as female crime.

The recent acknowledgement of female crime over the course of the last three decades has coincided with broader gender-specific changes, such as the entry of women into the economic workforce, media representations of and emphasis on female sexuality, and the promotion of female empowerment and gender equity (see Gavey, 2012; Gill, 2012; Lamb & Peterson, 2012). However, as previously indicated, publicly circulated images and messages of female empowerment through various media, political, legal, and educational communication channels often function to legitimise the continued surveillance, regulation, and control of femininity through the implicit heteronormative assumptions that frame these communications (Shaw, 2010). In fact, this discursive explosion concerning female sexual, political, and economic empowerment is the very technology through which the female body becomes the site of a deepening surveillance. The apparent rise of female criminality is a key example of this. Over the course of history, the accent on the 'natural' association of femininity to nurturing, caregiving, attachment, and passivity resulted in limited reporting and incarceration of female offenders (Denov, 2003). However, as discursive frameworks for female subjection began to include the 'thinkability' of female sexual prowess, desire, and liberation, so the number of female sex offenders began to 'rise'. The public emphasis on and promotion of female sexuality provides the impression that female empowerment and gender equity are superseding gender roles that emanate from the hegemony of masculinity (Gavey, 2012). However, this sexual 'liberation' of the female is merely a commodity sold to women as a means to mask its function as a mechanism by which an increased number of (female) bodies are made subject to disciplinary power. This is evidenced by the sudden media exposure and legal prosecution in the last decade of female teachers who have sexual contact with their male students, beginning with the highly publicised case of Mary Kay Letourneau in the United States in 1997 (Knoll, 2010). Whilst these teacher-offenders are still framed within gendered terms (pretty, emotional, harmless), their media and public exposure did provide the foundation for the acknowledgement of female sex crime (Chan & Frei, 2013). In turn, the last decade has seen an explosion of academic, legal, and medical interest in the area, with research expanding beyond the teacher-offender type to include a more heterogeneous categorisation scheme of female sex offenders as previously discussed (see Brockman & Bluglass, 1996; Gannon, Rose, & Ward, 2008; Miller, Turner, & Henderson, 2009; Nathan & Ward, 2002; Sandler & Freeman, 2007; Turner, Miller, &, Henderson, 2008; Vandiver & Kercher, 2004; Vandiver & Walker, 2002; Wijkman, Bijleveld, & Hendriks, 2010). The wider the conditions of possibility for female sexuality and transgression grow, the more cases of female-perpetrated sex crimes there seem to be. The exploitation of FSA as a taboo 'secret' and the adjunct discursive explosion on FSA through science aligns to Foucault's (1978) critique of the repressive hypothesis. In fact, the multiple categories and lists of FSA typologies offered by Vandiver and Kercher (2004) and Sandler and Freeman (2007) echo Foucault's (1978) list of emerging unorthodox and absurd sexualities in his discussion of 'the perverse implantation' as a mechanism through which perversity is produced against normalising power. Thus, in the same way that Foucault (1978, p. 49) shows how apparent prohibitions, silences, and taboos concerning these absurd sexualities in effect resulted in "a visible explosion of unorthodox sexualities", so too FSA, in all its disparate formations, begins to surface as a consequence of prohibition and ostensible 'repression'.

Recently, Chan and Frei (2013) conducted the first study on female sexual homicide. The combination of homicidal and sexually aggressive tendencies examined in their study would have been incompatible with femininity less than a decade ago. However, with society becoming ever more regulated and exposed to the diffusion of disciplinary power, it is unlikely that women would continue to remain outside of the historical constraints on female criminality. Rather, the presence of a growing network of disciplinary channels necessitates the provision of conditions of possibility for transgressive female behaviour. Such conditions (presence of female empowerment and promotion of female sexual liberation, for example) ensure the increased regulation of the female body, and consequently the manifestation of an epidemic of female (sexual) transgressions.

Conditions of possibility for the male victim

Until recently, rape was understood as the forced penetration of a vagina by a penis, and feminist writers asserted that this act was thus a representation of male sexual dominance (Freeman, 1996). This understanding of rape, which is still highly pronounced in public consciousness, implies that a woman is harmless because she lacks a dangerous phallic weapon, the penis. Even when a woman is convicted of rape, it is still perceived as less emotionally and physically damaging than penile penetration. This dismissiveness is present, even when the sexual perpetration occurs between a mother and a child. It is, however, most pronounced with male victims, as men are believed to always desire and enjoy sexual interaction with a woman, even under forced circumstances (Bourke, 2007). It is perhaps for this reason that male victims are more likely to report a sex offence when the perpetrator is male rather than female and are less likely to utilise the term rape, despite the event's alignment with the current legal definition (Weiss, 2010).

In much the same way as the female perpetrator, the male sexual violence victim is made invisible through various intersecting gendered structures and discourses, despite the possibility that the consequences of any form of abuse may transcend gender roles (Vandiver, 2006). This invisibility is primarily a result of discursive codes placed on the body that denote the phallus as a weapon capable of violation and the vagina as vulnerable to it (Woodhull, 1988). In his discussions on the legal system's conceptualisation of human sexuality, Foucault (1988) questions why rape, defined by penile penetration and assault at the time, should have different legal consequences to an assault performed by any other body part. In asking this question, Foucault (1988) interrogates the definition of rape as penile and therefore masculine, and implies that other parts of the body and other genders may also be imbued with the capacity to rape. However, given Foucault's (1978) overall lack of specific interest in gender politics and the differential effects of power on the masculine and feminine body (Dean, 1994), he does not venture further than this. Nonetheless, Foucault's (1988) questioning does point to the way historical productions of the body have ensured that certain body parts are oversexualised. Cahill (2000) advances this by noting how rape, often defined as something a woman, rather than a man, experiences, is reflective of a culture that promotes women as victims; thus, when a man is subjected to an act of sex abuse such as rape, he is feminised. This is because masculinity remains irreconcilable with victimhood and vulnerability. So, definitions typically attached to sex abuse in medical and legal documents tend to centre on female victimisation and ignore male-specific factors. As a consequence, men take up a masculine identity, and those implicated in FSA often do not consider themselves to be victims or the event to be criminal. Male sexual violence victims thus have very few subject positions available to occupy, and these are often limited to being identified as weak, homosexual, or feminine (Barth, Bermetz, Heim, Trelle, & Tonia, 2013), and as having failed to meet the standards of hegemonic masculinity (Weiss, 2010). This heteronormative gendering of sexual violence results in sociocultural barriers to the possibility of male sexual victimisation and a sense that, unlike in the case of the 'normalcy' of female victimhood, male victimisation is abnormal.

Male victims are also constructed as potential future perpetrators (victim-offenders), which is rarely the case with female victims (Schaeffer, Leventhal, & Asnes, 2011). In fact, despite there being scant research in the area of male sexual victimisation, there appears to be an abundance of studies that have set out to prove that the cycle of sexual violence in male victims (e.g. Duncan & Williams, 1998; Glasser et al., 2001; Lambie, Seymour, Lee, & Adams, 2002; Salter et al., 2003; Thomas & Fremouw, 2009) is attributable to the victim's mother (Lambie et al., 2002) or another female (Duncan & Williams, 1998; Salter et al., 2003). This has the effect of regenerating the vicious cycle whereby male victims are reluctant to report their experiences, which results in a significantly small measured prevalence of male sex abuse. In response, fewer studies are conducted on male victims (Finkelhor, 1994), which is evidenced by the discrepancy between the vast available research on female sexual victimisation versus the scant literature on male victims (Weiss, 2010). Given all of these legal, academic, and public constraints, men subjected to sex abuse are unable to easily position themselves within the possibilities of victimhood. Even when men are able to self-identify as victims, they tend to draw on other discursive codes for masculinity in delineating their experiences of victimisation in order to "repair, reclaim or reassert masculinity" (Weiss, 2010, p. 289) and counteract the feminisation associated with victimisation. Thus, typical narratives relayed by male victims often emphasise alcoholic or substance intoxication at the time of abuse, and other ways in which his capacity to offer resistance was compromised (Weiss, 2010). This demonstrates the stability of gendered discourses – despite evidence for extremely high rates of various types of masculine victimisation in South Africa (Kramer & Ratele, 2012), the impossibility of masculine victimhood continues to be perpetuated, even by male victims themselves. Through the very act of being sexually victimised by a woman, the male victim threatens masculine discourses, as he can no longer be structured as sexually potent and assertive. As Weiss argues (2010, p. 293),

> when men report sexual victimization [by women], they are publically admitting that they were not interested in sex, were unable to control situations, and were not able to take care of matters themselves – all statements that run counter to hegemonic constructs of masculinity.

Those men that do occupy a victim subject position, and thus acknowledge lack of consent for sexual interaction, violate gender codes that imply that only women can and want to exercise sexual restraint. The violation is often renegotiated at the level of the legal system, where it is upheld that men are incapable of being "aroused if they are unwilling participants" (Giguere &

Bumby, 2007, p. 3). Thus, FSA male victims that have experienced arousal or ejaculation are often regarded as consenting parties rather than as victims, and their experiences are frequently used in court as evidence that female sex crime perpetration is not possible in such cases (Bourke, 2007). Adherence to gendered and (hetero)sexual norms that imply that women are sexual gate-keepers and men are incapable of sexual restraint thus assist the legal system in maintaining that these are not 'real' crimes (Weiss, 2010). This is further supported by social constructions of victims as innocent, passive, and incapable of self-defense, which are attributes reserved for women rather than men. It thus seems that sexual violence is understood in relation to who the victim is, rather than according to the situation in which the violence occurred (Richardson & May, 1999).

FSA represents a challenge to the dichotomy of the sexes, especially because it serves as a reminder that "not only the female body, but the male body as well, is violable, penetrable" (Bourke, 2007, p. 212). Whilst the discursive associations between masculinity and victimhood are still vague and are primarily excluded from sex abuse discourses, the international recognition that lower-income countries such as South Africa have higher prevalence rates of male sex-abuse victims (Barth et al., 2013) does provide a platform for interrogating the emergence of both male victims generally and FSA victims particularly. This surfacing will surely disrupt the recalcitrant image of the male perpetrator and female victim and, by extension, male victims and female perpetrators will more readily occupy subject positions currently incompatible with their gender stereotypes (Weiss, 2010).

This chapter's evaluation of the material, political, and historical conditions of possibility for gender and sexuality has illustrated how sexuality, as a socio-historical construction, has come to occupy a powerful position in circulated knowledge. Sexuality is thus able to prescribe available subject positions and, in consequence, subjectivities that can be taken up or resisted by individuals. By questioning the exclusion of FSA victimhood in modern discourse, I intend to begin a process of what Halperin (1989, p. 273) has referred to as de-centring sexuality so that the "historicity, conditions of emergence, modes of construction, and ideological contingencies" of sexuality can be examined. This will present an opportunity to detail the ways social science, at particular points in history, has thus far constructed sexuality; and how, given the recent shifts in the possibilities of gender as demonstrated by the rise of female criminality and the surfacing of the male victim, the current South African and global context provides a historical moment for the emergence of the FSA victim and points of possible identifications of the self-therein.

Notes

1 Biopower refers to diffuse techniques that regulate and control the population.
2 LGBT is an acronym that stands for lesbian, gay, bisexual, and transgender.
3 The use of the word 'man' has obvious gender implications in the context of a book that aims to demonstrate the implications of widely circulated constructions of masculinity and femininity. The use of this word in no way implies that 'man' encapsulates humanity. Rather, it simply alludes to the comment put forward by Winnubst (1999).

References

Adler, F. (1975). *Sisters in crime*. New York, NY: McGraw-Hill.

Alcoff, L., & Gray, L. (1993). Survivor discourse: Transgression or recuperation? *Signs*, *18*(2), 260–290.

Ariès, P. (1973). *Centuries of childhood*. New York, NY: Jonathan Cape.

Armstrong, D. (1986). The invention of infant mortality. *Sociology of Health and Illness*, *8*(3), 211–232.

Barth, J., Bermetz, L., Heim, E., Trelle, S., & Tonia, T. (2013). The current prevalence of child sexual abuse worldwide: A systematic review and meta-analysis. *International Journal of Public Health*, *58*(3), 469–483.

Bartky, S. L. (1988). Foucault, femininity, and the modernization of patriarchal power. In I. Diamond & L. Quinby (Eds.), *Feminism and Foucault: Reflections on resistance* (pp. 93–111). Boston, MA: Northeastern University Press.

Bem, S. L. (1993). *The lenses of gender: Transforming the debate on sexual inequality*. New Haven, CT and London: Yale University.

Bourke, J. (2007). *Rape: A history from 1860 to the present*. London: Virago Press.

Bowman, B. (2010). Children, pathology and politics: A genealogy of the paedophile in South Africa between 1944 and 2004. *South African Journal of Psychology*, *40*(4), 443–464.

Brockman, B., & Bluglass, R. (1996). A general psychiatric approach to sexual deviation. In I. Rosen (Ed.), *Sexual deviation* (3rd ed.) (pp. 1–42). New York, NY: Oxford University Press.

Butchart, A. (1997). Objects without origins: Foucault in South African socio-medical science. *South African Journal of Psychology*, *27*(2), 101–110.

Butler, J. (1989). Foucault and the paradox of bodily inscriptions. *The Journal of Philosophy*, *86*(11), 601–607.

Butler, J. (1999). *Gender trouble*. New York, NY and London: Routledge.

Butler, J. (2004). *Undoing gender*. London: Routledge.

Cahill, A. J. (2000). Foucault, rape, and the construction of the feminine body. *Hypatia*, *15*(1), 43–63.

Cauffman, E. (2008). Understanding the female offender. *Juvenile Justice*, *18*(2), 119–142.

Chan, H. C. O., & Frei, A. (2013). Female sexual homicide offenders: An examination of an underresearched offender population. *Homicide Studies*, *17*(1), 96–118.

Chesney-Lind, M. (1989). Girls' crime and woman's place: Toward a feminist model of female delinquency. *Crime & Delinquency*, *35*(1), 5–29.

Collins, P. H. (1998). It's all in the family: Intersections of gender, race and nation. *Hypatia, 13*(3), 62–82.

Collins, R., Saltzman Chafetz, J., Lesser Blumberg, R., Coltrane, S., & Turner, J. H. (1993). Toward an integrated theory of gender stratification. *Sociological Perspectives, 36*(3), 185–216.

Connell, R. W. (1993). The big picture: Masculinities in recent world history. *Theory and Society, 22*(5), 597–623.

Connell, R. W., & Messerschmidt, J. W. (2005). Hegemonic masculinity: Rethinking the concept. *Gender & Society, 19*(6), 829–859.

Dean, C. J. (1994). The productive hypothesis: Foucault, gender, and the history of sexuality. *History and Theory, 33*(3), 271–296.

Demetriou, D. Z. (2001). Connell's concept of hegemonic masculinity: A critique. *Theory and Society, 30*(3), 337–361.

Denov, M. S. (2003). The myth of innocence: Sexual scripts and the recognition of child sexual abuse by female perpetrators. *The Journal of Sex Research, 40*(3), 303–314.

Digeser, P. (1992). The fourth face of power. *The Journal of Politics, 54*(4), 977–1007.

van Dijk, T. A. (2001). Critical discourse analysis. In D. Tannen, D. Schiffrin & H. Hamilton (Eds.), *Handbook of discourse analysis* (pp. 352–371). Oxford: Blackwell Publishing.

Donaldson, M. (1993). What is hegemonic masculinity? *Theory and Society, Special Issue: Masculinities, 22*(5), 643–657.

Donzelot, J. (1979). *The policing of families.* New York, NY: Pantheon Books.

Duncan, L. E., & Williams, L. M. (1998). Gender role socialization and male-on-male vs. female-on-male child sexual abuse. *Sex Roles, 39*(9–10), 765–785.

Finkelhor, D. (1994). Current information on the scope and nature of child sexual abuse. *The Future of Children, 4*(2), 31–53.

Fisher, B. S., & Cullen, F. T. (2000). Measuring the sexual victimization of women: Evolution, current controversies and future research. *Criminal Justice, 4*, 317–390.

Foucault, M. (1977a). *Discipline and punish: The birth of the prison.* London and New York, NY: Penguin Books.

Foucault, M. (1977b). *"Society must be defended." Lectures at the College De France, 1975–76.* New York, NY: Picador.

Foucault, M. (1978). *The history of sexuality: An introduction.* Canada and New York, NY: The Penguin Group.

Foucault, M. (1980). *Power/knowledge: Selected interviews and other writings, 1972–1977.* New York, NY: Random House LLC.

Foucault, M. (1981). The order of discourse. In R. Young (Ed.), *"Untying the text": A post-structuralist reader* (pp. 48–78). London and Boston, MA: Routledge & Kegan Paul Ltd.

Foucault, M. (1988). Confinement, psychiatry, prison. In L. D. Kritzman (Ed.), *Politics, philosophy, culture: Interviews and other writings, 1977–1984* (pp. 178–210). New York, NY: Routledge.

Freeman, M. (1996). Sexual deviance and the law. In I. Rosen (Ed.), *Sexual deviation* (3rd ed.) (pp. 399–451). New York, NY: Oxford University Press.

Fuss, D. (1989). *Essentially speaking: Feminism, nature and difference*. London: Routledge.

Gannon, T. A., Rose, M. R., & Ward, T. (2008). A descriptive model of the offense process for female sexual offenders. *Sexual Abuse: A Journal of Research and Treatment, 20*(3), 352–374.

Gavey, N. (2012). Beyond "empowerment?" Sexuality in a sexist world. *Sex Roles, 66*(11–12), 718–724.

Genel, K. (2006). The question of biopower: Foucault and Agabem. *Rethinking Marxism: A Journal of Economics, Culture and Society, 18*(1), 43–62.

Giguere, R., & Bumby, K. (2007). *Female sexual offenders*. Silver Spring, MD: Center for Sex Offender Management.

Gill, R. (2008). Empowerment/sexism: Figuring female sexual agency in contemporary advertising. *Feminism & Psychology, 18*(1), 35–60.

Gill, R. (2012). Media, empowerment and the "sexualization of culture" debates. *Sex Roles, 66*(11–12), 736–745.

Gilman, S. L., King, H., Porter, R., Rousseau, G. S., & Showalter, E. (1993). *Hysteria beyond Freud*. Berkeley, CA: University of California Press.

Glasser, M., Kolvin, I. Campbell, D., Glasser, A., Leitch, I., & Farrelly, S. (2001). Cycle of child sexual abuse: Links between being a victim and becoming a perpetrator. *British Journal of Psychiatry, 179*(6), 482–494.

Graves, K. N. (2007). Not always sugar and spice: Expanding theoretical and functional explanations for why females aggress. *Aggression and Violent Behaviour, 12*(2), 131–140.

Gubrium, J. F., & Holstein, J. A. (1994). Grounding the postmodern self. *The Sociological Quarterly, 35*(4), 685–703.

Halperin, D. M. (1989). Is there a history of sexuality? *History and Theory, 28*(3), 257–274.

Halperin, D. M. (1998). Forgetting Foucault: Acts, identities, and the history of sexuality. *Representations, 63*, 93–120.

Hearn, J. (2004). From hegemonic masculinity to the hegemony of men. *Feminist Theory, 5*(1), 49–72.

Higgs, D. C., Canavan, M. M., & Meyer, W. J. (1992). Moving from defense to offense: The development of an adolescent female sexual offender. *The Journal of Sex Research, 29*(1), 131–139.

Holden, M. (2009, November 9). Sex attacks by women on children soar. *Reuters*. Retrieved from http://news.uk.msn.com/uk/articles.aspx?cp-documentid=150771474.html

Hopper, J. (2007). *Child Abuse: Statistics, Research and Resources*. Retrieved from www.jimhopper.com/abstats.html

Jewkes, R. K., Penn-Kekana, L., Levin, J., Ratsaka, M., & Schreiber, M. (1999). *"He must give me money, he mustn't beat me": Violence against women in three South African provinces*. Pretoria: Medical Research Council.

Klein, D. (1976). The etiology of female crime: A review of the literature. In L. Crites (Ed.), *The female offender* (pp. 5–31). Canada and Lexington, MA: D.C. Heath and Company.

Knoll, J. (2010). Teacher sexual misconduct: Grooming patterns and female offenders. *Journal of Child Sexual Abuse, 19*(4), 371–386.

Koss, M. P. (1992). The underdetection of rape: Methodological choices influence incidence estimates. *Journal of Social Issues, 48*(1), 61–75.

Koss, M. P. (2011). Hidden, unacknowledged, acquaintance, and date rape: Looking back, looking forward. *Psychology of Women Quarterly, 35*(2), 348–354.

Koss, M. P., Heise, L., & Russo, N. P. (1994). The global health burden of rape. *Psychology of Women Quarterly, 18*(4), 509–537.

Kramer, S. (2010). *Discourse and power in the self-perceptions of incarcerated South African female sex offenders.* Unpublished Masters thesis. University of the Witwatersrand, Johannesburg.

Kramer, S., & Ratele, K. (2012). Young black men's risk to firearm homicide in night time Johannesburg, South Africa: A retrospective analysis based on the National Injury Mortality Surveillance System. *African Safety Promotion: A Journal of Injury and Violence Prevention, 10*(1), 16–28.

Kruttschnitt, C., Gartner, R., & Hussemann, J. (2008). Female violent offenders: Moral panics or more serious offenders? *The Australian and New Zealand Journal of Criminology, 41*(1), 9–35.

Lamb, S., & Peterson, Z. (2012). Adolescent girls' sexual empowerment: Two feminists explore the concept. *Sex Roles, 66*(11–12), 703–712.

Lambie, I., Seymour, F., Lee, A., & Adams, P. (2002). Resiliency in the victim-offense cycle in male sexual abuse. *Sexual Abuse: A Journal of Research and Treatment, 14*(1), 31–48.

Levett, A. (1992). Regimes of truth: A response to Diana Russel. *Agenda, 8*(12), 67–74.

Lorber, J. (2000). Using gender to undo gender: A feminist degendering movement. *Feminist Theory, 1*(1), 79–95.

Lützen, K. (1995). La mise en discours and silences in research on the history of sexuality. In R. G. Parker & J. H. Gagnon (Eds.), *Conceiving sexuality: Approaches to sex research in a postmodern world* (pp. 19–31). New York, NY and London: Routledge.

McFadden, P. (2003). Sexual pleasure as feminist choice. *Feminist Africa, 2,* 50–60.

McNay, L. (1991). The Foucauldian body and the exclusion of experience. *Hypatia, 6*(3), 125–139.

McWhorter, L. (2004). Sex, race and biopower: A Foucauldian genealogy. *Hypatia, 19*(3), 38–62.

Miller, E. (1986). *Street women.* Philadelphia, PA: Temple University Press.

Miller, H. A., Turner, K., & Henderson, C. E. (2009). Psychopathology of sex offenders: A comparison of males and females using latent profile analysis. *Criminal Justice and Behaviour, 36*(8), 778–792.

Miller, P. A. (1998). The classical roots of poststructuralism: Lacan, Derrida and Foucault. *International Journal of the Classical Tradition, 5*(2), 204–225.

Mohanty, C. T. (1988). Under western eyes: Feminist scholarship and colonial discourse. *Feminist Review, 30*(1), 61–88.

Moi, T. (2004). From femininity to finitude: Freud, Lacan, and feminism, again. *Signs, 29*(3), 841–878.

Morrell, R., Jewkes, R., & Lindegger, G. (2012). Hegemonic masculinity/masculinities in South Africa: Culture, power, and gender politics. *Men and Masculinities, 15*(1), 11–30.

Muehlenhard, C. L., & Kimes, L. A. (1999). The social construction of violence: The case of sexual and domestic violence. *Personality and Social Psychology Review, 3*(3), 234–245.

Muftić, L. R., Bouffard, J. A., & Bouffard, L. A. (2007). An exploratory study of women arrested for intimate partner violence: Violent women or violent resistance? *Journal of Interpersonal Violence, 22*(6), 753–774.

Murnen, S. K., Wright, C., & Kaluzny, G. (2002). If "boys will be boys," then girls will be victims? A meta-analytic review of the research that relates masculine ideology to sexual aggression. *Sex Roles, 46*(11/12), 359–375.

Naffine, N. (1987). *Female crime: The construction of women in criminology.* Sydney, Wellington, London and Winchester: Allen & Unwin.

Nathan, P., & Ward, T. (2002). Female sex offenders: Clinical and demographic features. *The Journal of Sex Aggression, 8*(1), 5–21.

O'Sullivan, L. F., Harrison, A., Morrell, R., Monroe-Wise, A., & Kubeka, M. (2006). Gender dynamics in the primary sexual relationships of young rural South African women and men. *Culture, Health and Sexuality, 8*(2), 99–113.

Petchesky, R. P. (2008). The language of "sexual minorities" and the politics of identity: A position paper. *Reproductive Health Matters, 16*(33), 1–6.

Phelan, S. (1990). Foucault and feminism. *American Journal of Political Science, 34*(2), 421–440.

Phillips, L., & Jørgenson, M. W. (2002). *Discourse analysis as theory and method.* London: Sage.

Posel, D. (2005). Sex, death and the fate of the nation: Reflections on the politicization of sexuality in post-apartheid South Africa. *Africa, 75*(2), 125–153.

Pryce, A. (2000). Frequent observation: Sexualities, self-surveillance, confession and the construction of the active patient. *Nursing Inquiry, 7*(2), 103–111.

Ratele, K. (2009). Watch your man: Young black males at risk of homicidal violence. *SA Crime Quarterly, 33*, 19–24.

Rawlinson, M. C. (1987). Foucault's strategy: Knowledge, power and the specificity of truth. *The Journal of Medicine and Philosophy, 12*(4), 371–395. Rich, A. (1980). Compulsory heterosexuality and lesbian existence. *Women, Sex and Sexuality, 5*(4), 631–660.

Richardson, D., & May, H. (1999). Deserving victims? Sexual status and the social construction of violence. *The Sociological Review, 47*(2), 308–331.

Salter, D., McMillan, D., Richards, M., Talbot, T., Hodges, J., Bentovim, A., Hastings, R., Stevenson, J., & Skuse, D. (2003). Development of sexually abusive behavior in sexually victimized males: A longitudinal study. *The Lancet, 361*(9356), 471–476.

Sandler, J. C., & Freeman, N. J. (2007). Typology of female sex offenders: A test of Vandiver and Kercher. *Sexual Abuse: A Journal of Research and Treatment, 19*(2), 73–89.

Sawicki, J. (1999). Disciplining mothers: Feminism and the new reproductive technologies. In J. Price & M. Shildrick (Eds.), *Feminist theory and the body: A reader* (pp. 190–202). New York, NY: Routledge.

Schaeffer, P., Leventhal, J. M., & Asnes, A. G. (2011). Children's disclosures of sexual abuse: Learning from direct inquiry. *Child Abuse & Neglect, 35*(5), 343–352.

Shaw, J. J. A. (2010). Against myths and traditions that emasculate women: Language, literature, law and female empowerment. *Liverpool Law Review, 31*(1), 29–49.

Shefer, T. (2010). Narrating gender and sex in and through apartheid divides. *South African Journal of Psychology: Facing the Archive-Living Through and With Apartheid: Special Issue, 40*(4), 382–395.

Shefer, T., Stevens, G., & Clowes, L. (2010). Men in Africa: Masculinities, materiality and meaning. *Journal of Psychology in Africa, 20*(4), 511–517.

Simon, R. (1975). *The contemporary woman and crime.* Washington, DC: National Institute of Mental Health.

Staunæs, D. (2003). Where have all the subjects gone? Bringing together the concepts of intersectionality and subjectification. *NORA, 11*(2), 101–110.

Steffensmeier, D., & Allan, E. (1996). Gender and crime: Toward a gendered theory of female offending. *Annual Review of Sociology, 22*, 459–487.

Stoler, A. L. (1995). *Race and the education of desire: Foucault's history of sexuality and the colonial order of things.* Durham, NC: Duke University Press.

Sutherland, E. (1924). *Criminology.* Philadelphia, PA: Lippincott.

Swartz, L., & Levett, A. (1989). Political repression and children in South Africa: The social construction of damaging effects. *Social Science & Medicine, 28*(7), 741–750.

Terre Blanche, M. (2002). Book review: The anatomy of power: European constructions of the African Body. *African Safety Promotion: A Journal of Injury and Violence Prevention, 1*(1), 65–67.

Thomas, T. A., & Fremouw, W. (2009). Moderating variables of the sexual "victim to offender cycle" in males. *Aggression and Violent Behaviour, 14*(5), 382–387.

Travers, O. (1999). *Behind the silhouettes: Exploring the myths of child sexual abuse.* Belfast, CA: The Blackstaff Press Limited.

Turner, K., Miller, H. A., & Henderson, C. E. (2008). Latent profile analyses of offense and personality characteristics in a sample of incarcerated female sexual offenders. *Criminal Justice and Behaviour, 35*(7), 879–894.

Vandiver, D. M. (2006). Female sex offenders: A comparison of solo offenders and co-offenders. *Violence and Victims, 21*(3), 339–354.

Vandiver, D. M., & Kercher, G. (2004). Offender and victim characteristics of registered female sexual offenders in Texas: A proposed typology of female sexual offenders. *Sexual Abuse: A Journal of Research and Treatment, 16*(2), 121–137.

Vandiver, D. M., & Walker, J. T. (2002). Female sex offenders: An overview and analysis of 40 cases. *Criminal Justice Review, 27*(2), 284–300.

Weedon, C. (1987). *Feminist practice and poststructuralist theory.* London: Blackwell Publishers.

Weeks, J. (1981). *Sex, politics and society: The regulation of sexuality since 1800.* Essex and New York, NY: Longman Group Limited.

Weeks, J. (1995). History, desire and identities. In R. G. Parker & J. H. Gagnon (Eds.), *Conceiving sexuality: Approaches to sex research in a postmodern world* (pp. 33–50). London and New York, NY: Routledge.

Weiss, K. G. (2010). Male sexual victimization: Examining men's experiences of rape and sexual assault. *Men and Masculinities, 12*(3), 275–298.

White, J. W., & Kowalski, R. M. (1994). Deconstructing the myth of the nonaggressive woman: A feminist analysis. *Psychology of Women Quarterly, 18*(4), 487–508.

Wijkman, M., Bijleveld, C., & Hendriks, J. (2010). Women don't do such things! Characteristics of female sex offenders and offender types. *Sexual Abuse: A Journal of Research and Treatment, 22*(2), 135–156.

Wilbraham, L. (2004). Discursive practice: Analysing a *Loveliness* text on sex communication for parents. In D. Hook, P. Kiguwa, N. Mkhize & A. Collins (Eds.), *Critical psychology* (pp. 487–521). Landsdowne: UCT Press.

Winnubst, S. (1999). Exceeding Hegel and Lacan: Different fields of pleasure within Foucault and Irigaray. *Hypatia, 14*(1), 13–37.

Woodhull, W. (1988). Sexuality, power, and the question of rape. In I. Diamond & L. Quinby (Eds.), *Feminism and Foucault: Reflections on Resistance* (pp. 167–176). Boston, MA: Northeastern University Press.

3

DISCURSIVE POSSIBILITIES FOR FEMALE-PERPETRATED SEX ABUSE VICTIMS

This chapter builds on Chapter 2's demonstrations of how particular gender and sexuality constructions are contingent on material, political, and historical conditions by applying this framework to the specific example of FSA victimhood. FSA victimhood is thus understood as (im)possible in light of specific institutionalised discourses that are very evidently entrenched in a grid of gender and sexuality constructions. For example, psychological discourses concerning trauma and victimhood, and legal discourses in the form of laws, statutes, and judicial and law enforcement principles and attitudes, are imbedded in gendered philosophies that limit men, women, and children to particular roles in a sex abuse event. These institutionalised discourses are further understood in terms of their reciprocal relationship with public discourses, promulgated by media messages and images that sexualise the female perpetrator and invisibilise her victims. The chapter concludes by showing how the use of a theoretical framework that understands FSA victimhood as contingent on particular conditions provides an impetus to disrupt normative categories of gender and sexuality through the critical exploration of discursive coordinates employed by self-identified FSA victims.

Victim subject positions: the role of gender, power, and sexuality

In line with Foucault's understanding of the discursive constitution of subjectivity, this text treats subjects as constituted in discourse through power (Foucault, 1978) and configured through technologies of the self (Foucault,

1985). Thus, an individual is formed and shaped through subjection; however, it is the practices of the self that sustain subjectivity. For Foucault (1985), these technologies of the self are the subject's compliant behaviours and manners that yield to an ensemble of regulatory discursive codes. Foucault (1985, p. 25) refers to these codes as 'moral orthopaedics', and describes them as "a set of values and rules of action that are recommended to individuals through the intermediary of various prescriptive agencies such as the family ... educational institutions, churches, and so forth". The inference is that those individuals that do not comply with this 'moral code' are drawing on technologies of the self to practice resistance. This echoes Butler's (1997) contention that performativity is discursively constitutive in either the reproduction or resistance of authoritative codes. It is thus through the application of the principles of the technologies of the self or performativity that the occupation of an FSA victim subject position could be understood as a form of resistance.

'Subject positions' exist within discourse as a system of concepts that are historically and culturally supported by various authoritative institutions (Weedon, 1987). Thus, knowledge about sexual abuse, the conditions of possibility for which are enabled, consolidated, and perpetuated by the social and medical sciences, provides the grounding for potential subject positions, which includes a victim that is often female and an aggressor that is almost always male (Levett, 1990). While the possibility of male victim subject positions and, more recently, female aggressor subject positions are rare, they are possible at the periphery of normative discourses. However, other than the potentially conceivable child victim, the subject position for an FSA victim is almost completely excluded from discourse. Butler (2004) proposes that gendered and sexualised normative discourses are unable to encapsulate the full range of potential human identities as they are constrained by boundaries that exclude particular subjects from the given organisation of 'truth'. However, normative gender and sexuality discourses stand against abnormality (Dean, 1994). Thus, reading non-normative victim positions will always provide some insight into the way normative positions are constituted. This is the underlying logic supporting the exploration of non-normative self-identifications of subjects, such as FSA victims. A focus on these peripheral and largely excluded forms of victimhood points very precisely to the way that gender, sexuality, and abuse are constituted in the construction of FSA and in sexual violence more broadly.

Given the widely circulated discourses that imply that the female is passive and maternal, not only is FSA itself considered a rare practice, but the potential for it to be harmful and therefore produce trauma is also regarded as unlikely (Denov, 2001). However, for Butler (1997, 1999), performativity implies that these normative discourses are not absolute. While performativity refers to a means of reproducing discourse and the consequent disciplining of bodies, it also refers to forms of subversion of discourse and thus the enabling of different bodies and subjects. Although sexual and gender norms have the power to shape self-knowledge and consequently subjectivity, this shaping is neither monolithic nor impervious to multiple contestations. This is primarily because the production of subjects is always in flux and so never delivers a final end point or product. Rather, gender and sexual identity formation is a dynamic process subject to both production and reproduction. Additionally, sexuality and gender are relational and can only be understood as performances in social interaction and in terms of the meanings attached to them by individuals (Weeks, 1981). As such, social structural forces operate in concert with individual psychological forces in producing the subject (Bem, 1993). As argued by Butler (2004, p. 15), "norms do not exercise a final or fatalistic control . . . [and] sexuality is never fully captured by any regulation". In fact, Butler (2004) proposes that sexuality can and often does surpass norms, regulation, and naturalised discursive practices by taking on alternative forms in response to these normative rules. Butler (2004, p. 29) cites the examples of

> drag, butch, femme, transgender, transsexual persons . . . [who] make us not only question what is real, and what "must" be, but they also show us how the norms that govern contemporary notions of reality can be questioned and how new modes of reality can become instituted.

In light of this, the subject is not entirely determined, but its possibilities are at least constrained by the normative sex and gender discourses that precede it. It is here that performativity's productive function becomes significant – while there is currently a limited frame of reference for FSA victims, the subversion of gendered and sexualised discourses that imply the impossibility of these victims must de facto surface alternative arrangements of sex, gender, and abuse in the contemporary world. In the act of discursively renegotiating their subjectivities, persons subjected to FSA perform an alternative discourse that opens up the possibilities for a victim subject position. By giving 'testimony' about their abuse at the hands of women, these performances are then acts of resistance that disrupt the institutionalised discourses that limit the sexual and gender diversities of human identity (Gregson & Rose, 2000).

Institutionalised discourses and FSA victimhood

A Foucauldian position views "power as a productive and creative force that fabricates individual and collective human bodies through the microtechniques of the social-medical sciences" (Butchart, 1997, p. 102) and other authoritative institutions such as religion, the law, and the media. Discourses on gender, sexuality, and other identity constituents are circulated by these institutions, relayed onto bodies, and incorporated into various subjectivities. However, these discourses exclude victimhood from FSA. This exclusion occurs primarily through an interlocking network of discourses that constrain the meaning, severity, and seriousness of the consequences of female sex acts and what can and cannot be considered 'victimisation' (Muehlenhard & Kimes, 1999). South African discourses that exclude FSA victimhood do, in some ways, overlap with Euro-American discourses. However, South African discourses are likely to be further complicated by their uneven dispersion across a context characterised by multiple inequalities. It is therefore necessary to further explore the particular ways that race, power, pathology, gender, and sexuality intersect and take shape across the racialised context of post-Apartheid South Africa.

Acts of transgression, such as FSA, provide evidence for an entrenched ontology of gender because these events so obviously oppose those gender constructions declared by discourse as 'real' (Butler, 2004). The 'truth' about sex and sexuality, therefore, is not necessarily about objectivity and neutrality, but rather about what is available in discourse. Parker (2005) stresses that 'truth' is grounded in language rather than in seemingly 'natural states', and subjectivity is thus a social construction rather than an ontological fact. However, as a consequence of these constructions, subjectivities become "materially effective in the way that people use and are used by language" (Parker, 2005, p. 165). Given the FSA victim's invisibility in currently circulated discourse, the opportunity for persons subjected to FSA to take up a victim subject position is limited and therefore he/she cannot exist in discursive 'truth'. In order to bring the FSA victim into the realm of discourse, an incitement to discourse is necessary. This is traditionally achieved through the mode of the confession.

Psychological discourse: trauma and the role of the confession

For Foucault (1978), one of the primary means of self-making occurs through the process of confession. This process dates back to the traditional penance and "the obligation to admit to violations of the laws of sex" (Foucault, 1978, p. 20). In the act of confession, the speaker's actions are transformed from illegitimate to legitimate and his "subjectivity from bad to good, from outside law and truth to inside" (Alcoff & Gray, 1993, p. 270). These confessional requirements have become so deeply engrained in the structure of modern societies that the confessional context has become both normative and one of the primary means of producing discourses on sexuality. This has resulted in the invisibility of the disciplinary obligation to confess and, in turn, the invisibility of the role of power in such obligations (Foucault, 1978). Furthermore, the apparatus of the confession implies that 'truth' is hidden within a given subject as an assembly of secrets that must be liberated (Phelan, 1990). So, "the self is not disclosed by confession, it is constituted by confession" (Tell, 2007, p. 4). Thus, Foucault (1978) argues that confessions are critically constitutive of sexual and gender subjectivities.

Today, the therapeutic context has replaced the church as an appropriate space for confession. The therapeutic model thus provides a means for the production of sex abuse categories in concert with the constitution of sex abusers and victims thereof as particular subjects that 'inhabit' sex abuse subjectivities. This is possible because the historical constitution of sexual deviancy has implicated the psychotherapeutic model as a therapeutic confessional site that facilitates healing[1] (Pryce, 2000). The confession functions to incite discourses that are legitimated or corroborated by 'expert' listeners. Through its normalising potential, the confession is thus central to the production of sexual norms and transgressions thereof (Alcoff & Gray, 1993).

For Foucault (1978), the confession is an essential relay in the surveillance of the subject. There are specific rules that apply to confessions that may be considered to reflect the traumatic or are *trauma-related*. Individuals that identify as sexually abused expect to be traumatised, "although they may be unclear as to what exactly this 'damage' would involve" (Levett, 1990, p. 43). Discourse on sexual trauma also implies that there must be a victim (usually female) and an aggressor (usually male). Thus, sex traumas replete with 'discourses of damage' (Levett, 1990) circumscribe victimhood as an inevitable outcome of abuse. Addressing this 'damage' requires consistent surveillance of the self so that the minutiae of the act and its impact can be disclosed to the 'expert' – most usually construed as a mental health practitioner or psychologist. The psychologist expert is therefore key to the incitement to sex that is taken up as an object for study and treatment by the human sciences.

Trauma is thus arguably the product of intersecting social processes and definitions rather than an outcome of any particular event (Swartz & Levett, 1989). Furthermore, trauma due to sexual victimisation is often associated with subsequent cases of sexual revictimisation – a phenomenon whereby one instance of sex abuse is postulated to result in learned subordination, a victim identity, and thus exposure to further sexual assaults (Gidycz, 2011). This frequently cited 'finding' demonstrates both the power and durability of the victim subject position once it has been occupied. However, given that the gender of the aggressor in FSA is incompatible with constructions of sexual- and violence-related trauma, FSA victims tend to escape both the incitement to discourse in the confessional context and the related experience of being traumatised.

In the confessional context of the therapeutic space, sex abuse is a particularly powerful mode of relaying Foucault's (1985) practices of the self, as they do or do not comply with 'moral orthopaedics'. Because sex abuse and rape are primarily framed as experiences that occur on the body of the female subject, "the socially produced feminine body is precisely that ... of a *guilty pre-victim*" (Cahill, 2000, p. 56). If the female body is constructed as sexually penetrable, then this expectation renders the female subject potentially responsible – "she was somewhere she should not have been, moving her body in ways that she should not have, carrying on in a manner so free and easy as to convey an utter abdication of her responsibility of self-protection" (Cahill, 2000, p. 56). Constructions of rape require the identification of who is and/or is not accountable and deserving in the event, and therefore who has the adjunct responsibility to confess (Weiss, 2010b). This leads to victims actively seeking opportunities for disclosure both in private settings as well as on public platforms (Posel, 2005). This implied accountability is hypothesised to result in the typical feelings of guilt, shame, and self-loathing that arise in victims of rape and sex abuse. These feelings are particularly attached to beliefs that the act of rape defiles and tarnishes a female's sexuality and body that is often (although not universally) constructed as sanitised and pure (Weiss, 2010b).

The construction of rape as an event that occurs on a fragile and penetrable female body is reinforced by biological 'truths' inscribed on the gendered body that imply that, while all men may not be rapists, all women are potentially rape victims. So engrained is this discourse that rape has come to play a central role in the production of the modern female body, a body that is defined by its vulnerability and penetratability (Cahill, 2000). The construction of rape as particular to the female experience influences the subjection of both its victims and perpetrators (Ryan, 2011). According to early feminists (Brownmiller, 1975; Griffin, 1979; Riger & Gordon, 1981), rape has historically functioned as an instrument of social regulation whereby its threat ensures that all women are affected by it, regardless of whether they are actually raped or not. The construction of rape as something that is always a potential outcome for a woman's body results in women self-regulating their movements, appearances, and behaviours through space and time. Thus, the earlier traditional definition of rape ensures that women impose restrictions on their own behaviour, and thus remain passive and victimised (Riger & Gordon, 1981). Gavey (2013) thus argues that both subjectivity and culture are produced at the intersection of sex and rape. Gavey (2013) traces the construction of rape (and sex more generally) across time to demonstrate the way that social codes have transformed women into inevitable victims and men into innately aggressive sexual transgressors. Gavey (2013) thus questions how the productive power of gendered discourse constrains possibilities for sexual violence such that the construct of rape as something done by a man to a woman persists. These constructions tend to foreclose the possibility of a male rape victim.

Richardson and May (1999) argue that violence is always gendered and victimhood is always mediated through culpability. These two points, taken together, may explain why certain victims are treated as 'deserving victims' (Boonzaier, 2014). For example, a woman dressed in a 'provocative' way or a gay victim of homophobic violence (both subjects being threats to the heteronormative social order and perceived as promiscuous) "are unlikely to be construed as 'innocent' victims" (Richardson & May, 1999, p. 310). Studies have demonstrated that homosexual male rape victims are likely to be held more accountable for their sexual victimisation than their heterosexual counterparts. In addition, homosexual male victims are perceived to experience pleasure in the act of a sexual assault, especially if this act involved sodomy. Both hetero- and homosexual male victims are frequently considered less traumatised than female victims of the same sex crime (Mitchell, Hirschman, & Hall, 1999).

Children, however, are usually constructed as pure, naïve, and innocent (Ariès, 1973), and therefore their experiences are viewed as incommensurate with any conception of adult sexuality (Bhana, 2006). Children therefore are not often considered responsible for their victimisation (see Wyatt & Peters, 1986) and, in consequence, are regularly treated as powerless. However, this treatment of children is not entirely stable across history and context and, in some cases, children are made accountable for their experiences of violence. For example, under the South African Apartheid regime, black children were not necessarily constructed in the same way as their white counterparts. Whereas white children were imbued with innocence and defenselessness, black children, by virtue of their 'blackness', were constructed as always vulnerable to their innate violent impulses and thus not necessarily pure and naïve (Swartz & Levett, 1989). Whilst South Africa is no longer an Apartheid state, the social undercurrents of continued racial inequality as well as the powerful remnants of a previously politically violent landscape means that the country accommodates multiple modes of victimhood that may or may not overlap with social structures that construct victims in other countries.

In light of the exclusion of FSA (and its victims more particularly) from normative discourse, the confessional context remains largely inaccessible to FSA victims. This discursive exclusion and inaccessible confessional context has the effect of ensuring that persons subjected to FSA are unable to occupy a victim subject position and produce themselves as traumatised subjects. Recent understandings of sex abuse, sexual victimisation, and rape have asserted the importance of victims' own self-perceptions of a potentially abusive sexual encounter (Koss, 2011). Thus, instead of a heavy reliance on legal or medical definitions, current sex abuse assessments attempt to measure a given individual's self-perception of victimisation. Koss' (2011) review has demonstrated how apparent self-perceptions and consequent self-making are merely reflective of larger regulating institutionalised discourses. In fact, historical changes in the meanings of terms such as 'rape', 'sex abuse', and 'sexual victimisation' "filter into the culture at large", with the effect of subjects 'realising' the applicability of these new definitions to their experiences (Koss, Heise, & Russo, 1994, p. 510). Psychotherapy is readily available as a site of confession, and thus if it is to become accessible to FSA victims, it may provide the conditions for inciting the discourses that underlie self-identification for FSA victimhood.

Legal discourse: constraining reporting possibilities

Given the legal system's role as a powerful surveillance and regulatory mechanism capable of meting out punishment, legal discourse in the form of statutes, laws, and practices presents a particularly powerful resource for self-regulation by individuals (Richardson & May, 1999). Legal definitions limit and regulate behaviours so that they are consistent with what is socially acceptable, socially expected, and socially desirable. In view of the fact that the law is principally concerned with governing violence, sexuality, and gender, it is important that legal definitions of FSA and victimhood be further explored.

Violence risk is often understood in dichotomous terms using variables such as public (a place of risk) versus private (a place of safety) and male (agressor) versus female (victim) as a way to frame both the definition of violence and our understandings of acceptable versus nonacceptable social behaviour. Additionally, spatio-temporal markers of violence circumscribe how the legal system treats a victim thereof (Richardson & May, 1999). Muehlenhard and Kimes (1999) have proposed that, since definitions of violence are temporal- and context-specific rather than reflections of universal human experience, that which is considered violent and those who are considered victims of this violence are context-bound. This results in an array of behaviours being subject to scholarly analysis, medical examination, and legal penalty, while another set of behaviours (such as female sexual transgressions) escape such scrutiny and are thus not considered violent. In addition, despite the widening of legal definitions for rape, the residue of older laws (such as those prohibiting wives from making rape allegations against their husbands or definitions that include only penile penetration) continue to influence legal perceptions of who can lay a legitimate claim to victimhood (Weiss, 2010b). This has the effect of both invisibilising and condoning particular behaviours. For example, the lenient treatment of South African female sex offenders continues (Kramer, 2010, 2011), despite the amendment of the Sexual Offences Act to include women as potential sex offenders (Minister for Justice and Constitutional Development, 2007). Limited references to FSA in legal discourse also compounds this invisibility. Those victims that do, however, come forward have no legal framework to support their experiences and are thus treated completely differently to victims of male sex abuse. This differential treatment takes the form of dismissal, mistrust, doubt, or disbelief.

The legal system generally treats victims of any sexual violence differently from victims of other forms of violence. Victim discourse is typically constrained or prohibited in some way – reported sexual assault is often dismissed across the legal system, and this limited reporting to local police stations is reflected in the alarmingly low conviction rates across the criminal justice system. This disavowal and thus silencing of victims is most evident in cases that threaten to disrupt hegemonic structures. For instance, in cases of husband-rape, women are often accused of being mad or of lying. Likewise, in cases of incest, children are regularly viewed as being incapable of providing credible reporting. This exclusion of victims' accounts from legal discourse ring-fences the way narratives must be shaped in order to be recognised. Often, this practice of exclusion further ensures that victims do not identify as such and therefore fail to report a sex crime. As Weiss (2011, p. 447) argues, "vocabularies that excuse and justify unwanted sexual situations are so entrenched within the culture's language and belief systems that victims invoke them somewhat unwittingly". The pattern of excluding sex abuse victim discourse within the legal system is likely to be even more pronounced in FSA cases, especially where victims are male and reporting would disrupt the very meaning of both masculinity and sexuality.

Until very recently, at least in South Africa, the law held that men could not be raped. Whilst these legal frameworks have been revised, there continues to be legal reluctance to prosecute cases of male rape and public reticence to view them as harmful (Bourke, 2007). Thus, the reporting of FSA is particularly complicated when the victim is a male. Given the mostly unfathomable status of the male victim, men exposed to FSA often do not view themselves as victims or the event to be criminal. This results in limited reporting.

Early traditional theories focused on general female crime have offered a chivalry hypothesis to explain male victim reporting patterns. The theory assumes that where police are men, exchanges between law enforcers and offenders are transformed into exchanges between men and women, and thus gender roles and expectations become more salient than the offence. This gives rise to the more lenient and preferential treatment of female offenders in the criminal justice system. Male victims of female perpetrators are therefore reluctant to report their experiences to the police because law enforcers are unlikely to make arrests or to press charges (see Pollak, 1950; Visher, 1983). This pattern of (non)reporting is further exacerbated when the crime is sexual and the reporting of the crime would result in the male victim challenging his traditionally sexually potent and assertive forms of masculinity (Weiss, 2010a). Those male victims that do report FSA are challenged by the legal discourses which use arousal, ejaculation, or men's incapacity to exercise sexual restraint as evidence for its 'impossibility' (Giguere & Bumby, 2007; Weiss, 2010a). Whilst most men that experience erections or ejaculations in FSA cases express their shock at the betrayal by their own bodies, the courts use these examples as evidence of pleasure and desire (Bourke, 2007). In fact, the legal assumption that pleasure cannot be experienced during an act of sexual violence further constrains reporting, especially for male children, who experience themselves as shameful or deviant as a result of often typical experiences of pleasure during mother–son incest (Kelly, Wood, Gonzalez, MacDonald, & Waterman, 2002). Sexual violence is therefore legally constructed according to who the victim is and can be, rather than according to the nature of the reported case (Richardson & May, 1999).

As such, regardless of gender, victims are often unwilling or unable to report a crime (White & Kowalski, 1994), and thus the lack of access to reporting mechanisms for FSA victims further undermines institutional legitimisation of their victimhoods. In addition, sexual violence victims typically report experiencing shame, guilt, and self-blame as a consequence of participation in sexual transgressions that violate culturally acceptable and normative sexual moral codes. In fact, many female victims often resist reporting sexual victimisation by men in anticipation of the scrutiny of their behaviours at the 'pre-victim' stage (Weiss, 2010b). In light of FSA being both sexual *and* gender transgressive, this experience of shame is likely to be exacerbated, reducing the likelihood of reporting even further. The lack of reporting results in sustained victim invisibility through the implication that the perpetrator is not guilty and, in turn, the insinuation that there is no 'real' crime to report (Weiss, 2011). This has consequences for our ability to introduce FSA into broader discourse – the potential presence of a guilty female perpetrator (usually a male) and an innocent male victim (usually a female) completely disrupts our understandings of 'real' sexuality and thus reportable sexual violence.

Most of the historical legal discourse on sex abuse and forms of it such as rape has centred on the penetration of the vagina by the penis. The implication that rape is a potential threat to all female bodies not only isolates men as potential rape victims but also ensures that women are incapable of being viewed as potential rapists. This has obvious implications for the conditions of possibility for female perpetrators of rape and therefore the identificatory possibilities of their victims. Historically, by legal definition, because females did not have penises, they could not be considered rapists. Whilst legal reforms across the globe have recently begun to recognise FSA as a potential sex crime, the discursive organisation of these laws (the use of terms such as 'forcing sexual activity without consent' as opposed to 'rape') implies that the experience of FSA is less traumatising and significant than a male-perpetrated sex crime (Bourke, 2007). This discursive positioning also continues to constrain the possibilities of female sex crime to non-penetrative sex abuse. In South Africa, the legal amendments made to the Sexual Offences Act (Minister for Justice and Constitutional Development, 2007) appear to be slightly more progressive than other global reforms, given their inclusion of women as potential sex offenders across all types of sex abuse, including rape. However, the residue of more traditional laws and the gendered political landscape of the country appear to hamper these reforms from filtering into medico-legal and policing practices, as implied by the continued professional denial of female sex crimes (Kramer & Bowman, 2011).

The surfacing of FSA victims would necessitate legal redefinitions of rape (at least in contexts still reliant on traditional definitions) as well as shifts in the actual criminal justice practices and procedures. This in turn would constitute a major transformation in gendered discourses that circulate within and from the legal system. Such a redefinition would shift our understanding of the female body as (only) fragile and penetrable and extend this biological 'truth' to male bodies, and thus both into multiple fields of potential resistance.

Media discourse: the absence of FSA victimhood in the popular imagination

The media is one of the key vehicles for the circulation of discourses and is thus central to the construction, invention, and maintenance of public consciousness (Beckett, 1996). Gender and sexuality are enduring themes in the media that are produced through images, narratives, and stories, transmitted as either fact or fiction. This is significant given the media's tendency to produce gendered and sexualised content that aligns with orthodox views of men, women, and sexuality. For example, there is a proclivity for the media to publish images of objectified women and sexually preoccupied men. Further, the media is able to adjust the content so that the public consumption of it is received in particular ways. For instance, a sexually 'transgressive woman' is often constructed in a particularly negative way, thus assuring that the audience views her in the same vein (Ryan, 2011). Even more problematic is the ability of the media to reformulate particular events or to exclude certain images, so that taken-for-granted constructions of sexuality and gender remain unchallenged.

Female sex abuse has recently come into focus in the media, both globally ("Female teacher," 2009; "Hubby's penis put through garbage," 2011; Jones, 2012; Morris, 2009; Morris & Carter, 2009; Plefka, 2012; Sheridan, 2011; Thompson, 2011, 2012; Welch, 2012; Wilson, 2012; "Woman gets 15 more years," 2011; "Would be robber," 2011) and within the localised sub-Saharan African context ("Barbie 'not remorseful'", 2010; Conway-Smith, 2012; Masingi, 2011; "Nanny gets life," 2011; Nkomo, 2012; Rademeyer, 2010; "Visser to appeal", 2010). This relatively recent media attention on FSA and related crime is most likely the result of a combination of factors, including increased surveillance of women in general, more 'liberated' discourses targeted at women's sexual behaviour, and a heightened public focus on sexual violence. Whilst this increased visibility surfaces FSA, it also does so in ways that continue to replicate normative gender constructions. For example, a number of films have depicted situations where men are forced to have sex with women against their will; however, these situations are treated by the filmmakers (and thus the audience) as wry and humorous. Similarly, films portraying sexual relationships between an older woman and an underage boy are presented as desirable for all young men. Even in the act of being what is conventionally constructed as abusive in cases of male perpetrators, female sexual perpetrators are treated as desirable, erotic, or seductive objects by films and other forms of media (Bourke, 2007).

Newspapers reporting on FSA cases also tend to replicate normative discourses. For example, media detailing the famous United Kingdom nursery school sex-abuse case treats Vanessa George, one of the three accused, as "cuddly", "an angel", "a good mum", and an "emotionally vulnerable" victim of her male accomplice, Colin Blanchard (Morris & Carter, 2009). These comments are presented despite police evidence demonstrating that George physically perpetrated the abuse, whilst Blanchard was receiving digital images of it. Likewise, Cindy Clifton, an American teacher accused of having sex with her students, has been described as "a devoted wife, hardworking teacher, a faithful member of her church and a well-respected member of her community" who "wept in her police booking photo" (Thompson, 2011). Emily Thurber, an American woman convicted for her sexual abuse of minors, has been depicted by the media as having problems that "stem from serious trauma that probably occurred at a very young age" (Welch, 2012). This is in contrast to the media's treatment of male sex abusers, who are mostly defined as 'monsters' that cannot curb their innate aggression rather than as driven by some sort of psychological damage that is beyond their control. These male-female contrasts are particularly evident in the South African media recounts of Cezanne Visser's case.[2] In addition to providing Visser with the nickname 'Advocate Barbie', media reports have characterised her as having "blonde hair and surgically enhanced breasts" and as "severely depressed before and during the sexual offences" due to being a "battered woman" under the influence of her accomplice, Dirk Prinsloo ("Visser to appeal", 2010). Prinsloo, however, has been depicted in the media as having "depraved sexual needs" and whose last victim has described him as a "perverted bastard" and "a monster" (Rademeyer, 2010). Another example of the perpetuation of normative discourse by the news media is the way young boys are viewed as regarding "early sex with an older woman as an opportunity to boast" and assert their "manhood" (Masingi, 2011).

In cases of male-perpetrated sexual violence, the media has constructed victims as commodities to increase viewership and readership. Rape, sex abuse, and sexual violence victims are regularly represented as anguished, damaged, and violated. Victims' experiences are eroticised and sensationalised through the use of various angles and visual frames that characteristically encourage voyeurism and thus ensure increased audience numbers. These images are often supported by 'expert' interpretations, analyses, and comments (Alcoff & Gray, 1993). In addition, the victims' identities are often concealed (usually for ethical reasons), so that there is a proliferation of nameless subjects circulating as possible victims within the public imagination. This has the effect of amplifying typical constructions of sexual violence as shameful and humiliating experiences for the victims (Weiss, 2010b). It also anonymises the violent events such that limitless identification with gendered modes of victimhood is possible. Despite the media's constructions of sexual violence victims, FSA victims are mostly invisible. This is particularly true of male FSA victims. Thus, FSA reports tend to centre on the perpetrator and the crime, and whilst there may be mention of the age or gender of the victim, there is very little other representation of him/her. In contrast to other cases of sexual violence, very little 'psychologically dense' information is provided. Indeed, in the highly publicised case of Vanessa George and her accomplices, the victims remain completely unidentified by both the police and the media (Morris, 2009). While this may be the result of ethical obligations to anonymise sex abuse victims, it does stand in stark contrast to the way that the media attempt to detail as much victim information as possible in the description of male sex-abuse events. An apt example is the collection of media representations of the recent male-on-female gang rape of a South African girl, Anene Booysen, whose history, relationships, personality profile, and post-rape physical trauma has been related in detail by the mass media (e.g. Knoetze, 2013). In those rare reports where FSA victims are visibilised by the media, their stories and experiences are produced in ways that align with conventional frameworks for sexual violence. For example, despite the decidedly publicised character of the Cezanne Visser case, very little is mentioned about the victims (other than demographic details), and when they are surfaced in the media, readers are reminded that Visser is herself a "victim to manipulation by her then boyfriend, Dirk Prinsloo" ("Barbie 'not remorseful'", 2010). This is in stark contrast to a three-page article devoted to a summary of Dirk's victim, Anastasia, a "petite, 23-year-old green-eyed blonde" which includes a comprehensive description of the sex abuse from her perspective and a detailed review of the consequent emotional and psychological damage that she has endured (see Rademeyer, 2010).

The invisibility and/or conventional configuration of FSA victims in the media echo the mass media's earlier treatment of child sex-abuse victims. Up until the 'discovery' of child sex abuse in the 1960s, child sex-abuse victims were entirely invisible in the media. Even in the 1970s, the term 'child abuse' was often substituted with phrases such as 'cruelty to children'. However, despite the media's initial practice of configuring child sex abuse to conform to the normative discourses of the time, it was also the media that was key to driving public awareness about child abuse and shifting the global exercise of collective denial into a state of collective consciousness (Beckett, 1996). These reality-making activities by the media in this instance are likely to be replicated in the case of FSA, as more female sex crimes are 'discovered' and thereafter produced in the media en masse. This is likely to result in the eventual consistent visibilisation of FSA victims.

While it is noteworthy that the images and messages conveyed by and through the media are important relays for the channelling of institutionalised discourses, Gill (2012, p. 738) reminds us that it is equally important to acknowledge that the media is less a "homogenous, monolithic and all-powerful" entity and more a variety of combined and diverse platforms characterised by contradictions, differences, and context-bound particularities.

The media is typically heteronormative, classist, gendered, and racialised; however, its operation at the intersection of politics, culture, and economy, and the capacity and desire for subjects to critically engage with media-based material, does somewhat erode its totalising effects. This is evidenced by material on media platforms that allow readers to post comments about online article content. An apt example is the public response to an online article about a female caregiver who raped a five-year-old boy ("Nanny gets life", 2011). The readers' comments demonstrate a critical engagement with the way the media constructed the story – ranging from debates about the definition of 'rape' to discussions concerning the very possibility of FSA, the fairness of the caregiver's sentence given her gender, the quality of the perpetrator's legal representation, and a hypothetical gender-switching comparison. Likewise, an article written by Masingi (2011) during the Sixteen Days of Activism Against Gender Violence in South Africa, cautions readers against viewing violence in gendered terms and calls for the acknowledgement of female sex abusers and male victims. These comments represent the possibilities for counter-discourses and knowledge on FSA.

This chapter draws on psychological, legal, and media discourse to demonstrate the ways that gender and sexuality constructions are mobilised to limit and constrain possibilities for FSA victimhood. By establishing how FSA victimhood is contingent on particular historical and material conditions supported by institutionalised discourse, a rationale is presented for the critical exploration of FSA victimhood possibilities. Accordingly, this text aims to explore the role of power, gender, and sexuality in producing the conditions of possibility for victimhood in cases of FSA. Specifically, having outlined the history, aim, and politics of the text, the following chapter identifies those discursive coordinates by which persons subjected to FSA are able to identify as victims. In so doing, this text becomes yet another mechanism in the power/knowledge coupling that reifies this category of personhood. However, disrupting the normative flows of gender and sexuality as they take hold of the subject also promises to shift many of the taken-for-granted knowledge conditions that continue to define modern selfhood.

Notes

1 In South Africa, social and psychological healing may be facilitated by different cultural actors such as 'witch doctors', sangomas (Zulu term for South African practitioners of traditional African medicine), charismatic leaders, and other traditional healers.
2 Cezanne Visser, a well-known and respected South African advocate, was recently arrested and convicted for several child sex crimes as well as the manufacturing of pornography.

References

Alcoff, L., & Gray, L. (1993). Survivor discourse: Transgression or recuperation? *Signs*, *18*(2), 260–290.

Ariès, P. (1973). *Centuries of childhood*. New York, NY: Jonathan Cape.

Barbie "Not Remorseful". (2010, February 9). *News 24*. Retrieved from www.news24.com/SouthAfrica/News/Barbie-not-remorseful-20100209

Beckett, K. (1996). Culture and the politics of signification: The case of child sexual abuse. *Social Problems*, *43*(1), 57–76.

Bem, S. L. (1993). *The lenses of gender: Transforming the debate on sexual inequality*. New Haven, CT and London: Yale University.

Bhana, D. (2006). The (im)possibility of child sexual rights in South African children's account of HIV/AIDS. *IDS Bulletin*, *37*(5), 64–68.

Boonzaier, F. (2014). South African women resisting dominant discourse in narratives of violence. In S. McKenzie-Mohr & M. L. Lafrance (Eds.), *Women voicing resistance: Discursive and narrative explorations* (pp. 102–120). East Sussex and New York, NY: Routledge.

Bourke, J. (2007). *Rape: A history from 1860 to the present*. London: Virago Press.

Brownmiller, S. (1975). *Against our will: Men, women and rape*. New York, NY: Simon & Schuster.

Butchart, A. (1997). Objects without origins: Foucault in South African socio-medical science. *South African Journal of Psychology*, *27*(2), 101–110.

Butler, J. (1997). *Excitable speech: A politics of the performative*. London: Routledge.

Butler, J. (1999). *Gender trouble*. New York, NY and London: Routledge.

Butler, J. (2004). *Undoing gender*. London: Routledge.

Cahill, A. J. (2000). Foucault, rape, and the construction of the feminine body. *Hypatia*, *15*(1), 43–63.

Conway-Smith, E. (2012, May 3). Zimbabwe: "Female rapists" semen-harvesting case dropped. *Global Post*. Retrieved from www.globalpost.com/dispatches/globalpost-blogs/weird-wide-web/zimbabwe-female-rapists-semen-rituals-case-dropped

Dean, C. J. (1994). The productive hypothesis: Foucault, gender, and the history of sexuality. *History and Theory*, *33*(3), 271–296.

Denov, M. S. (2001). A culture of denial: Exploring professional perspectives on female sexual offending. *Canadian Journal of Criminology*, *43*(3), 303–329.

Female Teacher a "Predatory Paedophile". (2009, October 8). *Daily Mail*. Retrieved from www.iol.co.za/news/world/female-teacher-a-predatory-paedophile-1.460788?ot=inmsa.ArticlePrintPageLayout.ot

Foucault, M. (1978). *The history of sexuality: An introduction*. Canada and New York, NY: The Penguin Group.

Foucault, M. (1985). *The use of pleasure: The history of sexuality* (Vol. 2). New York, NY: Pantheon Books.

Gavey, N. (2013). *Just sex? The cultural scaffolding of rape*. New York, NY: Routledge.

Gidycz, C. A. (2011). Sexual revictimization revisited: A commentary. *Psychology of Women Quarterly*, *35*(2), 355–361.

Giguere, R., & Bumby, K. (2007). *Female sexual offenders*. Silver Spring, MD: Center for Sex Offender Management.

Gill, R. (2012). Media, empowerment and the "sexualization of culture" debates. *Sex Roles, 66*(11–12), 736–745.

Gregson, N., & Rose, G. (2000). Taking Butler elsewhere: Performativities, spatialities and subjectivities. *Environment and Planning D: Society and Space, 18*(4), 433–452.

Griffin, S. (1979). *Rape: The power of consciousness.* San Francisco, CA: Harper and Row.

Hubby's Penis Put Through Garbage Disposal. (2011, July 13). *Independent Online.* Retrieved from www.iol.co.za/news/world/hubby-s-penis-put-through-garbage-disposal-1.1098007

Jones, A. (2012, August 6). Female sex offenders: Rise in Wales from 78 to 193 in three years. *The Leader.* Retrieved from http://ecleader.org/2012/02/07/female-sex-offenders-more-prevalent-than-reported/

Kelly, R. J., Wood, J. J., Gonzalez, L. S., MacDonald, V., & Waterman, J. (2002). Effects of mother-son incest and positive perceptions of sexual abuse experiences on the psychosocial adjustment of clinic-referred men. *Child Abuse & Neglect, 26*(4), 425–441.

Knoetze, D. (2013, February 8). 150 rapes an hour. *The Star.* Retrieved from www.iol.co.za/the-star/150-rapes-an-hour-1.1466999#.UThg9qLviSo.html

Koss, M. P. (2011). Hidden, unacknowledged, acquaintance, and date rape: Looking back, looking forward. *Psychology of Women Quarterly, 35*(2), 348–354.

Koss, M. P., Heise, L., & Russo, N. P. (1994). The global health burden of rape. *Psychology of Women Quarterly, 18*(4), 509–537.

Kramer, S. (2010). *Discourse and power in the self-perceptions of incarcerated South African female sex offenders.* Unpublished Masters thesis. University of the Witwatersrand, Johannesburg.

Kramer, S. (2011). "Truth", gender and the female psyche: Confessions from female sexual offenders. *Psychology of Women Section Review, 13*(1), 2–8.

Kramer, S., & Bowman, B. (2011). Accounting for the "invisibility" of the female paedophile: An expert-based perspective from South Africa. *Psychology and Sexuality, 2*(3), 1–15.

Levett, A. (1990). Childhood sexual abuse and problems in conceptualisation. *Agenda, 6*(7), 38–47.

Masingi, M. (2011, December 9). Women who abuse boys. *Women 24.* Retrieved from www.women24.com/Wellness/BodyAndSpirit/Women-who-abuse-boys-20111209

Minister for Justice and Constitutional Development. (2007). *Criminal law (Sexual offences and related matters) amendment bill.* Republic of South Africa: Creda Communications.

Mitchell, D., Hirschman, R., & Hall, N. (1999). Attributions of victim responsibility, pleasure, and trauma in male rape. *The Journal of Sex Research, 36*(4), 369–373.

Morris, S. (2009, December 15). Vanessa George jailed indefinitely but victims of abuse remain unidentified. *The Guardian.* Retrieved from www.guardian.co.uk/uk/2009/dec/15/vanessa-george-sentence-child-abuse

Morris, S., & Carter, H. (2009, October 1). Vanessa George: From angel to paedophile. *The Guardian.* Retrieved from www.guardian.co.uk/society/2009/oct/01/vanessa-george-plymouth-abuse-background

Muehlenhard, C. L., & Kimes, L. A. (1999). The social construction of violence: The case of sexual and domestic violence. *Personality and Social Psychology Review, 3*(3), 234–245.

Nanny Gets Life for Raping Boy. (2011, February 28). *News 24.* Retrieved from www.news24.com/SouthAfrica/News/Nanny-gets-life-for-raping-boy-20110228

Nkomo, S. (2012, February 1). Woman jailed for raping disabled boy. *Cape Argus.* Retrieved from www.iol.co.za/news/crime-courts/woman-jailed-for-raping-disabled-boy-1.1225023#.UaNxy6LviSo

Parker, I. (2005). Lacanian discourse analysis in psychology: Seven theoretical elements. *Theory Psychology, 15*(2), 163–182.

Phelan, S. (1990). Foucault and feminism. *American Journal of Political Science, 34*(2), 421–440.

Plefka, K. (2012, February 7). Female sex offenders more prevalent than reported. *The Leader.* Retrieved from http://ecleader.org/2012/02/07/female-sex-offenders-more-prevalent-than-reported/

Pollak, O. (1950). *The criminality of women.* Philadelphia, PA: University of Pennsylvania Press.

Posel, D. (2005). Sex, death and the fate of the nation: Reflections on the politicization of sexuality in post-apartheid South Africa. *Africa, 75*(2), 125–153.

Pryce, A. (2000). Frequent observation: Sexualities, self-surveillance, confession and the construction of the active patient. *Nursing Inquiry, 7*(2), 103–111.

Rademeyer, J. (2010, February 5). Dirk's "sex toy" speaks. *Beeld.* Retrieved from www.news24.com/SouthAfrica/News/Dirks-sex-toy-speaks-20100204

Richardson, D., & May, H. (1999). Deserving victims? Sexual status and the social construction of violence. *The Sociological Review, 47*(2), 308–331.

Riger, S., & Gordon, M. T. (1981). The fear of rape: A study in social control. *Journal of Social Issues, 37*(4), 71–92.

Ryan, K. M. (2011). The relationship between rape myths and sexual scripts: The social construction of rape. *Sex Roles, 65*(11–12), 774–782.

Sheridan, M. (2011, June 16). Molly Jane Roe raped, killed boyfriend's 17-month-old baby girl, Maleeya Marie Murley: Cops. *Daily News.* Retrieved from www.nydailynews.com/news/national/molly-jane-roe-raped-killed-boyfriend-17-month-old-baby-girl-maleeya-marie-murley-cops-article-1.131092

Swartz, L., & Levett, A. (1989). Political repression and children in South Africa: The social construction of damaging effects. *Social Science & Medicine, 28*(7), 741–750.

Tell, D. (2007, November). *Michel Foucault and the Politics of Confession.* Paper presented at the annual meeting of the NCA 93rd Annual Convention, TBA, Chicago, IL. Retrieved from www.allacademic.com/meta/p187824_index.html

Thompson, P. (2011, November 9). Is this America's worst teacher? Middle school reading instructor, 41, "had sex with ELEVEN teenage boys in three month period". *Mail Online.* Retrieved from www.dailymail.co.uk/news/article-2059491/Teacher-Cindy-Clifton-41-sex-ELEVEN-teenage-boys-month-period.html

Thompson, P. (2012, August 14). Mother, 29, and her boyfriend, 62, "repeatedly raped her baby from birth until she was 18 months old." *Mail Online.* Retrieved from www.dailymail.co.uk/news/article-2188333/Mother-29-boyfriend-62-repeatedly-raped-baby-birth-18-months-old.html

Visher, C. A. (1983). Gender, police arrest decisions, and notions of chivalry. *Criminology, 21*(1), 5–28.

Visser to Appeal to Constitutional Court. (2010, December 24). *News 24.* Retrieved from www.news24.com/SouthAfrica/News/Visser-to-appeal-to-Constitutional-Court-20101224

Weedon, C. (1987). *Feminist practice and poststructuralist theory.* London: Blackwell Publishers.

Weeks, J. (1981). *Sex, politics and society: The regulation of sexuality since 1800.* Essex and New York, NY: Longman Group Limited.

Weiss, K. G. (2010a). Male sexual victimization: Examining men's experiences of rape and sexual assault. *Men and Masculinities, 12*(3), 275–298.

Weiss, K. G. (2010b). Too ashamed to report: Deconstructing the shame of sexual victimization. *Feminist Criminology, 5*(3), 286–310.

Weiss, K. G. (2011). Neutralizing sexual victimization: A typology of victims' non-reporting accounts. *Theoretical Criminology, 15*(4), 445–467.

Welch, L. (2012, December 19). Judge says female sex offender responding to therapy. *Times-News.* Retrieved from http://magicvalley.com/news/local/crime-and-courts/judge-says-female-sex-offender-responding-to-therapy/article_e46283d7-efc4-516a-b80b-df7e2c668966.html

White, J. W., & Kowalski, R. M. (1994). Deconstructing the myth of the nonaggressive woman: A feminist analysis. *Psychology of Women Quarterly, 18*(4), 487–508.

Wilson, R. (2012, January 10). Mum jailed for raping daughter. *Sunshine Coast Daily.* Retrieved from www.sunshinecoastdaily.com.au/news/a-mothers-betrayal-abuse-daughter-sex-court/1232844/

Woman Gets 15 More Years in Webcam Sex Abuse. (2011, March 23). *News 24.* Retrieved from www.news24.com/SciTech/News/Woman-gets-15-more-years-in-webcam-sex-abuse-20110323

Would-Be RobberTaughtHardLesson.(2011, July 13).*IndependentOnline.*Retrievedfrom www.iol.co.za/news/back-page/would-be-robber-taught-hard-lesson-1.1098335

Wyatt, G. E., & Peters, S. D. (1986). Issues in the definition of child sexual abuse in prevalence research. *Child Abuse & Neglect, 10*(2), 231–240.

4

ON BECOMING A VICTIM

Using the previous chapters as a platform, this chapter surfaces the particular discursive coordinates by which persons involved in FSA are able or unable to occupy a victim[1] subject position. Findings from my original research on FSA victims (see Kramer, 2014) are used to support the arguments put forward. Specifically, interviews with self-identified FSA victims provide some examples of the discursive coordinates through and by which the conditions of possibility for FSA victimhood are contoured. These interviews have been understood through Parker's (1992, 2004) critical Foucauldian-informed discourse analysis, which highlights the productive power of the apparatus of discourses, institutions, and knowledge in constituting 'truth' (Parker, 2004) in relation to FSA. Foucault's (1978, 1981) philosophy of history, sexuality, and power argues that discourse is both an effect and an instrument of power that operates through selection, exclusion, and inclusion. Parker's (1992) epistemological framework for discourse analysis aims to identify "contradictions, construction and functions of language" as a means to critically interrogate the constitution of the modern psychological subject and its location in regimes of power and knowledge (Parker, 2004, p. 310) by deconstructing emergent discourses. Parker's (1992, 2004) method therefore allows for a discursive analysis informed by Foucault's (1980, 1981) approach to language and power/knowledge. This text thus explores how the power/knowledge coupling both restricts and provides the conditions for a subject's identification as a victim of FSA. The FSA victim position is enabled by a particular arrangement of discourses on gender, power, and sexuality. This text thus explores how the organisation of discourses at a particular cultural moment provides the conditions of possibility for FSA victimhood, and the way particular discursive representations and practices of self-identified FSA victims materialise at the 'surfaces of emergence' of these discourses (Parker, 2004).

During the data-collection phase of my research, the framing of the interview context as a confessional site geared to extract victimhood, trauma, and the 'secrets' about FSA allowed for the emergence of *both* the institutionalised discourses that exclude FSA victimhood as well as those that make FSA victimhood possible. The emergent discourses therefore stand as an exemplar of the way the power/knowledge coupling targets the body politic (Foucault, 1978, 1981). In line with Butler's (1989, 1999, 2004) theories on performance, FSA victims mobilise discourses on gender, sexuality, criminality, and victimhood in producing the conditions of possibility for taking up victimhood. In particular, victimhood is built on specific discourses that provide victims with the means to construct a subjectively fathomable aetiology for their abuse. These discourses arise from victims' access to particular institutions and disciplinary frameworks, such as psychology, tertiary education, the Internet, and online media forums. FSA victimhood is negotiated as a condition arising from an 'impossible' or 'inconceivable' crime, and so my research interviews were thus a site for the construction of, resistance to, and ultimately reification of heteronormative constructions of gender and sexuality as they intersect with criminality and psychopathology. The emergent discourse on FSA thus demonstrates how speakers both police and are policed by language, and how they are active participants in either the reproduction of or resistance to dominant and/or oppressive discourses.

FSA victimhood: an emerging organisation of discourses

FSA victimhood is constructed through various discursive strategies and coordinates employed by self-identified FSA victims. Victimhood is itself a historical project that cannot be understood outside of the sociocultural context in which it has been both produced and reproduced. Widely circulated social constructions of victimhood are largely reflective of the male–perpetrator female–victim dichotomy (Gidycz, 2011; Koss, Gidycz, & Wisniewski, 1987), and are thus not easily aligned with FSA victimhood. Sexual violence is historically and socially constructed in relation to who the victim is rather than according to the situation in which the violence occurred. The consequent exclusion of particular types of victimhood has profound effects for sexual violence and victimisation, as it determines who can and cannot be considered a victim, and what does and does not constitute sexual violence (Richardson & May, 1999). Whilst FSA victimhood is conventionally excluded from discourse, there are individuals who occupy FSA victim subject positions. It is therefore essential to begin an analysis of FSA victimhood with an understanding of the types of people that self-identify as victims. This provides an initial illustration of some of the conditions that make FSA victimhood possible.

Most of the FSA victims that I have interacted with have tertiary educations and almost all of them have been exposed to some form of mainstream psychological discourse, whether in the practice of their own careers or as a result of attending therapy and/or support groups. Additionally, these victims are mostly from a middle-income context, which is in sharp contrast to the FSA offenders I engaged with in my earlier work, who were mostly uneducated and from a low-income context (Kramer, 2010, 2011). Given that my various studies have demonstrated that victims usually know their offenders and are often from the same backgrounds as their offenders (Kramer, 2010, 2011, 2014), it seems that subjects exposed to FSA in low-income contexts do not surface as victims. Further supporting this is the fact that despite multiple attempts at engaging with a range of community-based organisations, social workers, and mental health practitioners, I was unable to access FSA victims. It was only through the modes of social media, the Internet, and other text-based communication forums that self-identified victims emerged. This is a powerful indication that, at least in South Africa, victims are only capable of identifying as such if they have access to particular forms of knowledge. This could also be a function of 'class' or income level, as this directly impedes on or supports access to knowledge.

Another interesting difference is that the offenders that I have interacted with (Kramer, 2010, 2011) are primarily black, whilst the victims are mainly white (Kramer, 2014). Furthermore, the offenders do not perceive themselves as perpetrators, whereas the victims self-identify as such. It seems that the privilege of 'whiteness' allows for white-identifying subjects to occupy more socially marginalised positions without serious consequence, given their advantage and access to power simply by virtue of their position within hegemonic class structures. The same pattern has been demonstrated in the case of South African black homosexuality. Racialised discourses imply that homosexuality is 'un-African' and thus limit homosexual possibilities for black subjects, while 'mainstream' homosexuality continues to be typified by whiteness. This results in circulated constructions implying the conceivability of white homosexuality and the impossibility of its black counterpart (Kulick, 2013). Rudwick (2011) argues that this is an outcome of the Apartheid system, which regulated race through heterosexual assumptions and codes such that black subjects were treated exclusively as heterosexual subjects. The residue of these Apartheid constructions in post-Apartheid South Africa continue to constrain possibilities for black homosexuality, and this no doubt filters into (im)possibilities for any non-heteronormative black sexual subject positions. Thus, whilst these comments relate to homosexuality, they do shed some light on how whiteness presents a condition for subjects to move into more fluid sexual subject positions. In addition, they very clearly point to the intersectionality of gender, race, and sexuality (Collins, 1998), and how these complex intersections circumscribe possibilities for identity and, more importantly, for victim identities.

The ability to self-identify as a victim is conditional on possibilities that emerge through cultural discourses diffused across diverse and unequal contexts (Winnubst, 1999). Those victims that I have interacted with that were children at the time of their abuse also grew up under the Apartheid system – a context typified by the construction of white children as vulnerable. During this period, white children were subject to consistent surveillance, monitoring, and intervention (Bowman, 2010) such that these practices repeatedly implied the capacity of these children to be vulnerable and victimised. In contrast, black children, by virtue of their construction as dangerous and defiled, were often treated as threats and as such invulnerable Apartheid subjects (Swartz & Levett, 1989). The participants' characteristics may thus be reflective of the powerful remnants of earlier Apartheid conditions grounded at the intersection of race, gender, and sexuality.

During my research with FSA victims (see Kramer, 2014), subjects constructed their own understandings of male sexual violence, psychology, existing criminal taxonomies, and victimology to develop frameworks for understanding FSA perpetration and victimhood. Some of the victims were abused by their mothers, and one was abused by her domestic worker.[2] This is in keeping with Vandiver's (2006) suggestion that constructions of motherhood allow women unrestricted access to children during child-rearing activities such as bathing and clothes changing, which provides the important conditions of access to children in FSA cases. Of interest, despite the participants' abilities to classify their mothers as perpetrators, such abuse was never classified as incest. Female familial sex abusers thus seem to escape the accusations of incest that most male familial sex abusers are subjected to. The greater part of the literature on male paedophilia highlights incest as one of the primary categories of male child sex abuse (Araji & Finkelhor, 1986; Berlin & Krout, 1986; Fagan, Wise, Schmidt, & Berlin, 2002; Hall & Hall, 2007; Howitt, 1995; Kempe & Kempe, 1984). However, incest is rarely mentioned in the literature on FSA. The invisibility of female-perpetrated incest in the scientific literature is echoed by the fact that victims exposed to maternal sex abuse do not use the term 'incest' to describe female CSA.

Across my victim study (Kramer, 2014), most victims knew their perpe-trators and most were related to her (family friend, older sister, neighbour, girlfriend, aunt). The majority were exposed to multiple sex-abuse incidents, either by the same perpetrator or by a different perpetrator altogether. In fact, some of the victims identified multiple female sex abusers across their lifespans. This echoes the frequently cited 'scientific finding' of sexual revictimisation in sex abuse victims (see Gidycz, 2011). Given the power and the intractability of the victim subject position once it has been occupied, a common 'finding' is that sexual victimisation predisposes an individual to subsequent sexual rev-ictimisation. This is explored in detail later, especially with reference to how the identification with an FSA victim subject position provides the condi-tions for further sexual victimisation by female perpetrators. Victims reported a range of acts which they classified as sexually abusive. These included vaginal rape, anal rape, attempted rape, bondage–domination–sado–masochism, fon-dling, forced performance and reception of oral sex, child prostitution, child exposure to pornography, and molestation. Most of the victims' perpetrators reportedly acted alone. A female sexual perpetrator acting alone is consid-ered rare, and typical FSA categories and constructions infer the presence of an abusive male coercer (Freeman, 1996; Higgs, Canavan, & Meyer, 1992; Lawson, 2008). This is so engrained in legal understandings of FSA that all of the incarcerated offenders that I have engaged with (see Kramer, 2010) were described as accomplices to a male partner. It thus seems that while the jus-tice system's defining conditions of possibility for FSA cannot easily expand beyond those incidents characterised by male coercive instruction, FSA vic-tims occupy victim subject positions defined by perpetrators acting alone.

South African context-specific conditions for FSA victimhood

Modern sexuality, in whatever formation, is always located at the nexus of power relations, and is therefore the site for the contestation of hierarchies and differences such as race, class, socioeconomic status, and gender (Posel, 2005). The South African context is characterised by multiple and contest-ing, diverse identities as well as a current explosion of public and scientific possibilities for sexuality driven by social inequalities, high crime rates and sexual violence, and the HIV/AIDS pandemic (Bhana, 2006). Thus, it is use-ful to draw on both local and global FSA victim experiences in order to identify whether the particularly gendered and sexualised, as well as inequi-table political landscape of the country, shapes representations of and limits 'classed' possibilities for FSA victimhood in comparison to other countries characterised by different kinds of gender, sexual, socioeconomic, and racial relations. I have thus worked with international FSA victim comparison cases to juxtapose the local and global contexts and their specificities. The inclusion of international experiences provides a strategic starting-point for understanding just how differences in sociocultural contexts may specifically shape conditions of possibility for FSA victimhood.

One of the particularly noteworthy South African-specific accounts in my victim study belongs to Jane[3], who conveys how her domestic worker sexually abused her as a child. In the South African context, it is common for middle-income households to employ domestic workers who often serve as child caregivers. These women thus have unrestricted access to their employers' children and are expected to partake in particular child-rearing practices, such as bathing and clothes changing. As Jane indicates, these women are often considered to be "part of the family" and assist in raising the children. The identification of a child caregiver as a female sex abuser is in line with Vandiver's (2006) formulation that women in caregiver roles are allowed unrestricted access to children, thus providing opportunities for sex abuse. However, the presence of a live-in domestic worker is a specific South African characteristic that provides a particular condition of possibility for FSA to arise. In addition, these domestic workers are typically African women. Given racial constructions that imply that violence is perpetrated by non-whites (Gilliam, Iyengar, Simon, & Wright, 1996), it appears that a sexually violent event characterised by a 'black' perpetrator and 'white' victim further supports the conditions for this sort of emergent victimhood.

Another typically South African point made by Jane relates to the general lack of trust in the country's law enforcement, justice, and legal systems. The dismissal of FSA by police officers and legal representatives is a common function of both the global and South African exclusion of FSA from legal documents and practice (Brockman & Bluglass, 1996; Giguere & Bumby, 2007; Kramer & Bowman, 2011). However, the mistrust reported by Jane seems to speak to a general skepticism regarding the law in South Africa, regardless of the crime. Her discourse powerfully indicates the complex intersection of race, ethnicity, and power in South Africa. In our discussions, Jane, a young white woman, mockingly implies that most South African police officers are Africans that cannot speak English. In keeping with Butler's (1989, 1999, 2004) performativity, this statement suggests the superiority of English (or 'white') culture over 'African' (or 'black') culture and implies that access to the English language provides the speaker (or performer) with the sophistication to understand problems that non-English speakers cannot. However, Jane simultaneously acknowledges the power inherent in these law enforcers to invisibilise her FSA experience:

But then I mean going and sitting and explaining it to . . . a freaking cop who probably doesn't, doesn't even speak English (laughs), in our country, with our justice system. What's the point? He's gonna turn around and say, oh no it didn't happen . . . and at the end of the day the case is gonna get thrown out.

Regardless of their various backgrounds and distinct FSA experiences, most South African victims express both shock and horror when detailing accounts of their perpetrators (see Kramer, 2014). These expressions are particularly attached to the potentially sexually transgressive nature of women. However, Tanaka, a Zimbabwean, presents his narrative with very few expressions of surprise. Whilst he indicates that his FSA experiences left him feeling traumatised, this trauma appears to be rooted in the context of the rape experience rather than as a result of the rapist being female. In fact, Tanaka treats FSA as a fairly normative and regular type of sexual violence in Zimbabwe and indicates that he has often seen it reported and that "it happens a lot". This noteworthy difference concerning the plausibility of female sexual violence is a powerful instantiation of how particular cultural conditions operate at power/knowledge to produce expectations, norms, and 'truths' about sex and sexuality.

Another notable 'cross-cultural' difference is that for South African victims, access to class resources through academic or at least higher education discourses appear to be a necessary condition for the occupation of an FSA victimhood, as does a position within a middle-income system of symbols. This does not appear to be the case for American victims who cross class and income levels (Kramer, 2014). In South Africa, access to class resources (such as education, knowledge, and information), or the limit thereof, is a function of whether subjects are able to self-identify as FSA victims. It may well be that sex abuse definitions vary according to socioeconomic status and that FSA victimisation may not be defined as abusive in low-income contexts typified by high levels of ongoing crime and violence.

Aside from the above-mentioned context-specific conditions for the emergence of FSA victimhood, most other FSA victimhood emergent discourses resonate across global and local contexts. The following sections describe the discourses drawn upon by FSA victims in my victim study (Kramer, 2014) in their identification with and simultaneous production of FSA victimhood. These discourses crisscross over a complex continuum of coordinates (see Figure 4.1) that signal those discourses that exclude FSA victimhood from that which is deemed 'real', possible, or 'thinkable' and those that provide the possibility of FSA victimhood.

CONDITIONS OF (IM)POSSIBILITY FOR FSA VICTIMHOOD

DISCURSIVE THEMES

THE INCONCEIVABLE CRIME	GENDER CONSTRUCTIONS	'MAKING' AN AETIOLOGY	NEGOTIATING THE MALE VICTIM	THE INCITEMENT TO DISCOURSE – VICTIMS IN WAITING	THE CONFESSION AS APPARATUS: PRODUCING FSA VICTIMHOOD	SURFACING FEMALE SEX CRIMES

DISCOURSES

THE INCONCEIVABLE CRIME	GENDER CONSTRUCTIONS	'MAKING' AN AETIOLOGY	NEGOTIATING THE MALE VICTIM	THE INCITEMENT TO DISCOURSE – VICTIMS IN WAITING	THE CONFESSION AS APPARATUS: PRODUCING FSA VICTIMHOOD	SURFACING FEMALE SEX CRIMES
The impossibility of FSA: Women do not commit sex crimes	The Madonna whore complex vs. the masculine aggressor	Absent paternal figures	Repercussions for masculine heterosexuality	Access to psychologised discourse	The secret: Silence and non-disclosure	Tracing the history: Patterns of public knowledge
FSA denial: Invisibility and avoidance	Vulnerable vaginas; vulnerable females	FSA as a function of mental illness, damage, or previous abuse	Body betrayal	The Internet and media as incitements to FSA victimhood	Victimhood and trauma	Counter-discourse: The fluidity of sexuality and gender
The innocent and naïve child: A fathomable FSA victim	Male sexual violence as normative	The she-devil: Un-gendering the female sex abuser	The ultimate education in sex	Class resources: Access to forms of knowledge	Revictimisation: Victimhood as destiny	
		The turn against maternity		Alternative sexualities: Access to non-normative discourse	The inversion of the moral code: Guilt and self-blame	
		Pleasure or power?			Psychic damage	
					Becoming the abuser to become the victim	
					Self-depictions of perversity: 'Effects' on sexual and gendered behaviour	
					FSA as more emotionally damaging than male sexual violence	

FIGURE 4.1 Continuum of discourses that provide conditions of (im)possibility for FSA victimhood

The inconceivable crime

FSA is gradually emerging as an object of knowledge in the social sciences, and this is progressively permeating into legal, medical, and public discourses. However, it is still generally regarded with skepticism, disbelief, and incredulity (Denov, 2001; Giguere & Bumby, 2007; Kramer & Bowman, 2011; Lawson, 2008). This has the effect of ensuring that FSA as a crime category remains peripheral to mainstream criminal discourse and FSA victimhood as almost unthinkable. As a consequence, FSA victims themselves tend to rely on understandings of FSA as inconceivable. Individuals exposed to FSA continuously shift between unequivocally identifying as victims and negotiating their own disbelief about the 'real' existence of such a position. The moments characterised by unwavering FSA victimhood always seem to be coupled with statements that deny the possibility of FSA. It is thus evident that FSA victimhood is complicated by continuous discursive conflict – on the one hand, these subjects are exposed to conditions that make possible FSA victimhood; however, on the other hand, they are simultaneously exposed to widely circulated discourses that continue to deny these possibilities. Jane clearly grapples with this conflict:

> I probably would have said something [if my abuser was male] because that would be . . . almost more socially acceptable. . . . But I think because it's a woman it's so . . . bizarre. . . . It's not something you hear about all the time. You hear about men doing stuff like this all the time. But you don't hear women.

Victims' reported conflict is expressed through their recognition of overarching discursive strategies (such as gendering) that make FSA unlikely and lead to avoidance and denial in the public, legal, and medical spheres.

The impossibility of FSA: women do not commit sex crimes

In line with Denov's (2001) arguments concerning the intractability of maleness as a basis for sex crimes, the participants in my study reflect on social norms and discourses that foreclose the possibility of FSA. These reflections demonstrate that despite their identifications as FSA victims, social discourses act as a constant reminder that this type of victimhood is primarily unimaginable. The social discourses reflected upon by participants are better aligned to earlier definitions of sex abuse that rely on vaginal penetration by a penis (see Koss, 1992) than the more recent and progressive definitions that provide for the possibility of other types of sexual violence.

One of the male victims, Richard, maintains that "society wouldn't classify it as abuse", and Jane feels that

> [There is] a perception that society builds . . . that women aren't criminals. That women can't do anything wrong . . . [and you] grow up in a society where it's like it could **never** happen here.

Tanaka makes a similar comment that "we live in a world where people think that only men can abuse women". Tanaka contracted a sexually transmitted disease from his female perpetrator, and he explains that "the doctor was even shocked" and "some people . . . just laughed at me". Tanaka's reference to 'the doctor' is an interesting recourse to science — a science that continues to rely on heteronormatively gendered understandings of sexual violence. Other participants in my study, such as Anna, notes that when she disclosed she was sexually abused, "they just assumed it was a guy" and Charles received questions such as "but physically how do you allow that to happen?" It thus appears that the recent revisions to sexual violence definitions in the South African Criminal Law (Sexual Offences and Related Matters) Amendment Act (Minister for Justice and Constitutional Development, 2007) do not yet provide the discursive possibilities of an alternative to sex crimes perpetrated exclusively by men.

Of interest is that until victims are exposed to some kind of condition that makes way for the possibility of FSA victimhood, they perceive FSA in much the same way as the social discourses referred to above. Richard notes that "I didn't even classify that thing with that woman as, as abuse" and Charles feels that "with a female . . . being a male . . . you'd see it as a normal sexual interaction, even though it's abuse". For another participant, Ella,

> It was like this couldn't be called sexual abuse but I'm not sure if it is because this is so far out of my realm. . . . And because this was a woman and I didn't realise that it was sexual. I just thought it was horrible punishment. . . . So, I think that's the biggest thing about it being a woman versus a man is it's harder to identify it for what it is. You want to say it's everything else. You wanna make all kinds of excuses and say that's not what it is. But that's what it is.

Once victims are exposed to some form of incitement to discourse (Internet, therapy, class resources), they seem more easily able to occupy a victim subject position. For instance, Anna notes "when people have studies on it, or you read something, an article or movies or whatever and then you kind of read how, how to deal with it". However, because social codes uphold the impossibility of FSA, Anna feels that there are no available legal, medical, or public structures to support this subject position:

> I've **never** ever heard of, of girls being sexually abused by other girls. Never, ever. Although, I mean up until . . . me. (Laughs). Um . . . I've never ever heard of anyone talking about it. . . . But, um, it's, it's weird that it's, it's a woman because you don't hear about it. Um, often you don't read about it. . . . I think it's just a, it's not a more common thing . . . and there's not like much implements and stuff in place of how you react and how one thinks and does things and you know. Because you don't, it's not, it's not a norm in society.

For many of the victims in my study, the call for participants acted as an incitement to discourse. Thabo claims that

> I think for me . . . when I was, the ad I saw, I, I just was like, "**Wow!**" I was like . . . I had to send you an email.

The participants thus used the interview to identify and negotiate various discursive strategies used at the broader level of the public, academic, legal, and health institutions that reinforce the (im)possibility of FSA victimhood. These key strategies are primarily institutionalised practices of invisibilisation and avoidance activated by the production and reproduction of particular gender and sexual discourses.

FSA denial: invisibility and avoidance

Whilst FSA is certainly an emerging object of human science knowledge that is receiving greater attention across the globe, denial and avoidance are not uncommon within both the medical and legal system. Across various institutions, female sexual violence is treated as rare, trivial, and innocuous (Denov, 2001) to the extent that officers of the law often dismiss FSA perpetrators. If they are formally acknowledged by the legal system, they receive lighter sentences (if any at all) than their male counterparts. In addition, the social science and medical literature largely accounts for FSA through aetiologies inseparable from mental disturbances, substance abuse, and/or histories of previous abuse (Higgs et al, 1992; Travers, 1999). The same aetiologies are not applied to male perpetrators who are regularly treated as 'monsters' that cannot control their innate sexual urges. This institutionalised level of avoidance, denial, and invisibilisation filters into the public imagination such that they are reproduced and performed by individual subjects. The broader discursive exclusion of FSA manifests in comments such as "I've never ever heard of anyone talking about it" (Anna). This invisibilisation and denial filters into the daily practices and performances of victims. For example, Jim indicates that it is "best to forget it" and move on with his life. Reliance on this avoidance discourse echoes typical victimhood discourses that Weiss (2011) argues are so entrenched in the cultural narrative that victims unwittingly invoke them. This, then, is not unique to FSA, but is also practiced by victims of male sex abuse and is thus rather typical of sexual victimisation in general.

The broader institutionalised practices of denial and avoidance tend to inadvertently protect perpetrators. For example, Ella explains how her mother would anally rape her in shared family spaces (unlike in 'dirty' or hidden spaces reserved for constructions of male sex abuse) and how most people knew that her mother was abusing her:

> She didn't give a damn who saw . . . she would do these things in the living room. . . . Where anybody could walk in and see what she was doing . . . and you know, people knew that I was being abused. And people knew there was something wrong with my mother. And nobody ever did anything about it so I was led to believe that this was normal behaviour. Or acceptable behaviour.

Similarly, Jane explains that her domestic worker warned her not to disclose to anyone, as she would not be believed in any case:

> I was standing against, lying against my door . . . and she was like choking me and she was saying like, um, who are you gonna tell? What are you gonna do about it?

While these types of threats are also common in cases of male sex abuse, male sexual violence victims are less likely than FSA victims to encounter avoidance responses. For example, Jane goes on to report that her perpetrator's warning was realised when she attempted to tell her parents:

> And I remember like, afterwards going into my parents' bedroom, like knocking on the door, like can I come in? No, we sleeping . . . Like many times I would bang that door down. But they would not come out.

Jane's reference to her parents' bedroom signifies the Malthusian unit and the ways that avoidance and denial conceal the potential for FSA to disrupt the institutionally 'acceptable' and 'healthy' family. When Jane's behaviour began to change, her parents "looked for every single reason to blame each other and blame the environment or whatever else". Later, when her psychologist informed her parents about the sex abuse, they continued to completely avoid broaching the issue with her. In much the same way, Tanaka notes how his family explained away his gonorrhoea with "kid's play" despite their knowledge that he "wouldn't have caught [gonorrhoea] . . . from someone who is my age". Similarly, Charles indicates that he never fought off his sexually abusive girlfriend because he felt that "she would have turned the story around and said that I tried to do something to her instead" and that this version would be more plausible.

The denial and avoidance practiced by participants' various support structures results in the invisibilisation of their victimisation and the implication that FSA is an impossible event. Given that this 'impossibility' is incongruent with participants' narrated experiences, they attempt to identify conditions that would make this FSA experience (globally) imaginable. One discursive strategy to this end is to rely on constructions of childhood as a conceivable condition for FSA victimhood by intimating that childhood is the only victim category that gains any traction in constructions of FSA victimhood.

The innocent naïve child: a fathomable FSA victim

The socio-historical construction of the child as innocent, naïve, and vulnerable (Ariès, 1973), as well as desexualised and passive (Bhana, 2006), makes possible a victim-child subject. This is further supported by widely circulated constructions of the modern family as child-centred, and cultural values that imply the necessity of the child's ongoing protection (Carrington, 1991). In addition, and as mentioned previously, female-perpetrated sexual victimisation of a child is both possible and plausible as a result of gender stereotypes that imply that women should and do have more access to children (Vandiver, 2006).

FSA victims draw on constructions of child vulnerability and 'purity' to make sense of their FSA experiences and to attempt to explain the possibility of FSA. For example, both Anna and Jim suggest that children are naïve and cannot understand the implications of sexual victimisation. Jim emphasises that "at that age, you don't know what you're doing" and that he was "exposed to a certain situation that someone that age isn't supposed to know about". The construction of the child as vulnerable provides the logic for how a male could be sexually violated by a female. Despite being a teenager at the time of his FSA experience, Charles drew on discourses that stressed his youth and small physical size as compared to his perpetrator. He explains that "because I was younger . . . automatically she would think that she would take charge". His emphasis here is placed on age, implying that age hierarchies are capable of replacing the usual gender force. He also explains his conception of how FSA is possible:

> The females were older as well. Um, but the males were . . . physically much smaller. Um, so obviously in terms of the physical side of it, the females were able to take advantage of the male.

The construction of the innocent child does go some way to providing the conditions of possibility for FSA victimhood. This is particularly because, in the hierarchy of vulnerability, children are constructed as first and women second. Thus, while childhood FSA victims are conceivable, the possibility of adult victims, particularly male adults, disrupts this hierarchy of vulnerability. For example,

> I was **very** shocked to hear that there are actually other people out there, that it happens to them as well. Not as a kid. As an adult.
>
> *(Jim)*

Jim's juxtaposition of a 'kid' and an 'adult' is an example of the implied hierarchy of possibility between childhood and adulthood that reinforces the child as the only 'possible' and 'real' category of FSA victimhood. This hierarchy, and particularly its placement of women, is traditionally supported by heteronormatively gendered constructions of vulnerability.

Gender constructions that sustain the impossible crime

> I think people's perception of women is just that they're not capable of something like that. Because women are seen as the victims, always.
>
> *(Jane)*

Sexual violence is conventionally defined in dichotomised terms that imply the male aggressor and the female victim (Richardson & May, 1999), and has historically been essentialised as deriving from a 'natural' masculine aggression (see Gidycz, 2011; Koss et al., 1987). In order to explain their 'impossible' statuses, FSA victims tend to identify particular gender constructions that emphasise male aggression and female passivity. Some of these constructions are purposefully identified by victims and proposed as key to FSA victimhood impossibility. However, many victims also unwittingly engage with and actively draw on gendered discourse as a natural means to explain sexual and gender 'truths'. In both instances, there is a consistent discursive appeal to dichotomous gendering. Descriptors such as 'male', 'masculine', and 'men' are understood only in their antithetical relation to 'female', 'feminine', and 'women', without any consideration of alternative possibilities for gender. Whilst these discourses demonstrate the particular coordinates that make FSA globally inconceivable, they are simultaneously the coordinates through which at least female victims are able to occupy victim subject positions.

The Madonna-whore complex versus the masculine aggressor

Across all of my data, womanhood is consistently defined in narrow terms by FSA victims such that femininity is either coupled with discourses on victimisation and vulnerability, or with constructions of the woman as a 'whore'. This is further accentuated with juxtapositions to an aggressive and sexually violent manhood.

In line with widely circulated discourses that a woman's inappropriate dress code might instigate her sexual victimisation (Du Mont, Miller, & Myhr, 2003; Muehlenhard & Kimes, 1999), Heather places particular emphasis on the "shame of being female":

> The phrase that my husband actually used was 'jail bait' and it's like young women or teenagers who look older than what they are and it's like they're provocative and they're in some way responsible for making men feel temptation. That is what my mother had sort of communicated to me about the neighbourhood boys. That sense of . . . well, she called me a bitch on heat. And . . . it was my fault that these boys were doing this sort of thing.

These comments align to Cahill's (2000) suggestion that the female body is constructed as sexually penetrable, which renders the female subject responsible for her sexual victimisation, at least at the pre-victim stage. This extract thus alludes to engrained understandings of sexual victimisation whereby the penetrable rather than the penetrating female is possible. Despite self-identification as FSA victims, these particular coordinates in participants' discourses were still tied to the improbability of FSA. However, they also allowed female participants to position themselves as victims.

Whilst Heather draws on the 'whore' end of the spectrum in constructing femininity, other victims rely on women-as-victim gender discourses and explain, "women are expected to be caring and loving" (Thabo). In turn, the most appropriate explanation for FSA is that "a lot of these women are actually victims anyway" (Richard). Anna maintains that female-to-male sexual submission is normative with her comment, "I think if, if I had to meet someone that I respected and trusted enough I think it would be okay to kind of submit in a way". This conception of the victimised and passive female is supported by the following heteronormatively gendered constructions:

> I think women sometimes . . . because of their like nurturing instinct, that they are very protective and like . . . I think women maybe have an incredible instinct for justice and taking care of things and putting things right again.
>
> *(Jane)*

> Obviously within . . . society they [women] are seen as the weaker . . . sex.
>
> *(Charles)*

In order to support these claims as well as to explain why FSA is often considered harmless and innocuous (Denov, 2001), victims provide concrete examples of the differences between a sexually violent female and a sexually violent male. Jane explains that her boyfriend "wasn't as upset about it because it wasn't a man . . . so it was almost . . . not that severe". She goes on to identify how society actively gendered her experience:

> If it's a woman it's almost . . . but that's like a perception that society builds. . . . That women aren't criminals. That women can't do anything wrong. And that's the perception that I think you grow up with. . . . And it's kind of instilled in you.

Male violence is also explicated as a physical act whereas female violence is constructed as a mental and emotional form of abuse. For example,

> I remember that it's [the male abuse] . . . was **very** like forceful. Like **much** more forceful and much more like violent. And abusive. Ya. Um . . . but with her, it was a more emotional, manipulative thing. . . . Like if it's, if it's a male then it's the dominant figure and he's

overpowering you and then, you know, you're kind of like this timid, you're the lady then you're vulnerable but if it's a lady then I think it makes you think as if you could have done something to avoid it because that power struggle is not part of it.

(Anna)

I never ever look at a female now and undermine her size; first of all, um because I think at the end of the day it's not necessarily always a physical overpowering. It's more of a mental overpowering, um, psychological where you're broken down to a point where even physically you don't want to do anything.

(Charles)

These extracts are important examples of the gendering of violence. Anna's construction of her female sex abuser as emotional and manipulative is a key illustration of how, in the event of a sexually violent act by a woman, physical abuse is transformed into verbal or emotional abuse. Emotion is so deeply engrained in the construction of femininity that even where there is female-perpetrated physical violence, it is both normative and acceptable to explain this event by restructuring it as emotive. This is made easier by virtue of the physical domain being so readily aligned with masculinity and, in this way, so obviously opposed to womanhood. Anna provides illustrations of typical male gendering to demonstrate the normativity of male dominance and aggression:

I mean obviously in society the male is the dominant figure. And I mean he has the power and everything.

(Anna)

These gendered discourses are further explored in the following sections, with a particular emphasis on the vagina as a physical representation of female vulnerability and the 'normalcy' of male sexual violence.

Vulnerable vaginas; vulnerable females

[One can't] expect a male to understand what is to violate someone in a way they can't be.

(Heather)

Codes mapped onto the gendered body signify the phallus as a weapon capable of violation and the vagina as a vulnerable space capable of being violated

(Woodhull, 1988). So engrained is this discourse that it has come to play a central role in the production of the modern female body, a body that is defined by its vulnerability and penetratability (Cahill, 2000). Some of the female participants in my study intimate that the potential to be penetrated leaves them vulnerable, ashamed, and horrified at their own sexual anatomy. Given that pregnancy symbolises female penetratability, this vulnerability is often related to pregnancy and childbirth. For example:

> That horror at being a female . . . I think it's mainly biological and ana-
> tomical, the physical reality of being female. So feeling horrified at the
> female anatomy. I've actually got to a point where it was . . . crippling
> to me. Even to be pregnant . . . I think that being female . . . maybe it's
> shame . . . but because as a female you can be penetrated, you do give
> birth, there's a biological reality and the shame that, that is what our
> body does.
>
> *(Heather)*

> Well I have a big fear of having sex one day . . . well one thing I must
> tell you is I can't wear tampons. . . . Like I get tense or if I think about
> anything, I think related to someone or anything going up there or
> something being near there, or something that's not me or whatever,
> you know. It's, it's daunting. Ya, and I still, I've tried once or twice. But
> I can't, I get like nauseous and warm and I know the one time I even
> fainted.
>
> *(Anna)*

Pregnancy also signifies women's heterosexual reproductive 'requirement' and alludes to child caregiving and maternal constructions that again impede on the possibility or at least harmfulness of FSA.

Discourses that centre on the female capacity to be penetrated and to be 'filled' are linked to the overriding construction of rape as something a woman, rather than a man, experiences (Cahill, 2000). It is therefore these particularly gendered discourses that provide female victims coordinates for self-identification as such. However, in the face of these powerful discourses, female sexual violence is produced as an improbable and abnormal phenom-enon, and its counterpart, male sexual violence, is produced as both probable and normative. For female victims, it is therefore the integration of key FSA victimhood coordinates such as access to psychologised discourses and class resources (that are discussed later in the chapter) with these gendering norms that provides the condition for their identifications as FSA victims.

Male sexual violence as normative

> We live in a world where people think that only men can abuse women.
>
> *(Tanaka)*

Sex abuse discourses are rooted in gendering norms that imply female victimisation and male aggression. These discourses are so immutable that any alternative conception of sexual violence is rarely considered. Consequently, both male-perpetrated sex abuse and female experiences of rape are considered normative (Rutherford, 2011). Victims draw on these discourses to explain reasons for nondisclosure of their FSA experiences as well as reasons for their own ambivalence about claiming FSA victimhood:

> I guess I'd expect being abused by males is sort of normal and I had fitted that into a way of surviving in the world. But being violated by my mother, I actually . . . didn't **ever** qualify that as quite normal so it was my dirty little secret that I've never said to anybody whereas there was some knowledge about the male sexual assaults. . . . I think . . . in my mind I had an acceptance of male sexual abuse.
>
> *(Heather)*

Similarly, Jane explains how she would have treated the situation differently, had her perpetrator been a man:

> I think I probably would have spoken out about it. I probably would have said something because that would be . . . almost more socially acceptable. . . . But because of, ya, definitely because it was a woman, it definitely felt like you couldn't say something. Because it's your caregiver, you know. . . . I think it is different because the moment a woman is abused by a man, it's almost . . . it's so much more open. Like people speak about it all the time. It's almost like the everyday thing now.

Jane's comment alludes to "the repeated juxtaposition of child care and sexual abuse", which implies that these two objects are inevitably linked (Mazur & Pekor, 1985, p. 11), despite meanings of caregiving being antithetical to meanings of abuse. Given that gender constructions inextricably link caregiving to womanhood, the widely held belief that caregiving and CSA are tied begins to make FSA conceivable. However, as indicated by Jane, it is still easier to comprehend a male sex abuser, even when that male is occupying a female role such as that of a caregiver.

Male violence is regarded as so normative that its aetiology is considered irrelevant. Rather, men are treated as naturally sexually aggressive and unable to control their innate sexual urges. For example, Jane refers to "the dodgy man" that sexually abuses children, and Heather states that "I don't expect a male to understand what he's doing but I do expect a female to". The same treatment is not applied to female sexual perpetrators. Rather, FSA victims tend to develop an aetiological framework for why a woman might be sexually transgressive. This is particularly centred on the turn against maternity and the warping of a natural inclination to caregiving. This is significant, as in the same way that men are treated as naturally aggressive, so too are women treated as naturally nurturing.

'Making' an aetiology

While current FSA academic and legal discourses are focused on potential FSA categories and possible 'causes' of this phenomenon (see Brockman & Bluglass, 1996; Gannon, Rose, & Ward, 2008; Miller, Turner, & Henderson, 2009; Nathan & Ward, 2002; Sandler & Freeman, 2007; Turner, Miller, & Henderson, 2008; Vandiver & Kercher, 2004; Vandiver & Walker, 2002; Wijkman, Bijleveld, & Hendriks, 2010), FSA as an object of knowledge has not yet filtered into public consciousness. Consequently, victims have very little knowledge to draw on to explain FSA; thus, they utilise their understandings of other psychological and scientific objects of knowledge to develop aetiological frameworks. These frameworks emerge through four key discourses, which are that FSA is a result of absent paternal figures, that FSA is a function of some psychological disorder or previous abuse, that FSA is meted out by particularly evil and/or masculinised women, and that FSA occurs when a woman abandons her maternal duties. The construction of a coherent list of potential causes allows for a more conceivable set of conditions in which victims can firmly locate themselves as victimised. This tendency to look to causes prior to being 'able' to identify as an FSA victim is fundamentally a psychological practice, and thus links to access to psychologised discourse – a key condition for FSA victimhood (which is discussed later in the chapter).

Absent paternal figures

Almost all of the FSA victims in my study indicate that, in some way, their father was absent during their childhood, and they directly link this to their victim statuses. For those victims abused by their mothers, the absent paternal figure is treated as an absent source of surveillance. Both Heather and Ella claim that their mothers were able to be abusive because their fathers worked away from home. In some cases, victims indicate that this paternal absence is an intentional attempt to avoid being close to their mothers. For example, Richard feels that his father "ran away all the time" because he was trying to "avoid living with the she-devil". Similarly, Suzette states that "he didn't come home until like **really** late because he didn't want to fight with my mom".

FSA victims abused by someone other than their mothers also indicate that absent paternal figures were key to their victimhood. Thabo explains that he can barely recall his father living with him after he was ten years old and that he grew up in "a house of women". Jane explains that her father was always at work and thus incapable of identifying her domestic worker as a sex abuser. Likewise, Tanaka states that "because my father was working night shift, he never knew anything" and Anna explains that her father "moved to Namibia . . . he was there when it happened". This consistent pattern of paternal invisibility in FSA victim narratives points to the possibility that the lack of an obviously sexually aggressive male provides the conditions for a fathomable FSA event. It is only when the very gender that represents aggression and sexual violence is no longer visible that other genders are able to occupy those roles.

The discourse centred on the absent paternal figure is also representative of broader discourses focused on the child-centred modern family unit that imply that the father is responsible for the protection of his children, who are treated as vulnerable, innocent, and requiring ongoing protection (Carrington, 1991). The absence of the paternal figure is thus a particular condition that makes possible FSA victimhood, especially as it allows for the deconstruction of the institutionally 'acceptable' and 'healthy' modern family, or as Foucault (1978) terms it, the Malthusian unit. This aligns with Kruttschnitt and colleagues' (2008) suggestion that the existence of female transgressions results in the sense that women are no longer limited to gender-constraining roles (such as motherhood), and this generates the perception that there is a decline in the regulation and discipline of the nuclear family unit.

FSA as a function of mental illness, damage, or previous abuse

Current FSA typologies rely on psychiatric or psychological discourse to provide explanatory logic for FSA as an object of knowledge. This is particularly focused on mental illness discourse that draws on histories characterised by childhood or previous abuse (Higgs et al, 1992; Travers, 1999). FSA victims in my research treat their perpetrators in much the same way. Suzette, Heather, and Ella insist that their mothers were suffering from mental illnesses. Suzette reports that her mother is "mentally unstable" and "crazy" whilst Heather states that her mother "lost her mind". Ella goes so far as to diagnose her mother with paranoid schizophrenia. These diagnoses are detailed across the corpus of my data:

> My mom was like . . . in the beginning I didn't really like notice all the little signs that showed that she wasn't normal, mentally normal. But now I think back I can see it a lot clear[er]. . . . I kind of like feel sorry for her because what she did was wrong, but she doesn't understand that what she did was wrong.
>
> *(Suzette)*

> My mother was crazy. I believe she was a paranoid-schizophrenic. She has all of the symptoms and the paranoia and the um, delusions. You know, like thinking vampires were hiding in the shadows and things like that. Uh, that would tend to confirm that she was a paranoid-schizophrenic . . . she was a horrible, violent human being that hated me. Um, for no reason of my own. Because she just had psycho problems. . . . And also she would blame me for things that I didn't do which, in retrospect, I believe that she was having delusions and that these things she was accusing me of only existed in her own mind.
>
> *(Ella)*

It is interesting to note that this mental illness discourse is only drawn upon by those victimised by their mothers. It seems that the double-pathologising of the maternal figure provides the condition for victimhood because it offers explanatory logic for how a mother can subvert her maternal duties. It also allows victims to remain sympathetic towards their perpetrators and makes possible a concurrent mother/perpetrator subject position. This is particularly evident in Suzette's comments that she feels sorry for her mother and that her mother cannot grasp the implications of her own behaviour. These comments powerfully demonstrate the way gender shapes FSA victimhood, because engrained gender constructions would prevent this kind of sympathy towards a male sex abuser. Mother-blaming discourse is also characteristically present in psychological frameworks for mental illnesses (see Caplan, 2013), and these discursive strategies thus point to the victims' access to and reliance on psychologised discourse.

Other victims rationalise their FSA experiences by drawing on classic sex-abuse theory that upholds that perpetrators are often victims themselves and are thus engaging in a cycle of abuse (see Gomez, 2011; Ogloff et al., 2012; Ryan, Leversee, & Lane, 2011; Yun, Ball, & Lim, 2011). It also frames the perpetrator in gendered terms (victimised) such that her femininity, and thus vulnerability, is prioritised over her capacity to be violent. For example:

> Kind of makes me think that that's what she went through . . . she's repeating the pattern, maybe. Um . . . Because I know, at one stage she was . . . from what I remember, staying with her uncle. So you don't know. Look, there's possibilities there. Like . . . she could just be repeating the pattern, and imitating. . . . Like maybe this, a woman will sexually abuse another child because it happened to them and this is the way they justify it, you know?
>
> *(Jane)*

This clearly points to the infiltration of the 'cycle of abuse' narrative such that FSA victimhood is conditional on the perception of the abuser as a victim herself. The tendency to apply psychological or psychiatric explanations to their FSA experiences provides victims with a seemingly scientific sanction for their sympathies. However, when this type of discourse is impossible to apply to their narratives, victims turn away from scientifically loaded rationalisations and instead turn to moral loadings of FSA and characterise their perpetrators as depraved, bad, and evil.

The she-devil: un-gendering the female sexual abuser

One of the strongest victim discourses refers to the horror invoked by the possibility of a sexually violent woman. Women are rarely regarded as 'monsters', and the innate tendency towards aggression is usually reserved for aetiologies concerning male perpetrators. However, when victims are unable to draw on more female-aligned and psychologically informed aetiologies for FSA, the ability to identify depravity in their abusers allows for an un-gendering process whereby the perpetrators are masculinised, and thus monstrosity becomes a discourse in which to situate the horror.

Richard refers to his mother as the "she-devil", Anna perceives her neighbor-abuser as "dark", Heather describes her mother as "brutal", and Ella describes hers as "mean and evil". These descriptors are supported by accompanying accounts of fear:

> I used to think to myself, "God, just keep her out of here. Just keep her out". With my mom it was, it was like . . . fear. . . . She would come and

you would feel like a cornered rabbit. . . . Like you can't get out of the situation. You're there, you know it's going to happen.

(Richard)

Richard's expression, "God, just keep her out of here" is particularly reflective of the moral loadings of FSA in these depravity discourses.

Victims' reflections on constructions of women as victimised and weak seem to paradoxically protect abusive women and simultaneously provide the conditions for them to be dangerous. For example:

Women are like that wolf in sheep's clothes. . . . They are perceived to be these pretty little faces but actually behind it all, they can be really mean.

(Jane)

Descriptors such as 'brutal', 'evil', and 'devil' are usually reserved for the construction of male abusers. The identification of depravity in their perpetrators thus allows victims to deconstruct the FSA perpetrator's gender and, in a sense, un-gender her so that she becomes masculinised. In so doing, typical feminine traits are no longer applicable to her character. This has the effect of making FSA possible if the perpetrator is 'like a man'. It also results in the acknowledgement that, if she is like a man, she cannot be like a woman, and thus she cannot occupy a nurturing maternal subject position.

The turn against maternity

Mothers aren't supposed to do that to their children.

(Richard)

Constructions of femininity are imbued with images of the nurturing and caring maternal archetype. The possibility of a woman that sexually offends directly contradicts these, such that mother and female sexual perpetrator are incompatible. For Heather, this represents a complete "betrayal" of her understandings of womanhood and, by extension, motherhood. Victims account for this incoherence by demonstrating that their perpetrators are not typically feminine, and thus not typically maternal. For example,

I think the fact that it was my aunt. And the trust that that young person has towards an aunt. She abused that trust.

(Jim)

My mom really didn't take care of Louis. I had to take care of him. I had to change nappies. I had to feed him. I had to put him to bed. I, I had no free time to myself. . . . I know the one night, my [mother] . . . said to me, I think I'm gonna give Louis alcohol to make him sleep but I don't, I can't really remember a lot of that night because I as well got really drunk cause my mom said I had to drink so ya, I couldn't remember or stop my mother from giving my youngest brother alcohol.

(Suzette)

The house was chaotic. My mother couldn't keep things together. I mean she didn't clean. She didn't cook. She was really erratic. It was almost like we were left to run around on our own most of the time. . . . I was being neglected. I was dirty, I was messy, my clothes were in a horrible condition.

(Ella)

For victims exposed to a maternal sex abuser, this turn against maternity results in a complete breakdown of typical maternal-child relationship discourses:

You try and understand why you hate her. You're supposed to love your mother. . . . If she died tomorrow, I'd actually be happy.

(Heather)

I mean when she died I was really sad that she died because I always wanted a mother and I never had one. And when she died, I never would have one. Um, but I was also relieved because she was gone. I mean, the evil person was gone. Um, it was not a close relationship . . . it was almost like living with a complete stranger that don't give a damn about you.

(Ella)

Ella's reference to a stranger echoes classic and widely endorsed rape myths which suggest that sex abusers are strangers rather than acquaintances (Du Mont et al., 2003; Muehlenhard & Kimes, 1999). Ella's intimation that her mother was 'like a stranger' is thus a discursive strategy that makes the maternal sex abuser both conceivable and possible.

The reported perceptions that their experiences are contradictory to circulated images of the normative family allows victims to engage with counter-discourses and thus occupy the non-normative subject position of FSA victimhood. In line with Butler's (1989, 1999, 2004) performativity, the capacity for victims to view their perpetrators as anti-maternal and thus 'abnormal' provides the conditions for victims to subvert normative discourse on motherhood and the nuclear family, and thus disrupt and dislocate idealising discourses on motherhood. Consequently, victims are able to perform an alternative discourse on maternal–child relationships and occupy a victim subject position.

Pleasure or power?

Historically, women have been constructed as sexually submissive and passive. However, more recently, women are being constructed as sexually empowered and liberated, so long as this is practiced within socially sanctioned contexts such as the heteronormative relationship (Gill, 2012). Given that FSA aligns with neither older nor more recent constructions of female sexuality, the act of female sexual perpetration is rarely engaged with as sexual practice per se. Identifying the sexual nature of FSA would necessitate the acknowledgement that women can be sexually transgressive outside of other motivating forces such as male coercion, substance use, or mental illness. This is so antithetical to the 'natural' maternal and caregiving functions attached to the female gender that this would require a complete reframing of femininity (Kramer & Bowman, 2011). Thus, whilst the act of both FSA and female-perpetrated CSA may be acknowledged by academics, the sexualising of these acts is notably absent across all types of reporting. By virtue of their self-identifications, FSA victims seem to challenge these widely circulated FSA discourses and engage in alternative possibilities. These counter-discourses are primarily centred on a debate concerning whether FSA is concerned with pleasure-seeking or power-seeking.

Pleasure is regarded from both the perspective of the perpetrator and the victim. Victims tend to question perpetrators' desires and sexual identifications as well as their own potential to have engaged with the pleasure-seeking aspects of the sexual contact. For example:

> I think . . . her getting pleasure out of it, I started to wonder what is it, what is she feeling. You know, what is that feeling? And most, like I mean every time I was with her I never remotely even had an instance of pleasure in it.
>
> *(Thabo)*

> I could have been enjoying it. I don't want to think about it.
>
> *(Jim)*

Jane indicates that in some instances, it felt like her domestic worker was making a specifically homosexual choice when she chose to sexually engage with her rather than with her brother. However, later she impugns this by stating that her domestic worker was "very aggressive" and that "I don't think it was like a sexual thing at all . . . it was definitely like a power struggle". Similarly, Ella feels that "she like had the compulsion to do these things . . . so I think it was putting her temptation out of the way, is why she did that to me". However, she simultaneously spoke of her mother's sexual engagements as "punishments". This inconsistency in victims' narratives regarding whether the motives are pleasure-based or power-based may be a function of the limited range of discourses, explanations, and definitions available for FSA as an object of knowledge. However, it is also worth noting that the pleasure–power question is part of the broader rape debate and thus may also be another example of the ways that FSA is not dissimilar to male sexual violence.

Negotiating the male victim

Traditional social sexual codes entrench the image of an oversexed dominant male and an unassertive female succumbing to his needs, thus maintaining the legitimacy, 'normality', and social acceptance of male-to-female sexual coercion (Murnen, Wright, & Kaluzny, 2002). As such, female victimisation is normalised and male victimisation is treated as 'abnormal'. FSA is discursively problematic given that it does not neatly align to these gendered constructions that imply the unlikelihood of female sexual transgression. Where females are victims of FSA, this misalignment, and its potential threats to the biopolitics of the day, is central to the possibility of the emergence of FSA victimhood. However, where victims are male, conditions of possibility are dependent on both the discursive configuration of a violent female *and* a victimised male. For women to identify as FSA victims, they need only to challenge and resist discourses that limit the possibilities for female sexual transgressions. However, for men to occupy FSA victimhood, they must resist both the aforementioned discourses as well as those that limit the possibilities for male victimisation. Thus, while FSA female victimhood is complex by virtue of its improbable perpetrator, additional gendering barriers that infer the improbability of both perpetrator and victim further complicate FSA male victimhood. Despite this additional complexity, half of my victim study's participants comprised of self-identified male victims.

Gendered discourse implies the incompatibility of victimhood and masculinity, and thus results in a limited range of discursive possibilities for male victims (Eagle, 2006). Male sexual violence victims are limited to subject positions characterised by weakness, homosexuality, or femininity (Barth, Bermetz, Heim, Trelle, & Tonia, 2013), or a failure to meet socially acceptable standards of masculinity (Weiss, 2010a). As such, male victims draw on conventionally gendered discourses, despite the outcome of these discourses being identification as an FSA male victim, which is representative of a non-normative gender role. For example, regardless of the fact that male victims may not derive pleasure from an FSA experience, they tend to frame their understandings of its possibility through the sexualisation of the female perpetrator. This echoes Bourke's (2007) argument that men are constructed as always desiring and enjoying sexual interaction with women, even under forced circumstances. In addition, on contemplating their potential to be victimised by a woman, most men question the limits of their own masculinity, in both its physical and social form. The reliance on heteronormatively gendered frameworks results in the interrogation of their masculine identities and the acknowledgement of betrayal by their own masculine bodies. Such de-masculinising outcomes seem to be the condition that allows for the occupation of a male victim subject position, indicating that, at least in the case of male victimhood, the possibility of a sexually violent female requires the presence of an emasculated male victim.

Repercussions for masculine heterosexuality

Most male victims formulate the consequences of being sexually violated by a woman through heteronormative terms. These discourses are typically absent from female victims' discourses. For example, whilst female victims generally do not make mention of the potential sexual gratification for perpetrator or victim, many male victims feel that society expects them to derive pleasure from an FSA experience. Moreover, the absence of sexual gratification for these men means that their heterosexuality comes into question. As Richard indicates,

> The worst introduction to sex. It's absolutely like . . . gross. I remember going back to school and all the young boys . . . were saying "Hey, I got laid this weekend and hey, hey, hey these holidays . . . it was great!" And I'm going, "It was disgusting! Gross! Like the worst thing ever". And they all looked at me and were like, "Are you crazy?" And I go, "No, it was disgusting man! Geez. It was terrible". And then they started with all the nonsense, like because I didn't like it, am I gay.

For Thabo, these consequences are slightly more complex because he identifies as a homosexual man. He therefore draws on these sexualised constructions to question the possible links between his FSA experience and his sexual orientation:

Everyone around me was just like, "Yoh, you're gay"..... And I think for her as well, my sister, she also saw that and she, she, maybe on some level of her she was trying to fix me?

Did the molestation inform my sexual orientation? Did I become homosexual because a woman abused me?

The potential for FSA male victimhood to 'explain' homosexuality is grounded in particular patriarchal discourses that foreground 'typical' male traits. For example, Richard explains how his abuse came to an end because "I developed quite quickly and could be a man". He also notes that during sexual intercourse, "I need to be this stud that goes on for . . . like forever" and that when using urinals "I'd peek over and see, you know, see how I measure up". Similarly, Tanaka states that, "I always had a bigger pipi than most boys of my age group, I was also tall" and Charles comments that post his abuse, "I think I'd manned up to say the least". These are typical discursive strategies drawn upon by male victims as a means to 'repair' their masculinities and counteract feminine markers associated with victimisation (Weiss, 2010a). Furthermore, these strategies are used as a means to establish the innocuousness of FSA. The ability for men to identify as FSA victims appears to be contingent on the simultaneous ability to demonstrate their 'recovered' masculinities. Thus, FSA victimhood ironically emerges in part through the performance and maintenance of typical masculine constructions and roles.

Consequences to female sexual violation are also framed in heteronormatively gendered discourses rooted in what it means to occupy 'real' manhood. Most male victims indicate that their physical and social embodiments of masculinity are damaged through their FSA experiences. For example,

It makes me feel like I'm not a real man . . . part of it makes me feel embarrassed. . . . I mean for a man to just say these things: ya, you know, a woman abused me. I mean, because we live in a world where people think that only men can abuse women. . . . I mean women will look at you and say you're a sissy . . . because even my girlfriend, I almost slipped and told her. I don't think it's something that I want to tell her.

(Tanaka)

I haven't sat down and told her [my mom]. Um . . . I find that it may be a disappointment to her. As having a son, but wasn't able to do anything.

(Charles)

> Because obviously to ... tell a male friend that, um, males perceive it as being physically weak. Or mentally weak.
>
> *(Charles)*

> Sometimes I'd be anxious and ... she'd get disappointed that I did not have an erection.
>
> *(Thabo)*

By being sexually violated by a woman, these men contradict hegemonic constructs of masculinity because they cannot be simultaneously sexually potent *and* victimised (Eagle, 2006; Weiss, 2010a). The destruction of manhood and threat to heterosexuality appears to be central for male victims. This is perhaps because, as Charles indicates, "with a female, as being a male, is that you'd see it as a normal sexual interaction, even though it's abuse". He goes on to explain that he could not report the sexual violation or draw on his 'masculine' strength to "resist in terms of physically overpowering her is that I didn't want that story being turned around where I was the abuser," this being a far more plausible narrative. So engrained is the assumption of the impossible male victim that Anna, one of the female participants, completely disregarded this possibility and commented that "if like the study helps ... other girls, or other ladies, that would be awesome".

For men to frame themselves as FSA victims, they must actively violate gender norms that imply that women cannot sexually violate men. While male victims draw on gendered constructions of manhood as a strategy to reinforce their masculinities, discussions concerning actual FSA events and the consequent repercussions seem to reference an un-doing of gender such that the victims' maleness becomes 'undone'. This fluid gender dynamic and the continuous shift between maleness and 'un-maleness' appears to be the very node through which FSA victimhood finds traction.

Body betrayal

> Mind shuts down. The body is still doing what it's supposed to be doing.
>
> *(Jim)*

A key circulated discourse that upholds the invisibility of female-to-male sexual violence is the construction of men being incapable of exercising sexual restraint. Moreover, outside of its reproductive function, conventionally the erect penis has been constructed as serving one of two purposes during a sexual interaction – either to derive sexual pleasure or to use as a rape 'weapon' (Bourke, 2007). Due to widely circulated constructions of aggressive, virile, and sexually driven masculinity, male erections continue to be 'evidence' of either desire and enjoyment or danger and power during a sexual encounter, thus further invisibilising FSA male victimhood. Male victims that experience arousal or ejaculation during FSA are considered to be consenting and desiring parties, and this is used as key evidence that FSA is unfeasible in these cases (Giguere & Bumby, 2007; Weiss, 2010a). The possibility that a penis may be erect during the sexual violation of a male body is not easily assimilated into our discursive conditions for manhood. Male victims therefore construct their arousal and erections as a 'betrayal' by their bodies. For example,

> Your body betrays you. It definitely does . . . it's a natural reaction.
>
> *(Charles)*

Charles' comment that "it's a natural reaction" further solidifies the construction of the male body as incapable of controlling its sexual urges, regardless of the male subject's apparent 'psychological' desires. Ironically, whilst this experience of arousal threatens the possibility or 'proof' of male victimhood, victimisation requires an erect penis. As Jim notes,

> She told me to lie down and that's when she started fondling me. Obviously she had to do something to get it ready for the, the act.
> How does a woman rape a man? It's got to get . . . aroused.

The possibility of arousal and erect penises during FSA experiences appears to cause male victims extreme conflict – whilst society, science, and the law have insisted that male arousal and FSA are incompatible, their victimhood is defined by this compatibility. The male victim subject position is thus so strikingly irreconcilable to broader sexual 'norms' that male victims cannot make sense of this 'body betrayal'. This conflict is evident in Richard's comment:

> But she carries on tugging at the thing. And then your body betrays you and you kind of feel like . . . now I'm getting an erection. . . . And then she belittles you by laughing at it . . . it's kind of a gamut of emotions that you go through, that you can't understand.

The perpetrator's belittling response infers that Richard's erection is symbolic of desire rather than of victimhood, thus strengthening his reported conflict.

Body betrayal is therefore an extremely complex component of FSA – whilst male arousal is often used by science as evidence for the impossibility of an FSA event, it seems to be, at least in the case of penetrative rape, a material necessity for FSA male victimhood. A Foucauldian position would argue that "the body is a site where regimes of discourse and power inscribe themselves" (Butler, 1989, p. 601). Body betrayal discourse thus demands that we engage with the possibilities of the body 'in sex' in different ways. Both male and female bodies are rearticulated through FSA as equally penetrable and phallic. This rearticulation makes it difficult to continue to unequivocally equate the phallus with the penis, and thus sex is no longer reduced to male arousal and erection (Dowsett, 2002). This is not to say that a man cannot attain an erection during the act of rape. However, it does allow for a variety of body parts to become conceivably phallic and, in turn, for sexual transgressions such as FSA to become possible. Body betrayal discourse implies these rearticulations and is thus integral to FSA male victimhood.

The ultimate education in sex

The entrenched masculine norms that imply that male arousal and/or erection are evidence for an innate masculine drive for sex are also key vehicles for the image of the sexually voracious male, regardless of his age. Male victims who were abused as children or young teenagers claim that despite the prevailing belief that sexual interaction with an older woman provides "the ultimate educational experience" (Travers, 1999, p. 36), their individual experiences are not aligned to any form of sexual accomplishment. For example,

> Society dictates to me, "Geez, you got lucky, you've got this older girl teach you" . . . What a man! . . . And that's what everybody used to say to me but what I was feeling inside was like completely different. What I was feeling inside was like, disgusting.
>
> *(Richard)*

> You know, you think to yourself, shit, you were ten years old. You got laid. . . . It's like a, like an achievement type of thing. . . . But the more you think about it, you didn't get laid, you were raped.
>
> *(Jim)*

Both of these extracts foreground the oppositions that drive the discursive conflict reported by male victims. Social norms completely contradict these individual experiences as evidenced by dichotomies such as the pleasure/

disgust (Richard) and 'laid'/raped (Jim) polarities here. Richard's accent on 'disgust' also points to the moral loading of FSA.

Discourses concerning the 'ultimate education' in sex are absent for female victims who were sexually abused by a woman directly. However, Suzette, whose mother forced her to have underage non-consensual sexual interaction with various men, indicates that,

> I still went and did it. . . . Because it's my mom that said to me, "ya but you should drink this and you should go and do this with boys". I thought it was normal. I thought this is what every girl do, does with her mom. And what she teaches you.

It is interesting to note that Suzette views the sexual engagement with these men as a pedagogical event. It appears that the heteronormative assumption is so strong that victims can recast the sexual abuse into an educational experience that prepares for future heterosexual relationships characterised by violence of some kind. The assumption here is that heteronormative gender violence is, in some way, 'taught'. Where females are victims of FSA, this discursive condition cannot apply, as the possibility that this may be an educational experience towards a future homosexual orientation seems unlikely in a powerfully heteronormative context. Where prepubescent and adolescent males view FSA as educational, it is unlikely that these subjects would be able to see themselves as victims (Bourke, 2007). However, while FSA victims are cognisant of constructions of the female sexual perpetrator as sexual educator, their victimhood emerges through discursive strategies reliant on the perpetrator as sexual abuser. It thus seems that the recognition of these 'pedagogical' constructions coupled with an inability to identify with these norms results in the reliance on contradictory dichotomies (pleasure/disgust) and, in turn, a subjective conflict that surfaces FSA victimhood.

Creating conditions of possibility: the incitement to discourse – victims in waiting

Discourse has productive power and is thus the field in which the subject emerges (Winnubst, 1999). In order for subjection to take place, subjects must have access to the language of its production. For example, CSA is often only reported during late adolescence or adulthood. This late reporting is usually coupled with explanations that the seriousness of the CSA was only noted post exposure to particular media platforms, books, or conversations (Schaeffer, Leventhal, & Asnes, 2011). This incitement to discourse provides subjects the opportunity to construct their experiences as 'victims in waiting'. In much the same way as this CSA pattern, many FSA victims indicate that at the time of their FSA experiences, they did not self-identify as victims. Ella's comment that "it took me, you know, years and years and years to make that connection . . . [to] sexual abuse" points to this process of 'becoming' a victim. It is only after exposure to a particular condition or person, which or who incites FSA victim discourse, that victims are able to identify as such. For Suzette, this exposure was in the form of her father:

> I was really close to her, um until my dad kind of like explained to me that it was wrong, what she did and then I kind of like started realising, slowly but surely that my dad is right. . . . I started feeling really stupid that I didn't realise like my mom was actually abusing me and being really wrong compared to other mothers and what like the law said.

Once Suzette had self-identified as an FSA victim, she further consolidated this through other incitements to speak in detail about the abuse. For example, after disclosure to legal representatives, Suzette was asked to provide a detailed description of her experience, this narrative thus serving to further reify her subject position:

> I had to go into detail, what had happened. I didn't really want to do it. I was like, before the time I was like begging my dad, please don't let me do this, I don't want to do it and then my dad said "ya but you have to. Even I don't want you to do it but the court says, says you have to. You don't have that much of a choice in this".

Of interest is the perceived lack of choice identified by Suzette or, as Foucault (1978, p. 20) puts it, "the obligation to admit to violations of the laws of sex" and the injunction to do so by providing the most minute of details. This perceived obligation, as a consequence of the presence of legal structures and authorities, results in a 'confession' that provides coordinates for FSA victimhood. This is in line with Pryce's (2000) suggestion that the confessional vehicle (in this case a court case) is the standard device to elicit content to be interpreted, decoded, and comprehended. The incitement to discourse thus provides victims with an opportunity to 'confess' their FSA experiences, and in so doing, the self-identification as FSA victim is constituted (rather than disclosed) through confession. The current section identifies the mechanisms that provide the incitement to discourse that make confession possible. The mechanisms employed by victims include psychology and/or therapy, the Internet and media, cultural resources, and access to non-normative discourses on sexuality.

Access to psychologised discourse

Access to particular types of disciplinary discourses seems to provide an opportunity for subjects to occupy FSA victimhood. Unsurprisingly, the most salient of these appears to be the 'psychological'. During my research, this was easily surfaced due to the participants' awareness of my position in the field of psychology as well as the confessional architecture of the interview context. However, on the other hand, most of this psychologised discourse also appeared to be based on participants' previous exposure to therapy, psychological practices, or work in the actual field. It thus seemed that the interview, coupled with my status as a psychological researcher, assisted in the reification of discursive contours of the 'suspected' victimhood that preceded it. Most of the participants shared their own experiences of therapeutic contexts that provided the possibility for the emergence of FSA victimhood. Almost all of the participants realised or disclosed their FSA victimhoods inside a therapy, psychology, or counselling context. All of the participants discussed the value of therapy and how it has been particularly helpful in assisting them to 'deal' with their victimhood. For example,

> I also had a very big mental block when it came to it and the psychologist helped me get through that. . . . She says the more people I speak to, um within the future whether it be medically, in terms of more psychologists or just letting friends know is that it would definitely better me as a person.
>
> *(Charles)*

The implication by Charles' therapist that he should continue to speak about his FSA experience is a powerful example of the incitement to discourse proper. It also echoes Butler's (2004) argument that identity-making is dependent on a speaker repeatedly and consistently performing a particular discourse, in this case FSA victim discourse. Other examples of the way access to the 'psychological' incites FSA victimhood include:

> I think because I've shared it before, um, with a psychologist is that at the end of the day, it's a lot easier to speak about. The first time obviously definitely was not easy. Especially when speaking to another female . . . which I personally in my mind find odd, that I'm able to

speak to someone about a female problem. Yet she's a female . . . and I feel . . . threatened as such. But knowing that she was a psychologist and has dealt with these problems before is . . . [why] I haven't seen her as a threat.

(Charles)

And I know she [my stepmom] won't ever do the things that my mom did. Because I know she also did like, she wanted to become a sielkundige.[4]

(Suzette)

And when I started therapy and started to talk, actually started to use words rather than just enduring and surviving, I sort of began to piece together that there was a yesterday and there's likely to be a tomorrow whereas prior to therapy I'd never really been able to do that.

(Heather)

Charles' statement that "knowing that she was a psychologist and has dealt with these problems before" points to the requirement of an 'expert' listener to validate his FSA experiences as part of the incitement to discourse.

Some of the participants report that they have actually started to work in the psychological field, and that this too has provided them with an opportunity for understanding their situations. Richard is a support group leader for survivors of male sexual violence, Thabo is a psychological researcher in the field of sexuality and gender-based research, and Jane is a psychology student. It is quite evident that this work allows these three participants additional access to psychologised discourse that, in turn, further enables identification with victimhood. As Richard notes,

I do a lot of therapy online so I give a lot of people – I have a particular uh, empathy for survivors' wives and family. I kind of relate to them quite well because I know how badly I damaged mine, you know?

Victims also utilise their access to psychologised discourse to frame themselves in pathological terms. In doing so, victims are able to rationalise their FSA experiences as a function or cause of psychological pathology, implying that a condition for FSA victimhood is co-morbid pathology. For example, Heather explains how she has all "the unconscious stuff" that results in "dissociation". Another example from Ella is:

I have co-dependant personality disorder . . . [this] stems from my mother being so abusive and me basically doing anything so that I wouldn't get abused.

Whilst psychological discourse is one of the key mechanisms and outcomes of incitement, reference to traditional healing, such as ancestral healing, sangomas, and witch doctors, was completely absent from the South African interviews in my research (Kramer, 2014), despite the context. It thus appears that only particular types of 'healing' discourses are able to incite FSA victim discourse – those that are imbedded in the Malthusian unit, heteronormative monogamy, and the discourses of damage against which FSA can only be understood as transgressive.

The Internet and media as incitements to FSA victimhood

An interesting incitement to FSA victim discourse is access to online media forms. Internet access is a relatively recent phenomenon (especially in low-income contexts in parts of South Africa), and its wide range of easily accessible material allows for very rapid and efficient distribution of knowledge. The current global use of the Internet and media is thus a key driver of knowledge production and provides an optimal context for the incitement to peripheral gender discourses. Many FSA victims note that they did not self-identify as such until they had been exposed to material that availed this subject position to them. This demonstrates how conditions of possibility are temporally specific. For example, Ella explains how she did not really understand how to categorise her FSA experience until she "got this compulsion to get up on the Internet and um, look up BDSM-type videos". Richard also notes,

> I pushed the memories of my mother, I didn't remember them at all, I **really** didn't. Until I went onto the male survivor site, last, last year . . . I was reading, another guy, and he wrote this story and it was just . . . mad. It was like . . . my eyes closed and it was like this little movie playing and it just . . . **all** came back to me. It just . . . I could see myself sitting in the bath, I could see the bathroom, I could smell the soap and the shampoo. **Everything.** I could feel the warm water. And I sat there reading the story and everything he described in it was **exactly** how it happened to me. And I never remembered that. And all of a sudden it just came back. It was overwhelming.

Due to the general exclusion of FSA victimhood from available discourses on abuse, seeing 'oneself' as a victim of FSA in language is difficult. However, Richard's identification of the possibilities for his own victimhood is realised in the range of material available online and the ability for non-normative discourses to reify this subject position. For some victims, this means that the Internet provides an emerging discourse on curative and supportive options for FSA victims. As indicated by Jim:

> I think what made things easier for, for victims is the fact that we've now got internet. . . . We've got all these things that can help that person. . . . I mean from my phone. I can go into any site. . . . Like the . . . MatrixMen.[5] . . . I can do it right here.

This self-help discourse enabled by the Internet is a key example of the intersection of spoken and material conditions of possibility.

The call for participants for my research was presented on various media forums (radio, magazines, newspapers) and Internet sites. Ironically, this call for FSA victims appeared to be one of the very mechanisms that incited the participants to victim discourse. As Jim notes,

> I wouldn't say that, for me it wasn't that much of an issue. Um . . . until I heard the thing with DJ Fresh.[6] And . . . it just sparked a lot of memories regarding it. . . . I was listening to what you were saying. And all of a sudden, boom, shit, that happened to me.

This excerpt provides a powerful example of how my research is an incitement to FSA victim discourse and thus another cog in the discursive machinery through which FSA victimhood is further reproduced and reified.

Class resources: access to forms of knowledge

Access to class resources (in the form of social assets such as private and tertiary education) is a key mechanism that provides victims with a language from which to produce their FSA victimhood. This is a noteworthy observation, given that my research with incarcerated South African female sexual offenders demonstrated that nearly all of these women are from low-income contexts and consequently have very limited education (Kramer, 2010, 2011). Whilst my research (Kramer, 2010, 2011, 2014) on both FSA perpetrators and victims has demonstrated that perpetrators and their victims are acquainted and are of similar background, self-identified victim participants are from completely different socioeconomic contexts as compared to the incarcerated perpetrators. Despite the call for victim participants reaching an exhaustive list of contacts across a variety of socioeconomic contexts, I did not manage to elicit the type of victims identified by perpetrators in my perpetrator studies (Kramer, 2010, 2011) – those of low socioeconomic status (SES). It can therefore be assumed that the difference between these participants would signify some of the conditions that make FSA victimhood (im)possible. It appears that in order to self-identify as an FSA victim, subjects require some form of exposure to particular knowledge forms and discourses accessible through specific class vehicles, such as education. It is therefore possible that the victims of incarcerated female sexual perpetrators with limited access to education cannot yet access the domains that make FSA victimhood possible. However, given that the numbers of spaces that enable women to remain outside of new kinds of surveillance are rapidly decreasing, it is likely that as females become increasingly surveilled, FSA victims will become visible.

Throughout my FSA victim study (Kramer, 2014), participants spoke to their educational backgrounds and academic credentials. For example, Jane explains how she went to "posh schools" and that her brother is at a "very expensive private school". She also explains that her desire to study is based on her need to be academically stimulated and that "with school work, I was always academic colours, in the top ten". Thabo also identifies the value that his nuclear family places on education:

> My mother . . . was very hard working and she valued education. So, I think she was able to take us all to private schools.

Thabo's career as a researcher in the field of sexuality with a focus on sexual minorities not only provides him with academic discourse, but also with 'scientific' discourse on the particular subject area that is key to his self-identification as an FSA victim. As Thabo indicates:

> The more I read about issues like that, I tapped into things of, you know, you know, finding out what paedophilia is. I read about that . . . I'm a writer. And I've been published about certain things and whatever. But for me, it was, the thing it involves about sexuality findings. . . . The older I became and the more I read up on this thing, the more the world taught me things, the more I learnt from society. I got an awareness that that is actually not a nice thing to do to a kid.

Jane also actively draws on her access to academic language to explain her FSA experiences:

> I remember kind of feeling a bit paralysed. Definitely like that out of body experience. Like, the more I'm reading about it as well, it's like that's normal for like a situation like that . . . an interesting theory I actually picked up a month or so ago.

Anna utilises her access to academic discourse to indicate that she understands the necessity for the study of FSA victims and the value inherent in the research process:

> I am actually busy with my Masters in Law, so I know how difficult it can be to obtain all the info needed . . . anything I can do to help your studies and help with prevention I will.

Whilst prevention is not the objective of my work, Anna's assertion of its necessity is additional evidence of how the study of a construct such as FSA victimhood finds traction in health discourses preoccupied with preventability, regulation, and measurement. The above extract also demonstrates how the study of a particular subject has the productive power to reify sexual deviance. The production of FSA as an object that falls beyond the boundaries of our 'normal' social ontology creates the appearance of a potential pandemic (Bartky, 1988) and the object thus joins the 'prevention list'.

Alternative sexualities: access to non-normative discourse

The participants in my victim study were relatively young, and so it appears that being part of a generation that is widely constructed as increasingly sexually liberated and having additional access to online media, classed capital, and psychological discourse are pre-conditions for victimhood. Participation in a contemporary society characterised by 'sexual liberation' may thus be FSA victims' found way to circumnavigate conventional parameters and identify with alternative sexualities. For instance, some of the victims in my study are actively engaged with non-normative discourse that informs alternative sexualities, and they construct sexual victimisation from a fluid gender perspective (rather than in the binary terms offered by other participants). More specifically, these victims use their access to non-normative discourse as a means to pull gender and biological sex apart. For example, Charles reports how his group of friends identifies with a range of sexual orientations and beliefs such that it was unsurprising that he might date a much older woman. Thabo relays how his homosexual identity has allowed him to more fully engage with his FSA victim status:

> Very wide circle of friends. Um . . . majority females that were either lesbian or bisexual so very . . . open sexually but also majority of her friends were quite manly. . . . Um, there were some females that I had met in my life that I think they were more manly and more . . . they got more male testosterone in them than I do. Um, so ya, very open in terms of the sexual side. . . . I wasn't the only younger male within in the group, um . . . in terms of the older females dating younger guys.
>
> *(Charles)*

> I think that, it's probably different with gay people. It's sort of like we start to question our sexuality from a really early age so by the time we are in probably our middle ages we are sort of like so much more comfortable. It becomes like a normalcy to talk about sexuality . . . people of marginal sexualities are more comfortable talking about sexuality than the sexual majority . . . because we centralise it for ourselves. We gather. That's how you survive. You, you normalise it.
>
> *(Thabo)*

Thabo's link between survival and the normalisation of marginal sexualities implies that sex abuse is, in some ways, comparable to alternative sexualities. This is a powerful example of the ways that heteronormative standards produce and sustain 'non-normative' sexualities, sexual deviance, and sexual minorities such that the normal-abnormal binary is sustained. Thabo's particular emphasis on survival echoes Butler's (2004) suggestion that regardless of whether an individual submits to or resists the norms, all bodies are subjected to 'unfreedom' given their constant circulation in systems of surveillance and regulation.

The tendency to split discourses on gender from the constructions of biology as sex, along with access to a psychological vocabulary circulated via the Internet and other forms of media, seem critical mechanisms in the incitement of FSA victimhood confession.

The confession as apparatus: producing FSA victimhood

The confessional context is one of the primary means to the production of 'truth'. Foucault (1978) argues that sexuality is produced through the confession. The apparatus of the confession infers that 'truth' is concealed within a subject as 'secrets', and that these secrets must be liberated (Phelan, 1990). In this way, the self is constituted by confession, and the desire for disclosure is constituted as 'natural' (Tell, 2007). The psychological interview is undoubtedly an instantiation of this apparatus as it is used to draw out this 'secret' information to be interpreted. The presence of an 'expert' at the receiving end of this information is key to the incitement to discourse in gauging its 'truth value' (Pryce, 2000).

FSA victim discourse remains peripheral to the discourse on sexual violence in human science knowledge production. However, because FSA victim discourse emerges as a consequence of ostensible silences and prohibitions, this apparent 'exclusion' from discourse is reminiscent of Foucault's (1978) critique of the illusion of repression. Given that the interview context in my research was framed as a 'confessional' site to discuss the 'secret' of FSA victimisation, participants actively engaged with this space as a means to produce their victimhood. This production is centred on typical victim discourses, including references to nondisclosure, trauma, revictimisation, guilt, self-blaming, consequences, and emotional damage. Particular emphasis is placed on naming the FSA event as 'the secret' as well as a demonstration of the psychological trauma of victimisation. The participants' discourses are saturated with confessions of shame and the implication that disclosure of 'the secret' requires an expert listener that can 'understand' victimisation. Interestingly, these are not unlike the victim discourses arising out of male sex-abuse narratives (see Ahrens, 2006; Davis, 2005; Sturken, 1999). However, given the non-normative nature of FSA victimhood, these 'typical' discourses are embedded in complex intersections of sexuality, gender, and power that represent points of resistance and the promise of counter-knowledge at certain moments.

The secret: silence and nondisclosure

[I'm] a victim of the most undisclosed crime.

(Tanaka)

The implication that sexual 'truth' is housed within subjects as secrets to be liberated is intrinsic to the logic of confession and the incitement to discourse. Throughout my research, victims drew on the confidential quality characteristic of the confessional space by indicating that their only concern about participation in my study was potential identification as an FSA victim. Victims also constantly spoke of 'a/the secret' with reference to their FSA experiences:

It was my dirty little secret that I've never said to anybody.

(Heather)

I had to learn how to . . . go on with life and . . . not . . . and keep my secret and not let people find out.

(Jane)

Can you, can you imagine the **burden** of walking around with a secret that big, that could destroy another family, that could actually eventually come out?

(Jim)

Jane's comment that she has to "go on with life" and Jim's reference to his secret "burden" are key markers of the centrality of sex to selfhood. In addition, these assertions that bind FSA victimhood to secrecy reflect the illusion of the 'repression' of FSA victimhood. The treatment of their FSA experiences as secrets results in victims opting for nondisclosure to authorities or family about their victimhoods. However, 'the secret' is also crucial to the incitement to discourse; thus, the treatment of an FSA event as a secret is also the very mechanism through which victims are able to occupy a victim subject position in the confessional context of the interview with an 'expert'.

Nondisclosure is related to shame and the fear of being blamed or not believed, and is rooted in cultural narratives that victims should remain silent. Nondisclosure is thus typical in sexual victimisation (Enns, McNeilly, Corkery, & Gilbert, 1995.). These fears are clearly evident in FSA victims' reported nondisclosure decisions; however, in addition to this, they lack access to a language that could frame their FSA experiences. For example, despite having disclosed her sexual victimisation by a male perpetrator to the legal authorities, Heather failed to report her FSA victimisation because "it never occurred to me". Likewise, Jane indicates that she would have reported the victimisation if her perpetrator was a male because it is "more socially acceptable". For those who can frame it, nondisclosure seems to be based either on the shame or the implausibility that a woman could sexually violate them. Given this implausibility, people subjected to FSA cannot identify themselves as victims, a prerequisite for disclosure of abuse. In addition, an incitement to discourse cannot occur without an 'expert' present that can validate victims' experiences. For instance,

[If it was a male] then you would have, then you probably would have said something about it and then you would have been able to sort it out as a kid. By the time you've grown up, you've dealt with it. It's gone already . . . but now because it's a woman, now you kind of . . . keep it in forever. And the scars grow.

(Jane)

I didn't really want to talk about it because I was like really embarrassed about it.

(Suzette)

I wasn't gonna admit that to anybody.

(Ella)

The emergence of these very specific confessional elements is central to the victims' framing of their experiences as secretive, abusive, and traumatic. These confessional elements are not particular to FSA victimisation. It thus seems that there are at least some discursive coordinates that drive sexual victimisation in general rather than FSA specifically. This is significant, because it implies that FSA victimhood emerges through some of the very same mechanisms that operate to produce male-perpetrated sexual victimisation and as part of the discursive explosion on sex.

Victimhood and trauma

Gendered discourses link femininity with passivity and so FSA is considered rare, and the potential for it to be harmful and thus produce both trauma and a victim position is regarded as improbable (Denov, 2001). Additionally, trauma discourse infers that there must be a victim identity (usually female) and an aggressor identity (usually male). As Jane notes, "women are seen as the victims, always". This pattern has generally resulted in the exclusion of FSA victimhood from widely circulated discourses on trauma and damage. However, through various incitements, people subjected to FSA are able to self-identify as victims and, consequently, as damaged and traumatised. As Jim reports, "the more you think about it, you didn't get laid, you were raped". Levett (1992) argues that constructions of trauma resulting from transgressive sexualities and their practices result in the perception that the 'victim' is invariably and indelibly damaged. In line with this argument, FSA victims draw on words describing their powerlessness and helplessness when asked to explain their understandings of victimhood. For example,

'Victim' . . . it suggests powerlessness.

(Thabo)

> Overpowered in I think in any sense of the word. Where you feel helpless.
>
> *(Anna)*

> Victim is what I was when I was a little kid and I couldn't fight back and I had to put up with it.
>
> *(Ella)*

Ella interestingly explains that the type of trauma response is particular to the type of abuse to which the victim has been exposed. Thus, physical abuse may produce a different type of response to sexual abuse. As she notes,

> And because this was a woman and I didn't realise that it was sexual, I just thought it was horrible punishment. Um . . . it probably saved me from some of the really screwed up psychological problems that people have from that. Not to say that I didn't have screwed up psychological problems, but it put my problems in a different realm.

Ella's disclosure links sex and trauma in very particular ways. Aligned to the logic of biopolitics, a transgression against sexuality seems more potentially damaging than a transgression against the mere physical integrity of the body. Another example is the way trauma resulting from sexual victimisation is commonly associated with subsequent instances of sexual revictimisation. Here, one instance of sexual abuse results in 'learned' subordination, a victim identity, and thus the 'possibility for exposure' to further sexual assaults (Gidycz, 2011). This is a recurring theme in FSA victim narratives.

Revictimisation: victimhood as destiny

The FSA aggressor is incompatible with gendered understandings of sexual- and violence-related trauma. Thus, most FSA victims tend to escape the incitement to discourse in the confessional context and hence the related experience of trauma, including the opportunity for revictimisation. The frequently cited 'finding' of revictimisation in sex abuse cases (Gidycz, 2011) reflects both the power and the longevity of the victim subject position once it has been occupied. FSA victims in my study grounded part of their subjection to this position through the reproduction of classic sex-abuse narratives, especially with regards to revictimisation.

For some FSA victims, being sexually violated by a woman is accounted for as an outcome of their learnt subordination resulting from previous abuse. As Heather notes, "I did have some understanding of sexual activity because of previous abuse with neighbours". Jim explains that, prior to the FSA event with his aunt, his father had always abused him:

> I was terrified of my dad. Um . . . having had all those physical abuse moments from him. I mean can you imagine being tied to a bed. And then being 'donnered'[7] is the word I'm going to use. You don't get smacked. You get beaten. With a belt. Much bigger than this [points to his belt]. And you're six years old.

However, while Jim explains that "physical abuse in my house [was an] everyday thing", his FSA experience is perceived as less normative and as something that has the capacity to "destroy another family . . . [if it] could actually eventually come out". This again points to the possible differentiation of the sexual and the physical, and the construction of sex abuse as potentially more damaging than physical abuse.

Other FSA victims feel that their FSA experiences 'groomed' them to become victims and as a consequence to be revictimised. For example,

> I think by the time the male perpetrators came along, I was kind of already . . . groomed. And that's the thing that I struggle with. Is that it's almost like my mother groomed me for this evil future that . . . she opened the door . . . she kind of . . . she started it . . . she . . . kind of lowered my standards and, and sort of made me think that it was okay to go with these men. . . . I resent the fact that she started it. She opened the door. So she initiated my life as an abuse victim. . . . So it starts with one guy touching you on your back and then you sort of let it happen and the next guy puts his hand down your pants and then you go, "Well kind of my mom does this, so, you know, what's the problem?"
>
> *(Richard)*

> When she [my mother] died, my father sexually abused me until he died so it sort of all rolled in together then so the whole sexual life is just, you know, a blur of abuse.
>
> *(Heather)*

Heather's comments imply that sexual damage is irredeemable and everlasting, unlike the damage experienced under other kinds of transgressions. Again, this reveals the permanence and power of the discourse of the inevitable trauma that must accompany sex abuse when compared to its physical, emotional, and psychological manifestations.

In addition to their own multiple victimisation experiences, FSA victims in my study also identified other victims in their families, thus constructing FSA victimhood as part of the 'epidemic' of victims. It also points to the sense that the family cannot be 'normal' if FSA is possible. Richard states, "I found out last year that both my brothers were actually sexually abused by neighbours as children so pretty cocked up family". Similarly, Anna reports that "I discovered that it happened to my mom as well but with, with a male obviously". While most of the participants simply use these discourses to relay their victimhood, Jane reflects on its instrumentality, again instantiating its power:

> Like what does the pattern do? Like I'm always interested to find, like to figure it out because like do people sometimes, if they like get abused once, feel like they need to . . . go with it again?

Jane's reflections of this "pattern" is indicative of the way revictimisation is produced within sex abuse discourses such that it is reified as unshakeable, recalcitrant, and forever marking of the inversion of normality. Other engrained victim discourses are those centred on shame, guilt, and self-blaming.

The inversion of the moral code: guilt and self-blame

Foucault (1985) argues that subjection is sustained through technologies or practices of the self within historicised forms of moral government. This moral code is an ensemble of regulatory discursive codes or 'moral orthopaedics' that are recommended to subjects via the mechanisms of various prescriptive and authoritative institutions. Through the participation in sexual transgressions that violate culturally acceptable and normative sexual moral codes, FSA victims report feelings of shame, guilt, and self-blame. The inversion of morality is thus expressed through moral discourses that demonstrate a violation of the moral orthapaedics of selfhood. These are classic discourses that emerge in sex abuse narratives and are thus again indicative of the similarities between FSA and male-perpetrated sexual violence. However, the guilt and self-blame discourses are structured somewhat differently from those arising from male-perpetrated sexual violence. The shame associated with male-to-female sexual violation is typically attached to cultural beliefs that the act of rape tarnishes the female body (Weiss, 2010b). These cultural codes are relayed onto a female body, thus making it impossible for a male FSA victim to occupy this sense of responsibility and self-surveillance at the pre-victim stage. Most FSA victims (especially male victims) emphasise that their shame and guilt is compounded by the fact that they were sexually violated by female perpetrators (Kramer, 2014). Given the gendered construction of the weak and harmless female, FSA victims' guilt is directly linked to their inability to exercise power during an FSA event. This pattern of pushing guilt and victimhood against one another is important because the admission to guilt is irreconcilable with victimhood. These moral discourses are thus central to the (im)possibility of FSA victimhood.

Victimhood is always mediated through culpability (Boonzaier, 2014; Richardson & May, 1999), and this influences the structure of victim discourses. For example, the implicit obligation to confess a sexual victimisation experience results in the victim's acceptance of some responsibility for the incident (Posel, 2005; Weiss, 2010b). Richard describes feeling "shamed" and "belittled" while Tanaka indicates that he "felt **really** bad" and Anna says she was "vulnerable" and "ashamed". Charles reports that he felt "dirty" and "worthless" and Heather states that "there was just the most profound guilt". Jane comments that:

> Like people use the word "dirty", but that's not what it is. It's just … guilt, almost. It's like that sense of guilt that you felt, like when I was little. Like the sense of guilt of like, that happened. Even like when I got the flashbacks, thinking about it now, there was definitely like a sense of guilt there … it was definitely an intense sense of like guilt for letting it happen. And I think that was the biggest thing, that feeling.
>
> *(Jane)*

Jane directly links her experiences of guilt with "letting it happen". This is a powerful demonstration of the way female gender constructions imply that an FSA victim is a guilty victim because he/she should have the power to prevent a sexual violation by a woman. However, there are clear gendered differences in this particular guilt expression – male victims' guilt about the inability to prevent the FSA events is related to the shame of not 'being men', whereas female participants, in line with Cahill's (2000) suggestions about the guilty pre-victim, report feeling guilty for somehow eliciting the abuse.

The incompatibility of victimhood and guilt results in the continued exclusion of FSA victims from the lexicon of moral orthopaedics. Interestingly, Jane notes that her feelings of guilt are "not there anymore". It thus seems that moral discourses work to exclude FSA victimhood whilst the nonalignment with these discourses surfaces FSA victimhood. This tension between guilt and victimhood is frequently conflated with self-blaming. For example,

I eventually kind of got to a stage where you feel so powerless you actually start despising yourself. You know, you start thinking like, why couldn't I stop her from doing this?

(*Richard*)

Am I to blame for this? Or should I have done something earlier. . . . Are they gonna think that I . . . instigated it at all?

(*Jane*)

I still thought it was my fault. And I still thought that I had a role in it as well . . . I think that, that I could forgive them [my abusers] but I can never really forgive myself.

(*Anna*)

I thought he was going to be angry at me because I thought I was the one doing the wrong. Not my mom . . . I feel kind of like guilty that I, that I didn't stop it earlier.

(*Suzette*)

The way I understood it was that I was the guilty party and that I was dirty and bad and anything to do with anything below the chin, was my fault and it was wrong.

(*Heather*)

I was embarrassed and ashamed because I believed that I must have done something wrong enough to deserve all that.

(*Ella*)

These extracts demonstrate how the moral order shifts these individuals from victims into guilty parties who have not taken responsibility for their own complicity in their abuse. In keeping with the logic of sexuality and selfhood, the effects of these traumas are constructed as enduring and requiring constant management:

Sometimes I don't want to have sex at all and I feel bad after. I feel like I have committed a crime.

(*Tanaka*)

Tanaka's comparison of sexual interaction with criminal activity is a compelling example of the ways that the FSA victim is positioned in an adversarial relationship to the logic of a moral order in which victims of male sex abuse are arguably more centrally accommodated.

Psychic damage

One of the most cited and controversial findings in the sex abuse literature is that the trauma associated with sexual violence often results in repression, which is later transformed into recovered memories (see Brewin, 2012; Davis & Loftus, 2014; DePrince et al., 2012). Despite the controversy surrounding the recovered memory hypothesis, its central position in court cases and media reports on sex abuse has resulted in its production as a widely circulated psychological discourse. Most of my study participants had access to psychological discourse, and so it is unsurprising that their narratives were infused with both examples of their own memory losses and an indication of their psychological insights into these 'repressed' memories. It seems that following the incitement to discourse, consequent self-identifications with victim positions are further validated by expressions relating to memory loss:

> The abuse, in my childhood, a very difficult thing cause I just . . . I can't remember . . . like I have flashbacks. . . . I'm kind of trying to figure out if it actually happened, if the flashbacks are real or if they're just part of my imagination . . . there's a large part of my childhood that's just kind of blocked out.
>
> *(Richard)*

> It is quite fragmented. Um . . . I remember as a kid remembering **a lot** of it. But then kind of suppressing it, obviously. And then as I grew up through my teens, I think I just, it just disappeared, kind of? Although it was there. And then about . . . a year ago, it came back like quite vividly. In flashbacks. . . . She starts touching me and then at one stage just puts her hand down my pants. And then I can't remember what happened there . . . I don't remember how **exactly** it starts. I just know . . . but I don't know what happened after or how it stopped or anything like that. No, I just remember like, like in the middle.
>
> *(Jane)*

> I just remember that I have a fear of the garage and like I know that something happened there that I don't know why I can't remember it.
>
> *(Anna)*

It was one incident as far as my memory serves. I might have blocked it out. I don't know.

(Jim)

I'll put it as crude as possible. She was humping up and down. That's what I can remember. . . . Like you see in the movies when people go blank. That's basically what I've got. I've got a huge gap between 10, 11 years old, up to about 13 years old. There's, there's a bit of a gap regarding her. So I don't know if it happened after that. I can't tell you.

(Jim)

I don't actually know how it ended, I don't know . . . I think, in my mind what I remember is her rage and her . . . resent for [me] getting born. Um . . . once she bought out the kitchen equipment I don't have an ending of that memory. Like, I don't know what the end of it was. Like, did she just stop, did she carry on, did she. . . I have no idea.

(Heather)

Taking recourse to the problem of memory seems an attempt to validate the abuse. Interestingly, most of these recovered memories or 'flashbacks' surfaced recently in parallel to the emergence of broader global discourses on FSA. For example, Jim indicates that he only recalled his experience when he heard the call for participants for my victim study. For Richard, Jane, and Ella, their memories arrived in the form of flashbacks after exposure to similar material in a media format or on the Internet. Richard explains that "I call it my rebirth, when I discovered then that I was a survivor of abuse". Given that this occurred after exposure to information on FSA, this 'discovery' appears to be less the result of repression and more a function of the production of victimhood within which one could locate such repression. Additionally, in order to be a victim, one must be 'victim worthy' and demonstrate the invariable psychic damage that results from abuse. The turn to repression appears to be a precondition for describing the magnitude of the psychological burden resulting from an abuse that disrupts and damages personhood.

Participants in my victim study applied their own psychological insight into why their memories may have been repressed and then later 'recovered'. Richard indicates, "you might not remember but you never forget", and Jim explains that "a mental block may be in place". Jim goes on to clarify,

Think about it. If that, if that wall gets broken and all those memories come flooding out and all of a sudden it wasn't just once, it was 10, 20, 30 times, do I wanna know that? I don't think so.

While Ella reports not being able to name her experience as FSA until she was exposed to particular Internet material, she did construct it as being physically (rather than sexually) abusive within a particular (and less 'damaging') discursive framework that divides physical integrity from sexual destiny such that 'remembering' was possible:

> And the thing is I never forgot what happened. I know there's people that say that they blocked it out and they forgot what happened and then something triggered it and they suddenly remembered. I never forgot what happened.

Ella's extract presents as a startling counter-example to other victims' evocation of repressed memory discourse such that her victim worthiness becomes questionable.

The repressed/recovered memory discourse in the FSA victimhood narratives, along with victims' turn to the cycle of abuse theory, demonstrates how sex abuse constructions are so entrenched that the occupation of a victim position is immediately characterised by these classic victim 'traits'.

Becoming the abuser to become the victim

> I don't deserve to have a baby ... what if I hurt it?
>
> *(Thabo)*

The cycle of abuse is another psychological theory that is evoked to construct victim worthiness in victims' discourses. As with the turn to memory loss, the assumption that victims become abusers appears to be rooted in victims' access to psychological frameworks that guarantees that victimisation (especially sexual) may be linked to later perpetration (see Gomez, 2011; Ogloff et al., 2012; Ryan et al., 2011; Yun et al., 2011). So entrenched is this assumption regarding sex abuse that victims express concern regarding their own sexually violent capacities; this is yet another representation of the irredeemable and everlasting quality of sexual damage. In line with Schaeffer and colleagues' (2011) arguments that male victims are more likely to be treated as potential future perpetrators than female victims, the majority of participants in my victim study that occupied this victim-offender potential position were men (Kramer, 2014). Some examples of the cycle of violence discourse can be noted in the following extracts:

> I can remember changing her nappies and like looking at her fanny and going, "Don't you dare ever touch that. Don't you dare". And

I'd like clean it. You have to do that as a father, you have to clean it. And then I'd think, "Stop looking. Stop looking. You're going to hurt her. Don't you dare. You can't do this". You know? Then I used to bath her as well . . . I'd think constantly in my head all the time, you know, "Don't you forget what you're doing. You know that you're a little perv. You know that you're a sicko. Don't touch her. Don't touch her". You know. . . . So like eventually when she got to a point where she could actually bath herself, she was like five or six I think, then it was like thank god, you know, I don't have to do that anymore. But then I was totally divorced. I had one ritual that I did and I still, to this day, try and do it, she's twelve now. So I put her to bed. She's got her pyjamas on. The blanket's on. That's it. Just her little face that sticks out, you know? And I can love and kiss that face as much as I want to because there's nothing else happening. You know what I mean? It's all covered. It's protected by blankets, you know?

(Richard)

And the one cousin, I know for a fact, we were in the bushes and I was playing with her. Cause the aunt was doing it to me . . . so now I think in the child's perception is that, it's okay for her to do it to me so it should be okay for me to do it to her.

(Jim)

These comments demonstrate the 'curse' of victimhood through their implication that sexual transgressions are intractable and mark selfhood in perpetuity. In much the same way as victims speak to the inevitability of rev-ictimisation, the likelihood of becoming the abuser is a trope that appears to be a precondition for victimhood. These turns to the cycle of abuse are not expressed in isolation from the psychological frameworks that produce them. The gravity of female sexual transgressions is pronounced in the construct having to be underwritten by victim discourses itself:

You also get that horrible label that if you're abused you will go on to be an abuser.

(Richard)

I read about that. And cases of people saying they were paedophiles because they were abused. And it terrified me. Meaning, that does this mean I'm also gonna . . . I'm still terrified of it today.

(Thabo)

> Like maybe this, a woman will sexually abuse another child because it
> happened to them and this is the way they justify it, you know?
>
> *(Jane)*

Psychological explanations require a set of features for victimhood, and
potential offending is one of them. Victims' access to psychological discourse
allows them to construct victimhood and to demonstrate their victim worthiness. While the cycle of violence forms part of the discourses on sex abuse
in general (rather than FSA particularly), it is access to this type of discourse
that first provides the conditions of possibility for FSA victimisation, and
thereafter provides participants with a set of features with which to construct
their victimhood in perpetuity. The ability to occupy an FSA victim subject
position thus depends on its intelligibility amongst typical victim discourses,
albeit that in the case of FSA, the perpetrator must simultaneously share this
position.

Self-depictions of perversity: 'effects' on sexual and gendered behaviour

> I spent half my life thinking that I'm such a pervert that I avoid all people.
>
> *(Richard)*

For Foucault (1978), one of the key vehicles for biopower in the eighteenth and nineteenth centuries was the perverse implantation whereby an
explosion of discourses on sexuality came to produce a host of deviations
against the normalising sweeps of the Malthusian unit. These violations,
against the heterosexual couple and thus 'normal' sexuality, produced forms
of perversity that were to be annexed and implanted as population-wide
possibilities by medicine and the law. Foucault (1978) argues that this perverse implantation underlies the obligation to confess to sexuality. Given
the confessional context of the interview, my study participants' constructions of the perversity that must mark them emerged as a means to further
demonstrate the intractability of the inversion of sexual 'normality', and so
victim worthiness.

Access to particular discourses (psychological, Internet, media, and/
or non-normative sexual discourse) provides victims with a technology of
incitement to self-identify as FSA victims. One of the strongest claims to
this victim position is the reference to the 'perverse' sexual and gendered
consequences of FSA victimisation. All of my study participants constructed

themselves in an unquestionable relation to perversity. Participants drew on psychological discourse to frame their 'psychological insights' that linked 'perversions' directly to FSA. For example,

> There was this naked girl [the perpetrator]. As I said, she was quite chubby. To this day . . . I still have this thing about obese or overweight women. It freaks me out completely. My ex-wife when she like puts on weight I couldn't, I couldn't have sex with her. I just couldn't. She must . . . go away. You know? It's quite difficult. There's not too many anorexic women out there these days.
>
> *(Richard)*

> It's made me sexually aggressive. . . . It's a wonder I haven't got AIDS or . . . because the way I was going on, it was bad. I was literally sexually aggressive.
>
> *(Jim)*

> I think . . . her getting pleasure out of it [the FSA events] . . . I think I dived in pornography because it became – I started to even almost abuse it myself. Finding out that then I also became like quite . . . I'm not going to say addicted but I also became . . . the whole pornography of it also became my basis in terms of entertainment . . . I think in terms of sexuality because I got to realise, I got to . . . I think the, the molestation made me get onto sex way before I was ready.
>
> *(Thabo)*

Thabo's comment that his sexually precocious nature as a child was a consequence of his experience of molestation marks a lifelong deviation from 'normality'. Victims also infuse abuse into their reports on desire, sexuality, and satisfaction in their lives. In keeping with the centrality of sexuality to subjectivity (Foucault, 1978), this compromises and continues to mark their sexual selfhood and health more globally. For example,

> I've had more dirty sex and only with a handful of women so . . . like even **now**, when I have sex, I mean the actual penetration doesn't interest me. So, I would rather stimulate her orally or manually or whatever, then bring her to climax and then be quite happy just to leave it at that. It sort of becomes quite crazy in terms of like sex is not wrong as long as it's not satisfying.
>
> *(Richard)*

> When it comes to sex, I'm not a sex person. You know? I'm more, I'm very more sensual like with a partner and all that but with sex and whatever I still carry that whole thing of it being too intimate and I don't wanna, it's really difficult for me to share my, what pleasures me ultimately with a person because ... I don't know, does this make sense but I feel like they will see a connection to my sister.
>
> *(Thabo)*

> There were sexual problems in terms of, like very dysfunctional you know? Unable to perform, drinking and low self-esteem.
>
> *(Richard)*

> Well, when I first started having sex, I had a problem with um ... what is that called? Vaginismus?
>
> *(Ella)*

Again, this is not necessarily different from constructions of victims of male-perpetrated sexual violence – especially where the victim is a boy or man (see Myers, 1989). Discourses concerning nondisclosure, trauma, revictimisation, guilt, self-blame, memory loss, the cycle of abuse, and perversity are thus all mobilised to frame victimhood across the gender divide. However, in addition to these typical sex abuse discourses, one clear discursive theme that does not emulate classic sex-abuse narratives is victims' constructions of FSA as more emotionally damaging than sexual victimisation at the hands of a man.

FSA as more emotionally damaging than male-perpetrated sexual violence

> I know that that betrayal is there for my father as well, but it's not as bad. It's not as big.
>
> *(Heather)*

While victims take recourse to the construction of female sexuality as harmless in accounting for their reported reluctance to disclose abuse, their positions imply the inverse in their reflections on the emotional consequences of abuse that takes place at the hands of a woman. Rather than aligning their narratives to the conventionally imagined innocuous female sexuality, victims construct FSA as a special case of betrayal, damage, and disruption of selfhood. In short, FSA is constructed as hyper-damaging. Anna felt that if her perpetrator were male, she would have experienced less shame. She states that, "I can't explain why it's more shameful that it's, that it's a lady than with a man". Victims that had exposure to both male and female sex abusers (on separate occasions) maintain that the emotional damage is far worse under the sexual coercion of a woman. This is particularly confusing for Richard, who feels that the actual sexual violence was more injurious under his male abuser, yet his emotional response to the FSA event was more severe. Similarly, Heather compares her response to her mother's sex abuse to her response to being sexually abused by a group of boys with the following statement:

> I felt **much** more violated by my mother. I felt much more betrayed that . . . that she could hurt somebody . . . in a way that . . . it actually felt surreal. It's like I just started to think . . . this, none of this feels right. Whereas I don't think I had that thought for the boys.
>
> *(Heather)*

The tendency to view FSA as more emotionally damaging than male sexual violence can be understood as a function of the gendered constructions explored earlier in the chapter. Despite their FSA experiences, victims mobilise constructions of masculine aggression and virility, and feminine passivity and maternity, so that male sexual violence is thinkable and FSA is near impossible. FSA directly contradicts the essential 'truth' about women, and thus abuse by a woman is constructed as the embodiment of emotional betrayal and trust. In keeping with the discursive loading of women as caregivers, victims who report the most severe emotional reactions tend to be abused by their mothers (Kramer, 2014). Given the absolute 'unnaturalness' of a maternal sex abuser, these events are constructed as even more perverse and damaging. Reconciling the emotional custodianship of modern motherhood with the immorality and pathology attached to the sexual perpetrator seems impossible for FSA victims such that an everlasting hyper-trauma must mark their constructions of victimhood.

It therefore seems that the ability for subjects to occupy an FSA victim position requires casting female sexuality as potentially aggressive. This, in turn, is dependent on the integration of this knowledge into broader constructions of victimhood. Given that FSA remains peripheral to modern conceptions of sexual transgression, woman as abuser implies a very particular form of discursive arrangement in which the abuse represents not merely a transgression on the individual body, but perhaps, more specifically, a transgression on motherhood as the embodiment of custodianship and care, and ultimately the last bastion of human safety.

Surfacing female-perpetrated sex crimes

FSA victims draw on normative constructions of gender and sexuality as a means to demonstrate how FSA victimhood is 'abnormal' even in the context of sex abuse. However, given the contestations between FSA as either innocuous or hyper-damaging, FSA victimhood outcomes, such as tensions between the hypersexual man and an emasculated victimhood, and constructions of severe pathology and a compromised morality, serve as counter-coordinates for hegemonic constructions of gender and sexuality. Together, these counter-discourses may disrupt human science knowledge on sexuality in the further and refined production of the emergent female sexual perpetrator and her victims. As participants in my study progressed through their interviews, female sexual violence began to become increasingly thinkable, palpable, and dangerous. This thinkability and danger implies at least some disruption to our modern technologies of sex and subjectivity.

Tracing the history: patterns of public knowledge

Sex abuse knowledge has been subject to various definitions and frameworks across time according to prevailing cultural conditions that make aspects of sexual violence possible (Rutherford, 2011). The historical pattern of small and gradual developments of sex abuse human science knowledge governs that which is considered legitimate and relevant research subject matter in the discipline at a given point in time and, in turn, that which should be subject to surveillance and regulation. Whilst FSA was previously inconceivable, there is a current trend in academia, the law, and the health professions that is actively engaged with the 'discovery' of female sexual violence. This trend is a function of particular modern global and South African conditions that make FSA possible. Examples of these conditions include the current wave of panic and public concern in South Africa about sexual violence (see Abramjee, 2013; Bauer, 2013, Evans, 2013; Knoetze, 2013; Swart, 2013) as well as political and public calls, campaigns, and advocacy projects to counteract it. In addition, due to enhancements to birth control technologies and the increasing share of women in the economy (Collins, Saltzman Chafetz, Lesser Blumberg, Coltrane, & Turner, 1993), most Global North contexts and some Global South contexts are currently typified by a gradual erosion of the male-female binary that has neatly demarcated who can and cannot sexually transgress and be transgressed upon. This has resulted in female bodies now representing a greater threat to the order of things than they did before.

During the course of my victim study, participants noted how the emergence of FSA into circulated discourse parallels earlier trends in other types of sex abuse. Of particular interest was Jim's comments regarding why FSA is only emerging as an object of knowledge at this specific time in history:

> You know for those days . . . people just got away with that type of thing. . . . Those days . . . you don't talk about those types of things because it doesn't happen to people. . . . Today we are more, um, open about these type of things. . . . Um, as you said, there's, there's actually groups. Where people can go to. And they talk about it. Those days they wouldn't have . . . If it happened to you, you keep it to yourself. . . . Those days, you tell your mom, she'll probably beat the living shit out of you for lying.

Jim's comments on the increasing 'acknowledgement' of the possibilities for FSA show how the exclusion of a particular object of knowledge in discourse results in its invisibilisation and thus its 'un-truth'. Only by virtue of its ability to be 'written' into discourse, is an object of knowledge made real, possible, and conceivable. However, this easing of the parameters of who counts as a victim requires the alignment of new and alternative discourses (based on a body of scientific evidence) in order to be realised into the corpus of 'real' knowledge.

Counter-discourse: the fluidity of sexuality and gender

Given that the dominant cultural narrative on sex abuse depends on heter-onormative discourses, FSA – and more particularly FSA victimhood – lies at or beyond the boundaries of contemporary understandings of sex and sexuality. FSA victimhood discourse is, in this sense, a vehicle for counter-knowledge. Since the dominant narrative on sex abuse is constructed upon rigid and narrow definitions of gender and sexuality, the counter-narrative on FSA victimhood is likely to be dependent on discourses that support the fluidity of gender and sexuality. Breaking apart the binaries of modern heteronormativity thus seems to be a precondition for identifying as an FSA victim. For example, FSA is conceivable for Thabo because he is able to split sex from gender and desire from sexuality:

> As a homosexual man, there are certain women that I find attractive but I don't necessarily, I won't necessarily build a life with but I find them attractive. . . . I know I can be attracted to heterosexuals and some homo-sexuals actually enjoy it but hear what I'm saying, from that point of me being homosexual and having sex with a woman, I don't find it disgusting.

Likewise, for Suzette, to construct FSA requires restructuring our under-standings of men and women:

> I think personally that people should, that more people should know that women are capable of doing these kind of things. . . . And that they can, that they are capable of the same things that men are capable of . . . I want people to understand that it isn't just men that are doing wrong. It's women as well. And so that people have the voice to speak up and tell, tell someone if their mom or their, or a girl or someone is abusing them so that they don't go through the amount of pain that I went through when my mom abused me.

FSA victims' use of alternative discourse on sexuality and gender, coupled with their recognitions of historical patterns in sex abuse knowledge, are vehicles for the identification of FSA victimhood and further reification of this object in human science knowledge. In my study, victims' movements from FSA impossibility to possibility, and then in some cases probability, across their interviews, parallels the current emergent FSA victimhood discourse in the institutions of research and the law. In keeping with the logic of the confessional and its relationship to these institutions, participants were able to utilise the study interview as a context in which to perform gender and sexuality in ways that intersected and often produced new configurations of victimhood. Taken together, these discursive aspects of the interview material provide an overarching demonstration of those historical and material conditions that make FSA victimhood real and unreal, and possible and impossible. These discourses are, however, themselves now implicated in a reconstitution of these realities and possibilities.

Notes

1 Throughout this chapter, I refer to 'victims' because the participants in my original research self-identified as such. This does not mean to imply an essentialist under-standing of the participants as 'victims', nor does it mean to suggest that individuals subjected to FSA should be understood in dichotomous and narrowly defined terms.
2 South African women employed by households to perform domestic housework and chores. These women are also typically engaged in child caregiving and regularly live on the property with their employers. The South African domestic workforce comprises mainly of black women from rural areas with a low level of education.
3 All victims' names have been changed in order to uphold their anonymity.
4 Afrikaans word for psychologist.
5 MatrixMen is a website for male survivors of sexual violence (www.matrixmen.org).
6 Radio interview for the study call for participants.
7 Afrikaans slang meaning to beat up.

References

Abramjee, Y. (2013, February 12). Here's what we can do about rape. *Pretoria News*. Retrieved from www.iol.co.za/pretoria-news/opinion/here-s-what-we-can-do-about-rape-1.1468500.html

Ahrens, C. E. (2006). Being silenced: The impact of negative social reactions on the disclosure of rape. *American Journal of Community Psychology, 38*(3–4), 263–274.

Araji, S., & Finkelhor, D. (1986). Abusers: A review of the research. In D. Finkelhor (Ed.), *A sourcebook an child sexual abuse* (pp. 89–118). Beverly Hills, CA: SAGE Publications, Inc.

Ariès, P. (1973). *Centuries of childhood*. New York, NY: Jonathan Cape.

Barth, J., Bermetz, L., Heim, E., Trelle, S., & Tonia, T. (2013). The current prevalence of child sexual abuse worldwide: A systematic review and meta-analysis. *International Journal of Public Health, 58*(3), 469–483.

Bartky, S. L. (1988). Foucault, femininity, and the modernization of patriarchal power. In I. Diamond & L. Quinby (Eds.), *Feminism and Foucault: Reflections on resistance* (pp. 93–111). Boston, MA: Northeastern University Press.

Bauer, N. (2013, February 12). SA: A rape crisis, but no funds or will to fight. *Mail & Guardian*. Retrieved from http://mg.co.za/article/2013–02–12-f.html

Berlin, M. D., & Krout, E. (1986). Pedophilia: Diagnostic concepts, treatment and ethical considerations. *American Journal of Forensic Psychiatry, 7*(1), 13–30.

Bhana, D. (2006). The (im)possibility of child sexual rights in South African children's account of HIV/AIDS. *IDS Bulletin, 37*(5), 64–68.

Boonzaier, F. (2014). South African women resisting dominant discourse in narratives of violence. In S. McKenzie-Mohr & M. L. Lafrance (Eds.), *Women voicing resistance: Discursive and narrative explorations* (pp. 102–120). East Sussex and New York, NY: Routledge.

Bourke, J. (2007). *Rape: A history from 1860 to the present*. London: Virago Press.

Bowman, B. (2010). Children, pathology and politics: A genealogy of the paedophile in South Africa between 1944 and 2004. *South African Journal of Psychology, 40*(4), 443–464.

Brewin, C. R. (2012). A theoretical framework for understanding recovered memory experiences. In R. F. Belli (Ed.), *True and false recovered memories: Toward a reconciliation of the debate* (pp. 149–173). New York, NY: Springer.

Brockman, B., & Bluglass, R. (1996). A general psychiatric approach to sexual deviation. In I. Rosen (Ed.), *Sexual deviation* (3rd ed.) (pp. 1–42). New York, NY: Oxford University Press.

Butler, J. (1989). Foucault and the paradox of bodily inscriptions. *The Journal of Philosophy, 86*(11), 601–607.

Butler, J. (1999). *Gender trouble*. New York, NY and London: Routledge.

Butler, J. (2004). *Undoing gender*. London: Routledge.

Cahill, A. J. (2000). Foucault, rape, and the construction of the feminine body. *Hypatia, 15*(1), 43–63.

Caplan, P. (2013). Don't blame the mother: Then and now. In M. H. Hobbs & C. Rice (Eds.), *Gender and women's studies in Canada: Critical terrain* (pp. 99–103). Toronto: Women's Press.

Carrington, K. (1991). Policing families and controlling the young. *Journal of Australian Studies, 15*(31), 108–117.

Collins, P. H. (1998). It's all in the family: Intersections of gender, race and nation. *Hypatia, 13*(3), 62–82.

Collins, R., Saltzman Chafetz, J., Lesser Blumberg, R., Coltrane, S., & Turner, J. H. (1993). Toward an integrated theory of gender stratification. *Sociological Perspectives, 36*(3), 185–216.

Davis, D., & Loftus, E. (2014). Repressed memories. In R. L. Cautin & S. L. Lilienfeld (Eds.), *The Encyclopedia of Clinical Psychology* (pp. 1–3). Hoboken, NJ: Wiley-Blackwell doi: 10.1002/9781118625392.wbecp270

Davis, J. E. (2005). *Accounts of innocence: Sexual abuse, trauma, and the self.* Chicago, IL: University of Chicago Press.

Denov, M. S. (2001). A culture of denial: Exploring professional perspectives on female sexual offending. *Canadian Journal of Criminology, 43*(3), 303–329.

DePrince, A. P., Brown, L. S., Cheit, R. E., Freyd, J. J., Gold, S. N., Pezdek, K. B., & Quina, K. (2012). Motivated forgetting and misremembering: Perspectives from betrayal trauma theory. In R. F. Belli (Ed.), *True and false recovered memories: Toward a reconciliation of the debate* (pp. 193–242). New York, NY: Springer.

Dowsett, G. W. (2002). Bodyplay: Corporeality in a discursive silence. In K. Plummer (Ed.), *Sexualities: Some elements for an account of the social organisation of sexualities* (Vol. 2) (pp. 408–421). London and New York, NY: Routledge.

Du Mont, J., Miller, K. L., & Myhr, T. L. (2003). The role of "real rape" and "real victim" stereotypes in the police reporting practices of sexually assaulted women. *Violence Against Women, 9*(4), 466–486.

Eagle, G. (2006). Masculine victims: A contradiction in terms? *The International Journal of Critical Psychology, 17*, 47–76.

Enns, C. Z., McNeilly, C. L., Corkery, J. M., & Gilbert, M. S. (1995). The debate about delayed memories of childhood sexual abuse: A feminist perspective. *The Counseling Psychologist, 23*(2), 181–279.

Evans, J. (2013, February 8). Media united in outrage over rape. *Independent Online.* Retrieved from www.iol.co.za/news/crime-courts/media-united-in-outrage-over-rape-1.1467046#.UThgFKLviSo.html

Fagan, P. J., Wise, T. N., Schmidt, C. W., & Berlin, F. S. (2002). Pedophilia. *Journal of American Medical Association, 288*(19), 2458–2465.

Foucault, M. (1978). *The history of sexuality: An introduction.* Canada and New York, NY: The Penguin Group.

Foucault, M. (1980). *Power/knowledge: Selected interviews and other writings, 1972–1977.* New York, NY: Random House LLC.

Foucault, M. (1981). The order of discourse. In R. Young (Ed.), *"Untying the text": A post-structuralist reader* (pp. 48–78). London and Boston, MA: Routledge & Kegan Paul Ltd.

Foucault, M. (1985). *The use of pleasure: The history of sexuality* (Vol. 2). New York, NY: Pantheon Books.

Freeman, M. (1996). Sexual deviance and the law. In I. Rosen (Ed.), *Sexual deviation* (3rd ed.) (pp. 399–451). New York, NY: Oxford University Press.

Gannon, T. A., Rose, M. R., & Ward, T. (2008). A descriptive model of the offense process for female sexual offenders. *Sexual Abuse: A Journal of Research and Treatment, 20*(3), 352–374.

Gidycz, C. A. (2011). Sexual revictimization revisited: A commentary. *Psychology of Women Quarterly, 35*(2), 355–361.

Giguere, R., & Bumby, K. (2007). *Female sexual offenders.* Silver Spring, MD: Center for Sex Offender Management.

Gill, R. (2012). Media, empowerment and the "sexualization of culture" debates. *Sex Roles, 66*(11–12), 736–745.

Gilliam, F. D., Iyengar, S., Simon, A., & Wright, O. (1996). Crime in black and white: The violent, scary world of local news. *The Harvard International Journal of Press/ Politics, 1*(3), 6–23.

Gomez, A. M. (2011). Testing the cycle of violence hypothesis: Child abuse and adolescent dating violence as predictors of intimate partner violence in young adulthood. *Youth & Society, 43*(1), 171–192.

Hall, R. C. W., & Hall, R. C. W. (2007). A profile of pedophilia: Definition, characteristics of offenders, recidivism, treatment outcomes, and forensic issues. *Mayo Clinic Proceedings, 82*(4), 457–472.

Higgs, D. C., Canavan, M. M., & Meyer, W. J. (1992). Moving from defense to offense: The development of an adolescent female sexual offender. *The Journal of Sex Research, 29*(1), 131–139.

Howitt, D. (1995). *Paedophiles and sexual offences against children.* Chichester: John Wiley & Sons.

Kempe, R. S., & Kempe, C. H. (1984). *The common secret: Sexual abuse of children and adolescents.* New York, NY: W. H. Freeman and company.

Knoetze, D. (2013, February 8). 150 rapes an hour. *The Star.* Retrieved from www.iol. co.za/the-star/150-rapes-an-hour-1.1466999#.UThg9qLviSo.html

Koss, M. P. (1992). The underdetection of rape: Methodological choices influence incidence estimates. *Journal of Social Issues, 48*(1), 61–75.

Koss, M. P., Gidycz, C. A., & Wisniewski, N. (1987). The scope of rape: Incidence and prevalence of sexual aggression and victimization in a national sample of higher education students. *Journal of Consulting and Clinical Psychology, 55*(2), 162–170.

Kramer, S. (2010). *Discourse and power in the self-perceptions of incarcerated South African female sex offenders.* Unpublished Masters thesis. University of the Witwatersrand, Johannesburg.

Kramer, S. (2011). 'Truth', gender and the female psyche: Confessions from female sexual offenders. *Psychology of Women Section Review, 13*(1), 2–8.

Kramer, S. (2014). *Surfacing (im)possible victims: The role of gender, sexuality and power in constructing the conditions of possibility for victims of female sex abuse.* Unpublished PhD dissertation. University of the Witwatersrand, Johannesburg.

Kramer, S., & Bowman, B. (2011). Accounting for the 'invisibility' of the female paedophile: An expert-based perspective from South Africa. *Psychology and Sexuality, 2*(3), 1–15.

Kruttschnitt, C., Gartner, R., & Hussemann, J. (2008). Female violent offenders: Moral panics or more serious offenders? *The Australian and New Zealand Journal of Criminology, 41*(1), 9–35.

Kulick, A. (2013). *How gay stayed white: Millennial white gay men and the production of and resistance to racism, sexism, and heterosexism.* Unpublished Senior Honors thesis. University of Michigan, Ann Arbor.

Lawson, L. (2008). Female sexual offenders' relationship experiences. *Violence and Victims, 23*(3), 331–343.

Levett, A. (1992). Regimes of truth: A response to Diana Russel. *Agenda, 8*(12), 67–74.

Mazur, S., & Pekor, C. (1985). Can teachers touch children anymore? *Young Children, 40*(4), 10–12.

Miller, H. A., Turner, K., & Henderson, C. E. (2009). Psychopathology of sex offenders: A comparison of males and females using latent profile analysis. *Criminal Justice and Behaviour, 36*(8), 778–792.

Minister for Justice and Constitutional Development. (2007). *Criminal law (Sexual offences and related matters) amendment bill.* Republic of South Africa: Creda Communications.

Muehlenhard, C. L., & Kimes, L. A. (1999). The social construction of violence: The case of sexual and domestic violence. *Personality and Social Psychology Review, 3*(3), 234–245.

Murnen, S. K., Wright, C., & Kaluzny, G. (2002). If "boys will be boys," then girls will be victims? A meta-analytic review of the research that relates masculine ideology to sexual aggression. *Sex Roles, 46*(11/12), 359–375.

Myers, M. F. (1989). Men sexually assaulted as adults and sexually abused as boys. *Archives of Sexual Behavior, 18*(3), 203–215.

Nathan, P., & Ward, T. (2002). Female sex offenders: Clinical and demographic features. *The Journal of Sex Aggression, 8*(1), 5–21.

Ogloff, J. R. P., Cutajar, M. C., Mann, E., Mullen, P., Wei, F. T. Y., Hassan, H. A. B., & Yih, T. H. (2012). Child sexual abuse and subsequent offending and victimisation: A 45 year follow-up study. *Trends and Issues in Crime and Criminal Justice, 440*, 1–6.

Parker, I. (1992). *Discourse dynamics: Critical analysis for social and individual psychology.* London: Routledge.

Parker, I. (2004). Discourse analysis. In U. Flick, E. von Kardoff & I. Steinke (Eds.), *A companion to qualitative research* (pp. 308–312). London: Sage Publications Limited.

Phelan, S. (1990). Foucault and feminism. *American Journal of Political Science, 34*(2), 421–440.

Posel, D. (2005). Sex, death and the fate of the nation: Reflections on the politicization of sexuality in post-apartheid South Africa. *Africa, 75*(2), 125–153.

Pryce, A. (2000). Frequent observation: Sexualities, self-surveillance, confession and the construction of the active patient. *Nursing Inquiry, 7*(2), 103–111.

Richardson, D., & May, H. (1999). Deserving victims?: Sexual status and the social construction of violence. *The Sociological Review, 47*(2), 308–331.

Rudwick, S. (2011). Defying a myth: A gay subculture in contemporary South Africa. *Nordic Journal of African Studies, 20*(2), 90–111.

Rutherford, A. (2011). Sexual violence against women: Putting rape research into context. *Psychology of Women Quarterly, 35*(2), 342–347.

Ryan, G., Leversee, T. F., & Lane, S. (2011). *Juvenile sexual offending: Causes, consequences, and correction* (3rd ed.). Hoboken, NJ: John Wiley & Sons.

Sandler, J. C., & Freeman, N. J. (2007). Typology of female sex offenders: A test of Vandiver and Kercher. *Sexual Abuse: A Journal of Research and Treatment, 19*(2), 73–89.

Schaeffer, P., Leventhal, J. M., & Asnes, A. G. (2011). Children's disclosures of sexual abuse: Learning from direct inquiry. *Child Abuse & Neglect, 35*(5), 343–352.

Swart, H. (2013, February 15). Will Anene Booysen's brutal rape and murder shake the nation into action? *Mail & Guardian*. Retrieved from http://mg.co.za/article/2013-02-15-00-will-anene-booysens-brutal-rape-and-murder-shake-the-nation-into-action.html

Swartz, L., & Levett, A. (1989). Political repression and children in South Africa: The social construction of damaging effects. *Social Science & Medicine, 28*(7), 741–750.

Sturken, M. (1999). Narratives of recovery: Repressed memory as cultural memory. In M. Bal, J. Crewe & L. Spitzer (Eds.), *Acts of memory: Cultural recall in the present* (pp. 231–248). Hanover: University Press of New England.

Tell, D. (2007, November). *Michel Foucault and the Politics of Confession*. Paper presented at the annual meeting of the NCA 93rd Annual Convention, TBA, Chicago, IL. Retrieved from www.allacademic.com/meta/p187824_index.html

Travers, O. (1999). *Behind the silhouettes: Exploring the myths of child sexual abuse*. Belfast, CA: The Blackstaff Press Limited.

Turner, K., Miller, H. A., & Henderson, C. E. (2008). Latent profile analyses of offense and personality characteristics in a sample of incarcerated female sexual offenders. *Criminal Justice and Behaviour, 35*(7), 879–894.

Vandiver, D. M. (2006). Female sex offenders: A comparison of solo offenders and co-offenders. *Violence and Victims, 21*(3), 339–354.

Vandiver, D. M., & Kercher, G. (2004). Offender and victim characteristics of registered female sexual offenders in Texas: A proposed typology of female sexual offenders. *Sexual Abuse: A Journal of Research and Treatment, 16*(2), 121–137.

Vandiver, D. M., & Walker, J. T. (2002). Female sex offenders: An overview and analysis of 40 cases. *Criminal Justice Review, 27*(2), 284–300.

Weiss, K. G. (2010a). Male sexual victimization: Examining men's experiences of rape and sexual assault. *Men and Masculinities, 12*(3), 275–298.

Weiss, K. G. (2010b). Too ashamed to report: Deconstructing the shame of sexual victimization. *Feminist Criminology, 5*(3), 286–310.

Weiss, K. G. (2011). Neutralizing sexual victimization: A typology of victims' non-reporting accounts. *Theoretical Criminology, 15*(4), 445–467.

Wijkman, M., Bijleveld, C., & Hendriks, J. (2010). Women don't do such things! Characteristics of female sex offenders and offender types. *Sexual Abuse: A Journal of Research and Treatment, 22*(2), 135–156.

Winnubst, S. (1999). Exceeding Hegel and Lacan: Different fields of pleasure within Foucault and Irigaray. *Hypatia, 14*(1), 13–37.

Woodhull, W. (1988). Sexuality, power, and the question of rape. In I. Diamond and L. Quinby (Eds.). *Feminism and Foucault: Reflections on Resistance* (pp. 167–176). Boston: Northeastern University Press.

Yun, I., Ball, J. D., & Lim, H. (2011). Disentangling the relationship between child maltreatment and violent delinquency: Using a nationally representative sample. *Journal of Interpersonal Violence, 26*(1), 88–110.

PART III

Psychology and FSA victimhood

5
AN EMERGENT VICTIMHOOD
Implications for the psycho-political project

The 'confession': implications for the practice of psychology

Whilst victimhood and trauma are cast as rare in the aftermath of what is now constructed as FSA (Denov, 2001), the data emerging in this text largely suggest that FSA victimhood is thinkable under certain material and psycho-political conditions and that 'trauma' is volunteered. Key to surfacing these conditions is gender performativity (Butler, 1999) because in the context of a confessional interview, gender, sexuality, and power can be performed in unusual ways. Performance is inherent to subjectivity, and thus an interview constructed around FSA sexual victimisation allows for both the surfacing of FSA victimhood as well as an incitement to these performances via reflections on the gender of the self and the perpetrator. Performativity thus allows individuals to renegotiate their subjections, perform an alternative discourse, and consolidate an FSA victim subject position within the interview as an incitement to speak about sex. The interview context provides subjects with the vehicle to produce FSA victimhood in a way that clearly exposes those conditions that make such an object possible.

During the data collection phase of my project, the key thread across the interviews was the use of the format as a 'confessional' space by the participants. This was emphasised by the use of particular spaces for the interviews, which positioned me firmly in the field of psychology. Given the traditional ethical procedure that requires informed consent and assurance of confidentiality at the beginning of the research process, all of the participants related their stories, often for the first time, with the understanding that they were private and confidential. This ethical requirement inadvertently and ironically supported the confessional format and thus the incitement to sex abuse discourse. In almost all of the interviews, the participants referred to the FSA event as 'a/the secret'. Both the discourse voiced as well as that which remains silenced is socially produced in the interaction between researcher and participant, where "voice and silence are negotiated, imposed, contested, and provided" (Fivush, 2010, p. 89), especially as a function of larger cultural narratives that detail that which is considered normative and those experiences that are considered deviations from these norms. The continuous assertion of 'the secret' is a reflection of the institutionalised practice of excluding FSA victimhood from widely circulated discourses on sexual violence. Experiences that do not typically fit inside the dominant cultural narrative are silenced through the act of discursive exclusion (Fivush, 2010), and thus I used the 'confessional' context of the interview space as well as exploited this 'secret' in order to bring these apparently atypical experiences into discourse. This is not only evidenced by the content of participants' discourse, but also by the choice of discourse and the identification of excluded discourse (Weiss, 2010).

Given my position in the discipline of psychology, together with questions directly related to participants' sexuality, sex life, as well as the context of the interview as an anonymous and confidential space, participants felt not only the desire to speak, but also the obligation to do so. This is in line with Pryce's (2000) suggestion that the incitement to discourse operates at the nexus of the expert (or psychological) gaze and the implication that the interview is the standard device to elicit content to be interpreted and decoded. Furthermore, the interview, by virtue of its structure, implies that there is a value to confession, especially if there is an expert present. Thus, the interview itself is a key vehicle for the production and transmission of power/knowledge and the further refinement of FSA victimhood as a category of human science and (self)-knowledge. Additionally, the confessional context is typified by the 'expert' other's interpretation and evaluation of the status, identity, experiences, and speech of the confessor. Thus, although the confession appears to empower the victim through the provision of an opportunity to speak, it is the 'expert' listener who is able to determine the legitimacy and value of the victim's discourse (Alcoff & Gray, 1993). Whilst this text rests on my conceptualisation of what constitutes FSA victimhood and my identification of conditions of possibility for each victim's narrative, the 'expert' researcher is not all-powerful, as the opportunity to narrate an experience is dialectically related to the speaker's identity (Fivush, 2010). Thus, in the act of speaking, the participants construct their own sense of selves and subjectivities.

Given that the assumption of a victim position is an identity-defining experience that produces the subject as dependent and helpless (Furedi, 1998), an invitation to occupy and discursively negotiate a victim identity presupposes the possibility of disempowering the participants. The reification of a particular type of victimhood thus could result in potential subjective effects based on the participants' experiences of victimhood. This said, there is also an expectation that interviews constitute healing spaces. Thus, despite my concern that in the act of constructing a victim position, the participants would experience trauma or inevitable 'damage', as suggested by Levett (1990, 1992), participants, having already self-identified as victims, felt that this interview context would, in some sense, be therapeutic. This echoes Pryce's (2000) observation that the historical constitution of the (sexual) confession as an opportunity for reflexivity, growth, and catharsis has resulted in the expectation that it has curative, healing, and therapeutic benefits. This phenomenon was most likely emphasised by the statement in the participant information sheet that the research will contribute to the participants' own understandings of their circumstances. Such a statement inadvertently places me in a position of power through the implied suggestion that the participant will undergo a process of heightened self-awareness during his/her interaction with me.

Participation in the interview process is therefore itself indivisible from the discursive architecture that continues to construct and reify FSA victimhood as a possibility. In constructing FSA victimhood as the object of research and interviewing self-identified victims, this project participates in the refinement and further reification of this category. However, as is the case with all objects of power, it also creates new possibilities for rethinking gender, sexuality, and abuse in contemporary South Africa and globally.

Psychological theory and research as instruments of reification

Despite mainstreamed visibility of trauma and victim discourse globally, and in South Africa specifically, FSA victims have escaped academic, medical, legal, and public surveillance such that they remain invisible or at least peripheral. This text therefore both materialises and produces part of the emerging apparatus of discourses, scientific accounts, and theoretical propositions that surface the productive possibilities of FSA victimhood. The possibility for particular conditions to produce FSA subject positions thus highlights the politics of human science knowledge in its constitution of who qualifies for victimhood under current constructions of sex abuse. Accordingly, the exploration of conditions of possibilities for FSA victimhood represents a strategic point of entry into investigating how sexuality, gender, and identity intersect to produce a 'new' mode of social and sexual transgression that is itself both an instrument and effect of modern power. Because the social world is characterised by "implicit accounts of ontology" that determine which genders, sexualities, identities, and bodies can be considered 'real' (Butler, 2004, p. 214), this critical investigation reveals how discourse operates through selection, exclusion, and inclusion in the discursive fields of abuse, violence, sexuality, and gender. By specifically questioning the exclusion of FSA victimhood from modern discourse, this text actively engages in Halperin's (1989, p. 273) process of de-centring sexuality so that the "histrocity, conditions of emergence, modes of construction, and ideological contingencies" of FSA victimhood particularly, and gender and sexuality more broadly, can be identified. In so doing, I examine counter-discourses for sexuality and gender, and thus further refine, solidify, and reify new possibilities for thinking about gender, sexuality, and violence (Weedon, 1987).

The task of this text has been to identify and critique dominant narratives that exclude particular versions of victimhood from widely circulated discourses. This text is thus ultimately both the product of classical discourses on sex as well as potentially a springboard for the production of counter-knowledge on who may and may not be a victim or perpetrator of what can or cannot be considered sex abuse. The study of a particular construct is, in effect, the procedure through which that construct is partly being produced (Butchart, 1997). An inevitable consequence of this text's analysis is the reification of FSA victimhood as an object of knowledge through the definition, solidification, and visibilisation of this object as a scientific 'reality' (Bowman & Hook, 2010). It is therefore necessary to continue to treat our scientific discoveries in many instances as inseparable from the analyses that 'discovered them' (Armstrong, 1986). Victimhood is thus a product of the creative force of power and exists as an object of human science knowledge (Butchart, 1997). This text is but one node in a multifaceted matrix of both competing and corresponding discursive relationships that attempt to take hold of, release, create, and resist constructions of sex abuse.

In making FSA victimhood thinkable, this text no doubt further reifies this object of human science knowledge. This potential reification will certainly impact on a number of other institutional practices. For example, the possibility of an FSA victim will, in turn, shift policing and the criminal justice system, which currently reduce femininity to passivity and victimisation. This will influence FSA visibility such that there may be a rise in reporting and incarceration rates, and thus the appearance of a rise in rates of female-perpetrated sex offending. Science may declare that such abuse has always existed and it was merely waiting to be discovered, and the ever-expanding net of discipline will be cast wider. Whilst this expansion may still be constrained by a cultural fabric that cannot yet fully conceive of an agentic and sexually transgressive woman, the emergence of FSA victimhood will surely disrupt the gendering of sexual violence and trauma. Revisions to terms such as 'rape', 'sex abuse', and 'sexual victimisation' "filter into the culture at large", with the effect of subjects 'realising' the applicability of these new definitions to their experiences (Koss, Heise, & Russo, 1994, p. 510). It is thus likely that counter-knowledge on FSA victimhood will inform further revisions to understandings of sex abuse, and this in turn will provide conditions for a wider range of subjects to identify as FSA victims. This has theoretical, ethical, and political implications. First, whilst the aim of this text is not to provide a theoretical framework for understanding the psychological, biological, cognitive, or behavioural characteristics of FSA, the very act of surfacing these victims produces the adjunct possibility for these theories to arise. And no doubt, at least within the psychological field, they will. Thus, I am cognisant of how the production of a particular category of human experience will imply the need for further research in the area and how this future research will likely mould, categorise, and objectify the FSA victim. As a text closely aligned to Foucault's understanding of discourse, science, and the subject, this amounts to a committed acknowledgement that, as an author of a particular discourse, I am also a function of it (Phelan, 1990). Paradoxically then, this text participates in the very mechanisms it critiques by reproducing and reifying a particular human subject position and constructing the contextual, material, and temporal conditions for its possibility. Ethically, the manifestation of increased female sex offender incarceration rates may result in the construction of an FSA pandemic and consequently widespread moral panic. At least in South Africa, this will serve to amplify the recent surge in moral panic about rape and other forms of sexual violence, and in turn drive the increasing scrutiny and regulation of female (and other) sex offenders and the social regulation of sexual behaviour. More politically, the project of making possible a sexually violent female may serve to rationalise and fuel the continued pathologisation and repression of women's sexual agency. In the context of contemporary narratives on women's sexualities, feminist responses to this text may be concerned with the potentially antifeminist consequences of FSA reification. Specifically, the implication is that the production of a sexually violent woman aligns with dominant gender discourses that insinuate the corruptive potential of sexually agentic women. In turn, women become 'like men' (aggressive, sexually potent, for example), and female sexual agency is pathologised and punished. Thus, whilst the focus on female perpetration does well to provide possibilities for destabilising heteronormative gender binaries and binaristic positions on power and subjection, it also runs the risk of driving an antifeminist position.

Concluding remarks

Following Foucault's (1978) analysis of sexuality, by calling into question the universality of 'truths' about gender and sexuality, this text offers new possibilities for a reconstitution of these objects of human science knowledge. In tracing the conditions of possibility for subjects to identify as FSA victims, I have charted the coordinates of the discourses that constrain men to perpetrators and women to victims in a mutually constitutive production of sex abuse. In so doing, this text provides a compelling argument for rethinking the roles of gender and sexuality in outlining the parameters of 'truths' for sexual transgression, victimhood, and perhaps even sexual violence itself.

The FSA victim is produced in this text (for the first time) as possible, traumatised, and penetrable regardless of gender. In turn, the female sex offender herself is again recast. This invites a rearticulation of the female sex offender as an object and subject of human psychological research as well as the production and refinement of the psycho-political project of determining 'victim worthiness'.

References

Alcoff, L., & Gray, L. (1993). Survivor discourse: Transgression or recuperation? *Signs, 18*(2), 260–290.

Armstrong, D. (1986). The invention of infant mortality. *Sociology of Health and Illness, 8*(3), 211–232.

Bowman, B., & Hook, D. (2010). Paedophile as Apartheid event: Genealogical lessons for working with the Apartheid Archive. *Psychology in Society, 40*, 64–82.

Butchart, A. (1997). Objects without origins: Foucault in South African socio-medical science. *South African Journal of Psychology, 27*(2), 101–110.

Butler, J. (1999). *Gender trouble*. New York, NY and London: Routledge.

Butler, J. (2004). *Undoing gender*. London: Routledge.

Denov, M. S. (2001). A culture of denial: Exploring professional perspectives on female sexual offending. *Canadian Journal of Criminology, 43*(3), 303–329.

Fivush, R. (2010). Speaking silence: The social construction of silence in autobiographical and cultural narratives. *Memory, 18*(2), 88–98.

Foucault, M. (1978). *The history of sexuality: An introduction*. Canada and New York, NY: The Penguin Group.

Furedi, F. (1998). New Britain – A nation of victims. *Society, 35*(3), 80–84.

Halperin, D. M. (1989). Is there a history of sexuality? *History and Theory, 28*(3), 257–274.

Koss, M. P., Heise, L., & Russo, N. P. (1994). The global health burden of rape. *Psychology of Women Quarterly*, *18*(4), 509–537.

Levett, A. (1990). Childhood sexual abuse and problems in conceptualisation. *Agenda*, *6*(7), 38–47.

Levett, A. (1992). Regimes of truth: A response to Diana Russel. *Agenda*, *8*(12), 67–74.

Phelan, S. (1990). Foucault and feminism. *American Journal of Political Science*, *34*(2), 421–440.

Pryce, A. (2000). Frequent observation: Sexualities, self-surveillance, confession and the construction of the active patient. *Nursing Inquiry*, *7*(2), 103–111.

Weedon, C. (1987). *Feminist practice and poststructuralist theory*. London: Blackwell Publishers.

Weiss, K. G. (2010). Male sexual victimization: Examining men's experiences of rape and sexual assault. *Men and Masculinities*, *12*(3), 275–298.

INDEX